Dispersed Dispossession

Dispersed Dispossession

COLLECTIVE GOODS, APPROPRIATION,
AND AGENCY IN RURAL RUSSIA

ALEXANDER VORBRUGG

THE UNIVERSITY OF GEORGIA PRESS
Athens

© 2025 by the University of Georgia Press
Athens, Georgia 30602
www.ugapress.org
All rights reserved
Set in 10.25/13.5 Minion Pro by
Classic City Composition, Athens, GA

Most University of Georgia Press titles are
available from popular e-book vendors.

Printed digitally

Library of Congress Cataloging-in-Publication Data

Names: Vorbrugg, Alexander author
Title: Dispersed dispossession : collective goods, appropriation, and agency in rural Russia /
    Alexander Vorbrugg.
Description: Athens : The University of Georgia Press, [2025] | Series: Geographies of justice and
    social transformation | Includes bibliographical references and index.
Identifiers: LCCN 2025004403 (print) | LCCN 2025004404 (ebook) | ISBN 9780820363899
    hardback | ISBN 9780820363882 paperback | ISBN 9780820363905 epub | ISBN 9780820363912
    pdf
Subjects: LCSH: Rural development—Russia | Russia—Rural conditions
Classification: LCC HN530.Z9 C686 2025 (print) | LCC HN530.z9 (ebook) | ddc 305.50947—dc23
    /eng/20250414
LC record available at https://lccn.loc.gov/2025004403
LC ebook record available at https://lccn.loc.gov/2025004404

CONTENTS

ABBREVIATIONS AND RUSSIAN TERMS

ABD	Accumulation by dispossession
AKKOR	Russian Association of Rural and Farm Enterprises and Agricultural Cooperatives
BEF	Black Earth Farming (investment company)
CEE	Central and Eastern European countries
CIS	Commonwealth of Independent States
Dacha	Seasonal or year-round second home in the countryside
Duma	Russian legislative assembly
FAO	Food and Agriculture Organization of the United Nations
Hectare	Unit of land equal to 2.47 acres
Kolkhoz	Collective farm enterprise in the Soviet Union
Kolkhoznik	Member of a kolkhoz
LFE	Large farm enterprise
Mha	Million hectares
Minselkhoz	Ministry of Agriculture of the Russian Federation
Oblast	Administrative region in Russia
PA	Primitive accumulation
Pai	Land titles issued to workers during the land reform
Perestroika	Restructuring of the Soviet political and economic system during the late 1980s
Raion	Smaller administrative unit within an oblast, region, or republic, can be translated as district
RF	Russian Federation
ROIC	Returns on invested capital
ROE	Returns on equity
Rosstat	Federal State Statistics Service
RSFSR	Russian Soviet Federative Socialist Republic

SEK   Swedish krona
Sovkhoz   State-owned farm in the Soviet Union
USDA   U.S. Department of Agriculture
USSR   The Union of Soviet Socialist Republics, or the Soviet Union
WTO   World Trade Organization

For the romanization of Russian terms, I use the ALA-LC transliteration standard. In agreement with established conventions, I depart from this standard for words and names that are established in English and omit diacritics and two-letter tie characters. All translations from Russian and German are mine.

PREFACE

As I finalize this book in 2023, Russia's unjustified war against Ukraine has drawn new public interest to both states. Long labeled as transition economies, both countries have, in very different ways, again become places experiencing fundamental disruptions. Rightly, most attention has been on the destruction and human suffering in Ukraine.

I found it difficult to return to this project after Russia's 2022 full-scale invasion of Ukraine. The war has created much to react to, and my frustration and anger at the Russian establishment had grown to a point where I needed to accommodate it. Working on the manuscript helped me to remind myself and learn, in different ways, again and again, that the people of a country are of course not identical to a political system that often exploits and oppresses them—which does not resolve difficult questions of responsibility and complicity. I hope this book can contribute to a more nuanced perception of the social realities within Russia over a decade that seems central in the genealogy of the present historical moment: the 2010s.

I conducted fieldwork for this book in Russia from 2012 through 2014, and follow-up fieldwork in 2021, but most of it before the 2014 annexation of Crimea. I also did most of the writing before the 2022 invasion. I abstain from trying to (re)interpret this study in light of this war. However, I hope the book contributes to a better understanding of the place Russia has become, a question that has become more popular, as well as pressing, considering the wars its armies are waging. Furthermore, some of the main topics addressed in this book do speak to questions that have received broader interest under current conditions and deserve more attention.

When food exports from Ukraine and Russia became uncertain or stalled after February 2022, new international attention was brought to the extent to which both countries are global powerhouses of food production. This book tells a story about the conditions under which Russia established itself as a top wheat exporter—or as an agricultural "superpower," as the official rhetoric would have it. The formation of large agricultural companies is a central part of that. This study offers rare, grounded insights into the making and failing of such companies and their projects, and the contact zones between companies and rural actors.

The war further brought attention to how inhabitants of rural and marginalized regions within Russia, including so-called ethnic territories, are deprived of livelihoods and futures to the extent that they came to constitute a massive "reserve army" of soldiers more than workers. Besides direct coercion, including the recruitment of prisoners, it was economic deprivation in various peripheral areas that reportedly drove many to serve, and die, as soldiers in the war. Of course, this cannot justify the deaths or any other cruelties that Russian soldiers have inflicted on Ukraine. But it helps explain the circumstances that enabled the mobilization into the army and mercenary groups of people who could be sent into what journalists described as a "meat grinder."

Russia is among the most economically unequal of the former state-socialist countries. According to World Bank data, it is also one of the most unequal countries in the northern hemisphere, behind only a few other countries, including the United States. After the disintegration of the Soviet system, poverty and a lack of options have become particularly prevalent in rural areas. Most popular interpretations of what stabilizes the Russian political establishment, including the compliance or political passivity of rural populations, focus on propaganda, ideology, and nostalgia. *Dispersed Dispossession* focuses on material circumstances and economic conditions. It highlights the relationship between the deprivation of rural populations and the concentration of capital and power through often state-aligned businesses. It helps to explain how far these circumstances limit the agency of rural inhabitants, and how promises of stability and revival resonate with many of them. This does not justify support for or compliance with what an increasing number of observers describe as a totalitarian, or even fascist, political regime. But it may complicate the story of what led there. The economic violence throughout recent Russian history deserves recognition, including, of course, the staggeringly unjust political-economic system that emerged during market reforms. This book considers how Western business interests, reform agendas, and other transnational connections played a formative role in the Russian countryside, alongside domestic forces.

The concept of dispossession helps emphasize how widespread poverty and other forms of deprivation are not just unfortunate side effects of policies or the result of historical or environmental circumstances, but are linked to decisions taken and not taken, accountability denied, and powerful actors gaining profit based on others' deprivation. This book focuses on dispossession of a particular kind. What I conceptualize as "dispersed dispossession" articulates the separation of complex webs of relations and the deterioration of collective goods constitutive for well-being and agency. It implies the fundamentally unequal capabilities to navigate disruptive change and to repurpose, revalue, and appropriate devalued and degraded resources. It emphasizes drawn-out processes of dispossession in which preexisting harms and injustices, accumulated over historical periods and different political-economic systems, are perpetuated and exploited, and it helps us better understand how this affects social imaginaries. It further helps to grasp and theorize forms of agency that do not fit established understandings of resistance, complicating the cliché of rural inhabitants' general passivity and compliance.

This book is based on situated case studies. Over around ten months of fieldwork, I gathered insights from the contact zones between residents and workers, agricultural enterprises and companies, and representatives of the state apparatus. My aim was to demonstrate ways of thinking and conceptualizing from the Russian countryside, in conversation with the people I met. I am convinced that rigorous fieldwork-based studies offer unique possibilities for such theorizing. Yet I write this preface at a point in history when conducting such research in Russia has become extremely difficult for foreign researchers and, for different reasons, also for researchers with Russian passports or affiliations. In many ways, research conditions and freedoms had already gradually deteriorated throughout the 2010s. Since 2022, many of the remaining opportunities have been blocked.

In the first decade after the dissolution of the Eastern Bloc post-1991, fundamental systemic changes within former state-socialist countries coincided with new possibilities for research—or "freedoms," to echo some of the dominant rhetoric of those days. Through the lifting of state-dictated requirements and restrictions, researchers at Eastern European institutions gained freedom in what to study and how. As the collapse of the socialist state undermined research budgets and institutions, this freedom of choice and expression often coincided with being freed from the means to work in research, a situation akin to Marxian "double freedom." Many scholars left academia or left their institutions for others in the West. The situation was less ambivalent for more privileged Western scholars, who gained access to archives, fieldwork options, and various data in "the East" and returned to their institutional homes in "the West," reporting how they had been greeted enthusiastically by colleagues eager to collaborate. Publishing in English and other Western languages, these scholars were well equipped to satisfy the increased public and academic interest in stories from "behind the former Iron Curtain." Much has changed since the 1990s, of course—enough for scholars to suggest the necessity of entirely abandoning the idea that there still is, if there ever was, anything like a "postsocialist condition" that could characterize the complex and heterogeneous region of former Soviet and socialist states, or any single one of them.

As researchers, we also bring our own histories to the issues we study. I found a welcoming academic environment when I first traveled as an exchange student to Russia, to the Institute of Geography at Moscow State University in 2008, and three years later as a PhD candidate. I enjoyed the privilege of learning from, collaborating with, and building on the crucial help and support of Russian colleagues. Being a native speaker of Czech helped me to acquire proficiency in Russian relatively quickly during courses at the University of Tübingen, and later during long stays in Russia and Ukraine. My family background directed some of my curiosity and gave me a certain sensitivity to the heterogeneity of and sometimes violent history that shaped these countries. More recently, as for many others with research and biographical ties to Eastern Europe, Russia's ongoing war deeply affected my ways of relating to Russia. It is not that I have had romantic ideas about the Russian state, which has long waged wars and been highly repressive toward some groups. For instance, by the end of the period covered in this study, many if not most of the more prominent libertarian leftist activists whom I met during my first trips to Russia were in exile, imprisoned, or dead. After Russia's 2022 invasion of Ukraine, most Russian friends and colleagues with whom I continue to collaborate academically left Russia and are in exile. I stopped collaborations with Russian institutions from which my research, and this study, had greatly benefited in the past.

Russia's 2022 invasion of Ukraine, impactful and devastating in many ways, also became a brutal real-world demonstration of how "the region" is anything but homogeneous, as it is shaped by antagonistic and conflicting political and economic forces, including stark differences in relationships to the (state-socialist) pasts. While Putin uses various occasions for long and inaccurate lessons in Russian history, in many former state-socialist states outside of Russia calls for ideological distance from this past have been amplified. *Dispersed Dispossession* speaks to the newly heated battles of interpretation of the Soviet legacy but abstains from the often ideological stance of defending or despising state socialism. Rather, it traces how it matters in everyday situations and how the roots of dispossession may span different political-economic systems. The war also amplified calls by academics, artists, cultural workers, and others to decenter and decolonize knowledge production in and on "the region." This is because academic scholarship, cultural production, and public perception remain biased toward Russia. And, within this bias, the country's centers rather than its more peripheral territories (including much of rural Russia as well as Indigenous territories and so-called ethnic territories) are the focus. Many therefore call for a twofold decentering of knowledge production, away from the West and toward the former state-socialist East, including Eastern Europe, the Caucasus, and Central Asia, and away from the Russian center and toward various margins within this region.

This book is based on a study in Russia. It is, in some sense, even situated in the Russian heartland. I conducted fieldwork in the western regions of Lipetsk, Voronezh, Rostov, Perm, and the city of Moscow. All these regions have been part of Russia since the early decades of the tsardom in the sixteenth century, and most of its rural population is counted as "ethnic Russian." Even though this study is situated in rural areas, which differ greatly from urban centers, they are still relatively close to the country's center of power, symbolized by Moscow, in terms of geography and public perception.

This does not mean, however, that this book follows well-trodden paths in Western academic knowledge production. This is the first book on Russia, or any Eastern European country, published in this book series, and there are few such books recently published in geography and English overall. Book-length studies on rural Russia, based on in-depth fieldwork, have become rare across disciplines over recent years due to increasing challenges. Most books on Russia, and other Eastern European, Baltic, Caucasian, and Central Asian countries, have been published in book series with a regional focus. In this respect, I see it as a privilege and an opportunity to have this work published in a general human geography book series. I hope this signals a trend toward increased scientific interest in this region that will not be limited to Russia. I further hope it can contribute to the strengthening of relational perspectives that, rather than exceptionalizing Russia as a villain or victim, connect its imperial history and revival to imperialisms elsewhere, and its violent capitalism to varieties of capitalism elsewhere. Finally, I hope it can contribute to showing that some stories that emerge from Russia deserve a place in the broader thinking about and longing for a livable and more just future.

ACKNOWLEDGMENTS

The fieldwork underlying this study would have been impossible and much less pleasurable without the help and friendship of persons who accompanied and took care of me. I am grateful to many who offered their time and support during the fieldwork that underlies this study but who will remain anonymous. More than seventy interviewees offered their thoughts and insights, and many more in informal conversations. I also thank the many who hosted and accommodated me, gave me a ride and presents, and shared their personal stories.

I am particularly grateful to colleagues and friends in Russia who supported this project. Aleksandr Nikulin and Maria Savoskul accompanied me at times during fieldwork, hosted me in Moscow, mobilized friends and family members to support me, and offered me advice. Vera Bolotova was a crucial mediator for fieldwork in the Perm region. Aleksandr Kuzminov and Nina Kuzminova, Jan Pieter Rijpma, Nikolai and Sasha Nikulin and their families, Sergei Kasakov, and Valentina Petrovna hosted me several times and gave me further support. Aleksandr Nikulin, Dmitrii Bogachev, Maria Savoskul, Michelle Steggerda, Timur Sazanov, Vera Bolotova, and Viktor Shostko organized some interviews and travel arrangements.

I am grateful to several people for their mentorship and for providing resources. Peter Lindner introduced me to persons and sites that became core pillars of this project, and he provided freedom and support to develop it during work on my PhD. Stephen Collier invited me to the New School, where I developed some of the core ideas of this study, which helped with turning my PhD dissertation into a book. Susan Thieme supported this project during my postdoctoral phase, both morally and materially.

I thank everyone who provided feedback on text that went into this project at several stages. Iris Dzudzek, Nanja Nagorny, Peter Lindner, Stefan Ouma, and Vanessa Thompson discussed and commented on the underlying PhD thesis. Christian Berndt, Endre Dányi, Julian Stenmanns, Karin Schwiter, Marc Boeckler, Martin Müller, Nadine Marquardt, and Simon Noori offered feedback on individual chapters. Carole Ammann, Stephen Collier, and Susanne Wengle helped to turn my PhD dissertation into a book. Alexander Kurakin, Alexander Nikulin, Dace Dzenovska, Dominic Martin, Eszter Krasznai Kovács, Friederike Pank, Jevgeniy Bluwstein, Vera Smirnova, and Volodymyr Artiukh commented on the book manuscript, or substantial parts of it. I also thank Anastasia Nikolaeva and for their assistance, and Angelina Davydova, Luca Tschiderer, Natalia Shagaida, Elena Trubina, Mariia Tysiachniuk, Myroslava Volosko, and Stephen Wegren for feedback on specific questions and parts of the manuscript. Many more commented on this project at conferences, presentations, and research colloquia. Thanks to Natalia Taran, Viacheslav Lazarenko, Mark Borblik, Lena Ribe, and Michelle Steggerda for transcribing interviews, and to Peter Lindner and Evelin Moser for sharing three interview transcripts with me.

I gratefully acknowledge funding from the German Research Foundation (DFG) for most of the research underlying this study, and the Foundation for the Promotion of International Scientific Relations at Goethe University as well as the Vereinigung von Freunden und Förderern der Goethe Universität for several travel stipends. I enjoyed excellent working conditions and a friendly and inspiring environment in the Department of Human Geography at Goethe University Frankfurt, the Institute of Geography at the University of Bern, and the Institute of Advanced Studies at University College London. At a late stage in writing, I also enjoyed financial support from the Swiss National Science Foundation. Thanks to generous support from the University of Bern's Open Access Publication Fund, the electronic version of this book is available free of charge. I thank Joan Dale Lace and Leah Caldwell for copyediting, and everyone at the University of Georgia Press who supported the publication process: Bethany Snead, Lea Johnson, Mick Gusinde-Duffy, Rebecca Norton, among others, and the series editors Matt Coleman and Ishan Ashutosh. I am also grateful to three anonymous reviewers for their critical reading and helpful suggestions.

Special thanks to Julian Stenmanns, Stefan Ouma, and Vanessa Thompson for personal and intellectual companionship over extended phases of this project, and to Angelina Davydova, Jevgeniy Bluwstein, and Kateryna Polianska for helping me reorient after February 2022. Carolin Schurr, Iris Dzudzek, and Karin Schwiter helped me recharge through conversations and initiatives to make the university a better place. I am immensely grateful to Vanessa for what we shared.

Dispersed Dispossession

Introduction

A giant Russian sugar company had taken control of most of the six thousand hectares of farmland in a village where I had started fieldwork in 2013. From Moscow's "Shaninka,"[1] I called a friend living in the village to inquire about the event. He replied rather indifferently, "There's nothing new, nothing has changed, it's always the same here." This certainly was not the kind of answer I had expected, entering my second year of fieldwork at that time, tracing large investment projects across several Russian regions. Didn't the story sound like a massive land grab? Puzzled, I drove to the village.

What I encountered did indeed turn out to be surprisingly nondramatic, as the land deal has had little obvious immediate impact on the village or the lives of its inhabitants. There were no fences or other big infrastructure. The company, like many others at that time, had taken over land previously worked by other large farming enterprises, in often troubled economic conditions, rather than by smallholders. As Russian agriculture had been industrialized decades before, in Soviet times, it was not recent land deals that had displaced peasant farmers. Most of the village's farmland was located several kilometers away, accessed by dirt roads, partly across a highway. The portion of villagers employed in industrial agriculture had shrunk constantly since the 1990s, and subsistence or family farmers cultivated land that remained unaffected by the land deal.

By acquiring this huge land bank, the sugar company had not taken over something that would have been very close and dear to most villagers at that point in history. Rather, it had added a chapter to a longer story of reconfigurations and disconnections that had shaped the village over the past decades. I found traces of disconnections both in people's narratives and in village landscapes, where one could wander for hours around abandoned fields, stables, and other remains of former production and dwelling. Many villagers offered clearer and more lively accounts of the piecemeal demise of "their" former Soviet collective enterprises than of the more recent acquisition of enterprises and land from which they had already become alienated. And they described the apparent "land grab" as a continuation of deprivation, hardships, and uncertainty rather than as a novel event.

The concept of dispersed dispossession aims to illuminate such situations, which I found common yet often perplexing. It captures and relates five characteristics of a specific kind of dispossession. First, it captures the deterioration of state- or community-mediated collective goods, support systems, material infrastructures, social contracts, and the separation of further webs of relations constitutive for well-being and agency. Second, rather than through direct seizure, it works through the fundamentally unequal capacities to keep hold of resources, to navigate disintegration and to repurpose, revalue, and appropriate devaluated and degraded goods. Third, it captures drawn-out processes of dispossession in which preexisting harms and injustices accumulated over historical periods and political-economic systems are perpetuated and exploited. Fourth, dispersed dispossession shapes the horizon of conceivable alternatives and plausible promises. Finally, it comes with profound implications for the conditions and conceptualization of resistance and agency.

This book, and the idea of dispersed dispossession, build on a study of rural change in Russia within a specific period, the 2010s. I demonstrate how attention to dispersed dispossession is necessary to understand rural deprivation in this context, and how the context offers special opportunities for studying and thinking through related forms of dispossession. Yet dispersed dispossession is not unique or limited to Russia, nor is it the only form of dispossession one can encounter there. The concept supplements established conceptualizations and helps to grasp forms of dispossession that may otherwise elude our attention, in Russia and elsewhere.

Dispersed dispossession also offers opportunities for reflecting on the conceptual and political implications of the various ways of conceptualizing dispossession more broadly. The notion of dispossession is inherently critical. By calling something dispossession, you already criticize it. More fundamentally, critique constitutes dispossession. The language of dispossession translates what could otherwise be understood as bad fate or tragedy into a problem that necessarily relates to questions of (in)justice, power, and profit. Different concepts of dispossession involve different forms of critique. We may hence ask: How do specific concepts of dispossession emphasize certain processes with unjust effects but detract from others? Which dimensions of dispossession does a certain kind of critique problematize, and what is left out of the picture? This book offers answers to such questions in the context of rural change in Russia, but it also looks beyond. It reflects on forms of dispossession that may be rooted in state socialism and in its demise, in the successes and failures of the capitalist reforms that followed, and in the successes and failures of agricultural investment projects. Dispersed dispossession aims to make sense of complex and often ambivalent empirical realities, identifying patterns and contextualizing them in history and political economy, more than offering functional explanations of dispossession as an effect or integral part of the workings of one systemic cause alone.

This study combines extensive fieldwork with a sensitivity to complex histories and temporalities to better understand changing and disrupted "landscapes" (biophysical, economic, political, and social),[2] how actors navigate them, and how rapid and massive accumulation of agricultural assets occurs in parallel to the slower and often more complex processes of rural deterioration and persistence. It investigates the interactions, intersections, and relationships between different groups of actors—rural dwellers and large agricultural companies, company representatives and village administrations, workers and managers, managers and government representatives, local administrations and rural dwellers, large enterprises and family farmers. It is, in this sense, also a study of situated relationships between rural residents and state and economic actors, based on a total of ten months of fieldwork between 2012 and 2021, and in five Russian regions between Moscow, the Southern Steppes of Rostov Oblast, and the Urals in the east. It focuses on the concrete places where the connections that constitute rural worlds wither, are forged, and (re)negotiated.

In the following chapters, we will encounter familiar figures such as the ruling party, economically invested politicians, and politically involved businesspersons in less familiar settings: not in Moscow or other centers of power, but in mostly rural places across several regions. These situated insights, together with historical and political-economic contextualization and context-sensitive conceptualization, will provide insights on configurations and processes that often do not fit grand narratives of post-Soviet path-dependence or the (neoliberal) market economy. Yet I shall begin with some popular, spectacular, and partly problematic representations of the Russian countryside and agriculture to illustrate some tensions this study engages with and to introduce a discursive landscape that the following chapters aim to deconstruct.

Slow Crisis, Big Promises

"Agriculture has been the most troublesome sector of the Russian economy for as long as one can remember," write Ioffe, Nefedova, and Zaslavsky (2006, 44), echoing an opinion widely held even in the 2010s. "We are number one," claims Vladimir Putin in sharp contrast, commenting on Russian wheat exports in 2017.[3] The history of Russian agriculture is not short of dramatic episodes and has often been described in superlatives.

Russia's arable land is among the largest in the world. Agrarian lands have been repeatedly expanded far into northern forests and southeastern steppes, most famously during the so-called Virgin Lands campaign, which followed Nikita Khrushchev's 1953 plan to boost Soviet agrarian production by plowing up large areas of the Russian and Kazakh steppes. The Soviet countryside has witnessed some of the arguably most radical and large-scale agrarian reforms in world history—the collectivization under Stalin and later privatization encompassing millions of rural dwellers, thousands of large farms, and millions of hectares of land. Cropland abandonment that followed the disintegration of the Soviet agrarian system has been described as the most abrupt and widespread land-use change of the twentieth century in the northern hemisphere (Kurganova et al. 2014), and it is still seen by many as a symbol of a deep-rooted agrarian crisis.

In media, public, and policy discourses within the country and the West, the Russian countryside is often represented as a site of contradictions: spectacular despair and foreclosed future, but also and increasingly as a site of spectacular agricultural and economic potential. The first narrative describes a "mass exodus," "orphaned villages" (Strelnikova 2011), and "ghost villages" (Shapovalova 2011), as sites of "slow death" and without "much hope left for revival" (Nemtsova 2015). Images of social, political, and economic stagnation stand alongside more dramatic ones that describe a "struggle for survival" (Schepp 2010). For some, "the lifeblood of Russia's vast and fertile countryside appears to be draining away forever" (Shapovalova 2011). Such quotes echo a broader discourse on the Russian countryside as a place of hardship, poverty, alcoholism, and apathy that everyone who can, chooses to leave. Such representations tend to stereotype, blame, or victimize rural dwellers and places. But they also point to very real hardships, crises, and structural disadvantages. Up to 50 percent of rural households are estimated to have been around or below the official subsistence minimum in the 1990s, the decade after the Soviet Union's collapse, and a "ruralization of poverty" (Gerry, Nivorozhkin, and Rigg 2008) continued into the following decades (chapter 3).

The Yeltsin government in the 1990s was infamous for agricultural pessimism. Some of its representatives, including Yegor Gaidar and former minister of finance Alexei Kudrin, even described the post-Soviet agricultural sector as a "black hole" that will never become effective and will swallow all resources that governments or businesses invest (Wegren 2014, 84). In 2009, in contrast, President Dmitri Medvedev published a guest column in the German *Sueddeutsche Zeitung* that—against the backdrop of the food price crisis of that time—used Russia's record yields in 2008 to underline the country's unique agricultural potential: "Russia is number one concerning its farmland's area and quality," wrote Medvedev. He supported his claim with the fact that the International Bureau of Weights and Measures in Paris stores Russian Black Soil as a standard for soil structure and fertility (Medvedev 2009). In Medvedev's narrative, Russia's future agricultural potential is huge because—in contrast to most other countries—cropped areas can still be expanded and outputs enhanced. Here, the yet unused agricultural potential is described as a potential rather than a deficit.

Reclaiming Russia's place among the world's leading agricultural producers, and redefining domestic agriculture as a strategic priority, became a prominent narrative of that time. In January 2010, Medvedev signed a food security doctrine[4] that promised to "ensure food security as the essential component of the national security, predict and prevent emerging threats and risks to the country's economy, improve its stability, create conditions for a dynamic development of agri-industrial and fishery complexes and improvement of the population's welfare" (USDA Foreign Agricultural Service 2010, Article 26, p. 11). Vladimir Putin later declared that Russian agriculture had ceased to be a "black hole" and had become one of the "locomotives" for the development of the country (Moskvin 2012) and "one of the flagships of our economy," "developing actively and dynamically" (TASS 2021).

Increased business interest in the agrarian sector dates from the early 2000s. When legal restrictions on the land market were lifted in 2002, companies became aware of the country's low land prices and diagnosed yield gaps that investments could close. When from 2007 crop failure and global demand for food, fodder, and biofuel drove up market prices, domestic as well as international businesses began to sense "an investors' nirvana" (Lucas 2013). Some started ambitious business ventures, with one Western company priding itself on working a land bank not only twice the size of Hong Kong but also "endowed with some of the most fertile soils in the world" (BEF 2015). At the time, however, a Swedish business newspaper mocked the company that had "ploughed" millions of dollars "in the Russian soil" (cited in Lander and Kuns

2021, 22), and two years later, with massive losses on its books, it was sold to a Russian company. Other investors, too, spectacularly failed to deliver on promised targets. Indeed, only one of the four companies included in the initial sample for this study in 2012 still existed by the end of 2015—and they had been indebted and loss-making before—which echoes a more general tendency of that time in Russia (Luyt, Santos, and Carita 2013; Visser, Spoor, and Mamonova 2014). Some of these "disappearing" companies had controlled land banks larger than the territory of Luxembourg, which is home to more than half a million people. This reminds us that we should not simply equate size with power and stability. And yet the concentration of control over farmland and other agricultural assets continued. In 2020, more than sixty companies were reported to control land banks of more than one hundred thousand hectares each, with six of them controlling more than half a million hectares (BEFL 2020).

Since the 2010s, journalists and analysts within the country and the West have increasingly contemplated whether Russia may be "the emerging global 'breadbasket'" (Visser, Spoor, and Mamonova 2014) and the implications of a (re)emergent agricultural powerhouse or agro-superpower (Zhou 2022). Such aspirations have been evident in official statements emphasizing Russian agriculture's geoeconomic and political significance. For example, the Kremlin website quotes Putin saying that "we will need to conquer (*zavoëvyvat'*) foreign markets, and why not—with so much land, and such colossal arable land that can still yet increase. In this sense, we are the richest country—not in terms of oil and gas, but in terms of the possibilities for agriculture. And the need for food in the world will only grow" (Kremlin 2015). The issue acquired new meaning and urgency after Russia's full-scale invasion of Ukraine when, amid fears of rising food prices and food shortages around the globe, the volume of both countries' wheat exports became evident to a wider public.

Global heating, too, has increased speculation about Russia's potential agrarian superpower status. Assessments of the climate crisis have become less denialist and more nuanced among people in power in Moscow, and its projected devastating consequences have become somewhat more frequently and openly addressed (Conley and Newlin 2021).[5] Yet the prospect of agricultural frontiers being pushed north (Hannah et al. 2020), and related farmland gains in the midterm, foster expectations of relative future advantage on global grain markets. In an article titled "How Russia Wins the Climate Crisis," the *New York Times Magazine* echoed such expectations, noting that, as the "planet continues to warm, vast new stretches of Russia will become suitable for agriculture" (Lustgarten 2020). The effects of global heating in Russia are predicted to be mostly catastrophic, as in other parts of the world. Therefore, depicting it as a winner in absolute terms is misguided. But relative strategic advantages may well be expected. Persistent decline, pervasive abandonment, staggering potential and accumulation, strategic importance: representations of the Russian countryside are full of tensions, many of which this study attempts to unpack.

The Conundrum of Rural Dispossession

The concurrence of poverty and despair and stunning economic potential is not contradictory in principle, of course, but it may be just another instance of profiting from others' misery.[6] However, there is a tension between mundane forms of rural deprivation and episodes of spectacular degradation, huge land deals, or exaggerated development and business promises that can be problematic. Many rural communities around the globe repeatedly experience deprivation and dispossession. To date, the global poor are predominantly rural and mostly employed in the agricultural sector (World Bank 2016). Already disadvantaged rural populations are often particularly vulnerable to existential risks, dispossession, and exclusion (Dudley 2000; Gidwani 2008; Li 2014a; Watts [1983] 2013). Rural poverty and deprivation tend to be normalized, historically and into the present. They gain broader public attention mostly when culminating in disturbing images and episodes: like when farmer suicides rise sharply and come to symbolize prevalent conditions of rural poverty, indebtedness, and desperation, such as in India in recent years. Or when rural communities and organizations address deprivations publicly through protest and direct action, such as the popular Movimento dos Trabalhadores Rurais Sem Terra (MST) in Brazil. Or when reports about "land grabs" in countries of the Global South create powerful images of unjust seizure.

Making dispossession visible by turning it into a spectacle comes with analytical pitfalls, however. It may misrepresent rural populations one-dimensionally as either victims or heroic resistance fighters (Levien 2018). It may also focus too strongly on dramatic figures and images at the expense of sound evidence and analytical depth (Oya 2013). The quieter, more uneventful, and unspectacular forms of dispossession, by contrast, often remain invisible or are dismissed as less relevant than their "more attention-grabbing counterparts" (Stoler 2013, 5), such as land grabs that the media and policymakers but also social movements tend to focus on (Li 2014a; Vorbrugg 2022). Among other things, this lack of attention has to do with conceptual language. Although dispossession is one of the most important topics in critical agrarian studies, it is, maybe surprisingly, rarely defined as a concept in this literature (D. Hall 2021; Levien 2018).

The land grab trope, particularly popular in public, activist, and academic discourses in the early 2010s, is a well-known and much-discussed example of how rural dispossession may be presented as straightforward. Temporally and causally, dispossession here follows from the appropriation of farmland by powerful states or private investors, to the extent that rural dispossession and the land grab may appear synonymous. A narrow focus on dramatic episodes of land takeovers, especially during the early land-grab debate, has been variously criticized[7] and the debate has moved on. Yet the limitations inherent in the idea of the land grab can help illustrate the need for multidimensional concepts of rural dispossession.

For rural dwellers in Russia who are at the center of this study, land's usefulness and worth are contingent on bundles of relations and other resources that allow them to benefit from land access. Furthermore, while fundamental for some, and in some respects, land is only one among a variety of resources that support rural livelihoods. Hence land access alone is not a sufficient condition for securing rural livelihoods, and it is not always a necessary one (Dudley 2000; Li 2014a; Oliveira, B. M. McKay, and Liu 2020; Ribot and Peluso 2003). As land relations are complex, so are the processes of their breakdown and alienation, ranging from straightforward theft to the withering of opportunities to benefit from land access (Bluwstein et al. 2018; D. Hall, Hirsch, and Li 2011). This does not mean that land relations are irrelevant. But close attention is required to understand how land matters, in different ways, and to whom. Land's role in dispossession, then, should be seen as a question to investigate more than a given, and as one element within broader bundles of relations and resources (Ribot and Peluso 2003). This study thus contributes to a growing literature on rural change and dispossession in relation to complex, socially and geographically diverse, and historically contingent land relations.[8]

Concepts help us to grasp the nonobvious. For rural dispossession in Russia, one task is to address processes that are more mundane and, at the same time, systemic, than the dramatic episodes emphasized in popular discourses on the Russian countryside. This includes turning attention to forms of dispossession that often go unnoticed, whether by broader critical international audiences as they do not fit the more established framings of dispossession such as land grabbing, (post)colonial seizure, or neoliberal privatization; or because they are rarely met by organized and visible protests on the ground, or addressed by NGOs, international activist networks, and journalists. Understanding such forms of dispossession can be challenging if they unfold through complex historical temporalities and the reconfiguration of complex sets of relations. Yet the forms of dispossession addressed in this book are not invisible or marginal. Rather than bringing to light hidden realities, this study proposes ways of dealing with some of the analytical, representational, and political challenges of addressing, contextualizing, and criticizing well-documented forms of crisis and deprivation.

Rural Change

The 2010s, covered in this study, were a crucial period of rural and agrarian change in Russia in various respects. This was a period of continued agricultural reform and the consolidation of landownership and land markets. Large agricultural companies gained prominence in this period, including foreign investors and joint ventures. Government policies and programs often favored large producers that have further advantages in accessing credit and investing in new production technologies. Still, bankruptcies and sales of even large enterprises and companies remained common, and almost all foreign investors had quit Russian agriculture by the end of the decade. The adaptation of new farming technologies and large producers' pushes toward increased efficiency led to the continued decrease in demand for manual labor in agriculture. Some regional and local disparities kept growing during the period. While some regions experienced improved living standards due to government support schemes, increased productivity, or the diversification of rural economies, others experienced rural depopulation, the deterioration of social and material infrastructure, and a continuing lack of opportunities. State programs addressing rural unemployment, poverty, and infrastructural issues were consolidated in the 2010s with varying success, but, together with stabilization and even modest increases of wages and pensions, they had a significant impact on overall rural living conditions. At a national scale, Russia boosted agricultural production and exports, and from 2016 onward it regularly topped the list of the world's largest wheat exporters. In 2014, Russia imposed an embargo on agricultural imports from the United States, the European Union, and some other countries in retaliation for sanctions that these entities had imposed on Russia after its annexation of Crimea. This embargo further spurred the domestic production of certain agricultural products (Wengle 2016).

While this study is set in the 2010s, understanding the broader historical trajectory of these changes is important in grasping the specificities of rural landscapes and the agrarian economy in Russia more broadly. Large-scale industrialized agriculture was introduced to Russia, and many other state-socialist countries, with the establishment of collective and state farms (*kolkhozes* and *sovkhozes*) in the early Soviet period (chapter 3). The so-called collectivization and industrialization of agriculture implied a radical redesign of the countryside. New settlements, schools and cultural centers, roads and railroads, silos, machinery bases, irrigation systems and other infrastructure, multistory buildings, and large fields were created to realize a collectivized agrarian way of living and industrial mode of production (Josephson et al. 2013; Scott 1998).

The post-Soviet agrarian and land reforms, too, were an immense and, in some respects, unique socioeconomic experiment that aimed to reconfigure not only land access and ownership but also the established mode of agricultural production and rural way of living. Agriculture was to be modernized but also scaled down and decollectivized, and Soviet-style large industrial farms were to be replaced with private farms or farming cooperatives. In Russia and other former state-socialist countries, market reformers in the 1990s wanted to see large state-run farming enterprises, seen as notoriously inefficient and representatives of a failed agricultural system, replaced by Western-type private family farms (Rylko and Jolly 2005; World Bank 1992).[9] To this end, the state distributed entitlements (*pai*) to farmland and other assets among workers in the early 1990s. Document holders were entitled to a share of farmland of a certain size (e.g., four hectares) within a large farm's landbank, but the location of such a share would be unspecified. Relatively burdensome procedures were required to turn land entitlements into ownership of a specific piece of land, and many shareholders abstained from it.

However, this post-Soviet land and agrarian reform has been described as incomplete (Shagaida 2010; Volkov, Khlystun, and Fomin 2021; Wegren 2009). Family farming remained relatively marginal. More than policies and reform plans, the 1990s were shaped by a deep agrarian crisis, with Russia's "commercial agriculture being downsized in a way and at a rate that have no precedent in Russia's history" (Ioffe 2005, 200). Plummeting production, bankruptcies of enterprises, mass layoffs of workers, crumbling production infrastructures, abandonment of villages that had been built around single main enterprises, and widespread poverty were among the results. In many of these respects, the crisis resembled one in postindustrial settings more than peasant or smallholder agriculture (Hann 2003). But it also implied a "simplification" (Pichler, Schmid, and Gingrich 2022) of land use and economic activity that one may rather associate with industrialization: while most Soviet farming enterprise harvested a range of crops, kept livestock, processed some of their products on the farm, and further provided social and cultural services (chapter 2), rural residents often criticize their successors for concentrating production and

cutting many of these functions. Even though Russian agriculture began to recover from the direst phase of this crisis by the turn of the century, there remained a sense in the 2010s among many rural residents that the crisis had become permanent as poverty, precarity, and exposure to various risks became
an intrinsic part of rural life and the agrarian economy.

While the post-Soviet land reform has been associated with dispossession
(Allina-Pisano 2008), it is not a typical example of landed dispossession as rural dwellers were, formally, *granted* individual land rights (Wegren 2009).[10]
More than two decades later, land documents play a highly ambivalent role
for rural residents in Russia. This may seem surprising, given the importance
that both liberal (Soto 2001) and critical (Benjaminsen et al. 2009; Peluso and
C. Lund 2011; Pichler 2015) scholars in general ascribe to land rights in securing smallholders' land tenure or, conversely, depriving them of informal
land access. In interviews conducted for this study, however, rural dwellers explained how they hardly cared about land documents, which they may have
forgotten, lost, never claimed, or sold for some derisory amount (chapter 3).
Paper entitlements can even become a negative asset for rural dwellers, as they
can be taxed for land they do not use or fined for not using and thereby "de-
grading" farmland.

One reason is that an entitlement does not guarantee access to land or the
ability to derive benefits from it (Ribot and Peluso 2003). In some instances,
unfavorable regulations, bureaucrats, and local elites prevented rural residents
from exchanging their land entitlement for an actual piece of land (chapter 2).
Furthermore, in Russia as in other postsocialist countries, landed property often turned out to be an unattractive prospect for individual households for
economic reasons (Allina-Pisano 2008; Hann 2003, 2011). Lacking access to
machinery, credit, securities, lucrative markets, legal and technical expertise,
and facing complications in access to actual land, comparatively few individuals and households were ready, able, or willing to start small private farming
enterprises.

A second reason is that rural residents in this study use private plots around
their houses for household production rather than the large formerly collective
fields to which abovementioned entitlements apply. This means that subsistence farming was not directly affected by large land deals. Private household
plots, already established during the Soviet period, are usually close to homes,
relatively small, and suited for (semi)manual family agriculture. In contrast,
fields and production infrastructures related to the former state and collective farms have been designed for large-scale agriculture, which came to pose
hurdles for post-Soviet landholders lacking the machinery and further means

to operate at such a scale. In their capacity as smallholders, rural residents were alienated from much of the land surrounding them due to a large-scale landscape design and mode of production. They could continue to use such land if they stayed with large farming enterprises, and this is what often happened, at least for some time.

From the early years of agricultural reform, the dispersion and concentration of agricultural assets went in parallel. After the turn of the century, state legislatures and subsidies shifted back to benefiting large agricultural enterprises (Uzun, Shagaida, and Sarajkin 2012). Many small private farms disappeared a few years after they had been established (Wegren 2011). What emerged, rather than a family farming sector, was a dual agrarian structure (Spoor 2012) in which large agricultural enterprises and wage laborers do most commercial agricultural production while many rural households are engaged in subsidiary farming on plots around their houses (usually less than one hectare in size) to supplement their food supply. As the two forms of production remain closely entangled (Pallot and Nefedova 2007), many rural dwellers continue to depend on large farming enterprises not only for jobs but also for various technical or material support to maintain households and household production. In effect, large-scale agriculture remained prevalent in commercial farming. The accumulation of land and other agricultural assets by powerful businesses was relatively opaque and remains incomplete, with stark regional differences (Wegren, Nikulin, and Trotsuk 2023). While powerful companies and more successful private farmers have long consolidated control over most land in agriculturally favorable regions such as the Southern Steppes and Central Black Earth, less favorable regions experienced a much weaker or delayed increase of interest in agriculture, and dozens of millions of hectares of agricultural land remain abandoned in other parts of the country (Prishchepov et al. 2013).

Rural dwellers rarely see subsistence farming as endangered by agro-companies, which are not in direct competition with them for the same land or markets, and they do not always reject land deals and big investors (Visser et al. 2015). They do care, however, if there are jobs, schools, medical centers, and functioning social and institutional networks available in their village and whether a village is a place that allows them to live or start something new. Large agrarian enterprises play ambivalent roles in this regard. To different extents, they provide services that support individual villagers and communities: sending workers and tractors to clean the roads during winter; maintaining housing, water, and electricity infrastructures; and providing special support for pensioners who make up a large part of many villages' populations. Workers and villagers may borrow money from enterprises for weddings, funerals, or to cover medical costs (chapter 5).

Industrial agriculture also remains dominant in how rural inhabitants envision a good life. I have not met a single rural dweller who would have described living on private subsidiary agriculture alone as an acceptable, let alone desirable, option: It provides very little income, relies on much manual family labor, and often—far from peasant autonomy—goes along with unfavorable dependencies on large agricultural enterprises and middlemen for access to machinery and markets. It does not provide an escape from poverty. Thus, being thrown back into household production is often experienced as regression (Kalugina 2014, 118) while large-scale industrial agriculture is associated, by many, with modernization and progress (Smith 2014; Wengle 2022) and with being part of a working collective and the national economy. Such tendencies do not mean that land was irrelevant or that there were no alternatives to large industrial agriculture in the Russian countryside. Various forms of rural subsistence and smallholder farming practices exist, and some of them present themselves as such alternatives (Nikulin and Trotsuk 2016; Visser et al. 2015). However, thus far, they provide necessary subsistence or entrepreneurial niches for some rather than alternatives at a systemic level.

This study focuses on the deterioration of relational, collective, and institutionalized goods that is at the center of many rural dwellers' criticisms. Many criticize the devaluation of agricultural assets and labor; farm enterprises' recurrent bankruptcies and dismissal of workers; the loss of various forms of social, technological, and monetary support formerly provided by large-scale enterprises and the state; and the deterioration of various infrastructure and local institutions. Although established concepts of dispossession seem rather ill-suited to address many of these prevalent forms of deprivation in the Russian countryside, there are hardly any alternative concepts to make sense of the processes described here. *Dispersed Dispossession* attempts exactly this.

The book is concerned with the disintegration of valuable and supportive relations at various scales. Some of these transformations relate directly or indirectly to the demise of state socialism. I do not intend to propose any general concept of "postsocialist" dispossession here, however. Not only would this go beyond the scope of this study, it would also risk romanticizing state socialism, essentializing the postsocialist condition (Kangas and Salmenniemi 2016; M. Müller 2019), and sidelining how dispossession was and remains unequally distributed across these spaces. For instance, the historic suffering and the death toll caused by Stalinist agricultural policies for people in Ukraine and certain Soviet minorities was not only more severe but qualitatively different from that for most rural dwellers in the Russian Soviet Federative Socialist Republic (RSFSR) (Snyder 2012; see also chapter 2). Unequally distributed, too, were the benefits and losses during the postsocialist and all ensuing transitions. Yet, as I will detail in the conclusion, there remains a need to acknowledge, conceptualize, and work through forms of dispossession related to the postsocialist "condition" (Buck-Morss 2006), as well as an opportunity to pin down forms of dispossession that are particularly clear in such contexts but may not be unique to them.

As another potential pitfall, a focus on dispossession may emphasize losses over emerging possibilities, deterioration over improvement, and an orientation to the past more than the future. Hence, it could reproduce biases in academic and popular representations of the region in general and its countryside in particular, or economic determinism in studies of the region. This study is written with the aim to avoid such kinds of determinism while focusing on dispersed dispossession, to which I turn now, as one dimension of more complex political economic and lived realities.

Dispersal

Given the size of the companies, the pace of accumulation, and a massive concentration of agricultural assets in Russian agriculture today, the idea of dispersed dispossession may seem counterintuitive. Dispersion suggests diffusion rather than massive concentration, creeping rather than eventful transformation, and elusiveness rather than clear shifts. This tension, however, is essential for the argument put forward here and helpful to get to the subtler but also more systemic patterns of dispossession at the center of this study. To speak of dispersed dispossession is not to deny the magnitude of accumulation processes or the fact that some get rich while others become or remain poor. However, it refrains from taking the relation between these processes for granted and shows that a close analysis of dispossession may well open space for new questions and shed light on less-expected drivers and stakes and different temporalities.[11]

One finds frequent though semiconceptual uses of the notion "dispersed" in various recent social-scientific studies[12] that are often used to indicate conceptual and methodological challenges associated with a certain phenomena's relative elusiveness, apparent randomness, or dispersion across time and space. This book aims to develop dispersed dispossession as a concept rather than a metaphor, but it also works with the notion's imagery character. The Online Cambridge Dictionary defines the verb "disperse" as "to scatter or move away over a large area, or to cause this to happen." Dispersed dispossession speaks to scattering and disintegration.

In this sense, "dispersal" also reverberates with terms that are used as concepts in studies in postsocialist settings and relate to themes often voiced by inhabitants of the Russian countryside: disintegration, deterioration, discontinuity, decline, devaluation, deindustrialization, deeconomization, demodernization, decollectivization, depopulation, disorientation, or disenchantment.[13] In Russian, there is a comparable cluster of terms, many of them with the prefixes *ras/raz*, indicating the undoing, taking or falling apart of things, a lack, a rupture, or regression.[14] Thinking of them as a family of related terms is useful as it allows a clustering of related everyday and academic concepts—which we will encounter through the chapters—around a common theme to open new perspectives on the problem of dispersed dispossession.

Recursive Crises, Foreclosed Futures: The Temporalities of Dispersed Dispossession

Conditions for the types of accumulation and dispossession addressed in this study were shaped by context-specific crises that span the Soviet phase, the reform period, and contemporary hybrid or authoritarian state capitalism.[15] They led, among other things, to a massive devaluation and multiscale disintegration of agriculture that were not a mere function of capitalist accumulation but provided a basis for it. Crises and failures are not uncommon to this economic sector elsewhere. As Susanne Wengle (2022, 7) puts it, failures "are important elements of agricultural histories, and the list of vulnerabilities of industrial agriculture, in Russia as elsewhere, is long and growing." In this study, we encounter such failures at different scales, from technological disruptions to systemic crises, which are remarkably common subjects in rural dwellers' accounts. In our conversations, rural residents recalled poverty and mismanagement during Soviet times. They recalled how, in the early years of market reforms, new enterprises were unable to take off and old ones unable to carry on, pay wages, and continue production. They have seen the successive failures associated with state socialism and market reforms, each of them promising to undo the evils of the previous system. Politicians and investment companies often promise to fix the effects of past crises in one way or another, and they mostly fail to live up to any of these promises.

Such a sense of repeated and related crises is confirmed by analyses of the agrarian political economy. Under its relatively stable surface, the late Soviet agricultural system was strongly dependent on state budgets, which, in turn, strongly depended on revenues from oil and gas exports and thus were vulnerable to global market volatilities and further factors even before market reforms (Nefedova 2014, 76). When market reformers stressed that the Soviet agricultural system was far from sustainable—economically, politically, and environmentally—they extended a diagnosis and reform agenda that began under Soviet governments in the 1980s (Lindner 2007). However, reforms could not solve many of the problems and contradictions built into the system, and they created new ones. The Soviet agrarian system was based on logics of abundance, expansion, extraction, and intensification and resulted in massive ecological deterioration and waste of resources (Josephson et al. 2013; Wengle 2022). Market reforms provided little means to clean up the mess created in Soviet times or alternatives for workers who became "superfluous" as enterprises closed or were reorganized according to principles of efficiency. Decollectivization, too, has been an official reform goal that many still associate with crisis and dispossession: it involved material losses and was a process that eroded the very potential for collective agency. Decollectivization was meant to undo Soviet collectivization, which was, of course, a historic process that constituted another, more blatant form of dispossession. If we understand dispossession as unfolding in repeated spirals, it may seem ironic, but not necessarily surprising, that both collectivization and decollectivization can be described in terms of state-imposed, historic dispossession.

In emphasizing the interlocking of crises, alienation, and dispossession across historic periods, the idea of dispersed dispossession does not presuppose "integrity"—wholeness, intactness, authenticity, stability—as a reference base. Dispossession cannot always be attributed to one specific political system or period. Rather than identifying either state socialism or neoliberal capitalism as solely responsible for dispossession, the question to be investigated then becomes how it is rooted in and perpetuated through the succession of programs, regimes, and crises that caused a "multiplicity of destructions" (Gordillo 2014, 19) and created a condition in which dispossession is immanent. This has important implications for rural relations in former socialist contexts, while similar arguments have been made for (settler) colonial and other contexts as well (Bluwstein et al. 2018; León 2023; Mollett 2016; Nichols 2020; Watts [1983] 2013).

It is ironic that reforms that had promised agrarian, rural, and overall economic development were and often remain perceived as leading to regression and demodernization on the ground. This seeming contradiction is no coincidence, however. The disintegration of the old system was among the reform's intended aims, and many reformers presented it as a necessary brief phase of creative destruction that would be followed by new growth and prosperity. That's why critics labeled the reforms "shock therapy."[16] But against the idea of a brief, painful but salutary intervention, many rural dwellers today still emphasize the experience of a persistent shock over that of therapy. According to their accounts, the "therapy" led to dismantling more than maintaining or (re)building and did not fill many of the gaps it had created. Disintegration, and with it the "interstices of the old world and the new" (Dzenovska 2020, 23), turned out to be much more persistent than reformers had promised, and many expressed a sense that an old world had vanished and a promised new one failed to come about.[17] The idea of dispersed dispossession implies that this is more than a mere sentiment, shedding light on how certain futures were and remained foreclosed to certain people. This does not imply historic determinism, however, as some not only found ways to cope with difficult situations but also to open future pathways that would have been impossible in earlier years or decades.

Lived Realities of Disintegration: Disorientation, Disconnection, and Disenchantment

If we imagine dispossession as a drama, the idea of dispersion impacts the entire scene—its duration, subject matter, roles, and context. If dispossession results from recurrent crises more than from single actions and events, this has consequences for the figure of "the dispossessed," too. If the category should apply to all who live and act under these conditions, this would include large parts of entire generations. However, as the forms of and degrees to which people are affected depend on subject positions, such generic use of the category would make little sense. It is not necessary either. A focus on the mechanisms and effects of dispossession allows for acknowledging dispossession as a historic, and in this respect collective, experience without categorizing persons. Hence, and in contrast to some earlier work on post-Soviet dispossession (Humphrey 1996; Rigi 2003), I deliberately abstain from using the category of "the dispossessed."[18] Subjects are always more than merely dispossessed. Further, we also should be able to address dispossession even in instances in which it is difficult to identify the dispossessor, or a "villain to blame" (Li 2014a, 16). Dispersed dispossession does not always have a clear subject–object relation or manifest in clear dispossessive actions.[19] Rather than focusing on isolated goods that can be held in private property, it is about collective goods, infrastructures, and further relations that support and sustain social and economic life, the upkeep of village and household economies.

Dispersion evokes the image of a cloudy liquid or fog. This resonates with the persistent difficulties, described by many research participants, in navigating what appears to them as uncertain circumstances, recurrent and unpredictable changes, and unclear options. Rather than being deprived of one specific thing, many describe their situation as a mess with no identifiable way out (Li 2014a). The chapters detail various causes of this situation: a deep and enduring agrarian crisis; the piecemeal erosion of government and local support structures; reforms that have not filled the gaps created by the disintegration of the Soviet agrarian system; inaccessible or unpredictable agricultural markets; and laws and bureaucracies that aren't working in rural dwellers' interest. During the "dispersion of the people" (Marx [1867] 2015, 516) in which many have left the countryside or attempted to do so, those who stay are often faced with being stranded in a place without a future, where particularly older generations have long struggled with the sense of being left behind. In this and other senses, spatial fragmentation in the countryside has become part of an unsettling collective experience (Ioffe, Nefedova, and Zaslavsky 2004).

These conditions formed over drawn-out periods and sometimes in spirals, which makes it harder, even for those who live through them, to make sense of them. Also, these experiences are what people were often left with when development promises did not materialize, so the sense of being caught in a place without a future implies disenchantment. This does not mean, of course, that dispersed dispossession took away all of people's agency and vision, but it has impacted the conditions for developing agency and vision. In a fog, it can be hard to imagine the world beyond one's limited vision, or one may be distracted by false images of what lies beyond the fog.[20] Forces that curtail agency in such a way can be the unintended side effects of historical processes but also opacity and occlusion built into institutionalized processes and intentional obfuscation. Dispersion, or a fog, can benefit the interests of those better able to navigate it themselves or exploit others' disorientation, so there can be incentives to create or at least not dissolve it. Dispossession that unfolds under such conditions is not of the kind that would be obvious to "the dispossessed" or the analysts (Vorbrugg 2022), which is partly why dispersed dispossession requires a distinct conceptual vocabulary.

Dispossession, Appropriation, Agency

The concept of dispersed dispossession aims to extend understandings of dispossession to include aspects of dispersal. Questions may arise at that point: Taking seriously the described qualities of dispersal, is dispossession still the right concept to use? Why should we speak of dispossession if it is not necessarily the intended result of action or a function of capital accumulation? Also, isn't one political and analytical strength of dispossession as a concept how it allows for the clear and explicit calling out of instances of illegitimate theft? If this is the case, does the idea of dispersal water down this critical edge?

One may argue that such tensions could be avoided by simply using a different term such as deprivation, alienation, or abandonment. While I do use these terms in this study, I stick to dispossession as the overarching concept for several reasons. In Marxist and other critical analytical traditions, dispossession is conceptualized in ways that imply relating, dialectically or otherwise, the losses of some to the gains of others, deprivation and theft being linked with appropriation and accumulation. Dispersed dispossession also assumes that dispossession is best understood in *relation* to state coercion and capitalist appropriation on the one hand and the agency of the deprived on the other. As this book deals, inter alia, with the effects of a historic redistribution of wealth and control, goods and "bads" at a massive scale, such a relational perspective helps develop a critical understanding of the historical moment. Interpreting these processes of systemic change as implying dispossession is to insist that the deprivation of many is not simply an inevitable side effect of necessary reforms, but that it is bound to concrete decisions, policies, actions, nonactions, or willful withdrawal. It also means investigating the concrete relationship between gains for some and losses for others—and, indeed, investigating this relationship is even more necessary if it does not take the form of straightforward and obvious theft. It means insisting on asking questions about drivers and responsibility behind those forms of abandonment and neglect that do not immediately serve anyone's profit. To speak of dispossession in situations often interpreted as a historic tragedy means to insist that things could be and become otherwise and to hold those who shape them accountable. It also means insisting that deprivation is not simply a normal continuation of structural disadvantage that has been characteristic of rural life in Russia over most of the past centuries, but that it has been driven by dynamic forces of dispossession.

Given the variety of conceptualizations of dispossession and even more semiconceptual uses of the term, speaking of dispossession does not in itself provide conceptual clarity. This flexibility can be a strength, however, when it allows concepts to be adapted to the historic and geographic context. Following Robert Nichols (2020, 5), "As with most useful terms of political articulation, the concept of dispossession can be mobilized in a variety of manners, for diverse and competing purposes. Its appeal and utility resides precisely with its protean quality."

Appropriation

Historically and throughout the present, dispersed dispossession goes along with appropriation. It is well documented how many of the now wealthiest individuals and companies in Russia laid a basis for their power and fortunes by taking advantage of the "freeing up" of cheap assets that resulted from the disintegration of the Soviet political economic system (Barnes 2006; Dzarasov 2014; Kagarlicky 1992, 2002). A hunger for undervalued assets is not unique to Russian capitalists, of course, but it can be argued that many of them have specialized in exploiting opportunities to swallow the fruits of devaluation within their own country.[21] This occurred relatively late and slowly in agriculture, which drew the interest of big business gradually, at different times in different regions, but overall only by the turn of the century (Rylko and Jolly 2005) when the "redistribution" of the biggest pies was already relatively consolidated in many other sectors. The prospects for profitability of investments in agriculture were highly uncertain in the early decades of transition (Ioffe, Nefedova, and Zaslavsky 2006), and to some degree this remains the case. Investment projects investigated for this book were only partly a grab for land and often more of a gamble on future agricultural potential. The success of these gambles was determined not least by how far they could be hedged through state guarantees and supported by state programs.

The rapid and massive growth of large agricultural companies would not have been possible without the rounds of crisis, devaluation, and disintegration that made land, agricultural enterprises, and labor abundant, freely available, and cheap. These conditions partly persist both because of difficulties in solving them and the opportunities they provide to elites (chapter 4). Agriculture is a sector that has become clearly dominated by domestic businesses. Russia's ten most profitable agribusinesses are reported to have generated a total of $11.35 billion in revenue in 2019 (Large Scale Agriculture 2021). Although "only" four of Russia's 118 reported billionaires listed by *Forbes* in 2021 have made a larger share of their wealth in agriculture and food production, their existence shows that agriculture can bring a fortune to some. Most foreign investment into the sector, by contrast, was relatively short-lived.

Massive concentration notwithstanding, dispossession, as it is addressed by rural dwellers and conceptualized in this book, does not strictly follow, chronologically or causally, from companies' land deals and enterprise takeovers in a narrow sense. Agricultural assets and labor in post-Soviet Russia were heavily devalued before capital showed any appetite for investing in it. Consequently, rural dwellers will accuse investing companies of exploiting existing deprivations rather than creating them. Many rural dwellers are not opposed to, and even wish for, a "good" investor to revive villages and enterprises—a task many see as impossible to tackle without substantial state or company support. Disintegration and devaluation caused a fog that helps to conceal theft and created material conditions that make it easy to legitimize private investment and state interventions as corresponding with popular demands.

Under conditions unfavorable for smallholder farming for most, many rural dwellers heavily depend on large agricultural enterprises for employment. Agricultural enterprises, which often are the single significant employers in a village, can exploit this situation and sell poorly paid jobs as employment opportunities, as can politicians promising development to harvest votes. In this regard, dispersed dispossession created conditions to take from the rural deprived what is useful to the powerful: their land, their votes, their labor power, or even their lives when they are sent to war. Some rural dwellers address this as blunt exploitation and dispossession. But the story is complicated by how many enterprises fulfill social functions of the kind one may rather expect from the state—functions that make them appear as capitalist exploiters and provisioners of social support at the same time (chapters 2 and 5).

Reassembling

Dispersed dispossession erodes the conditions for many types of agency and results in increased vulnerability. Yet those who experience it are not passive victims of their circumstances. The chapters describe different ways of acting that respond to dispersed dispossession directly or that occur under conditions formed through it. Analogous to the family of de-/dis- terms that help characterize "dispersal," a family of re- terms offers an appropriate entry point to understanding such agency: relating, repairing, recreating, recombining, reviving, regenerating, redeeming, restoring, reproducing, reinventing, recycling, and renewing. The prefix re- points to doing something again or returning something to a former state. Few things can simply be returned, but variations can be reinvented and reenacted, as I detail in chapter 2. We find variations of this theme in studies in former state-socialist settings.[22] Empirically, we see it in attempts to maintain and revive reliable social contracts and material infrastructures, relations of support and care that have value in themselves and form the basis for individual and collective agency. We also see it in claims for necessary support from authorities. In this sense, they resemble notions of care that emphasize humans' general dependence on sustaining environments and relations of care (Tronto 2009 [1993]) and how these are impacted by conditions of damage and precarity (Kovács 2016; Puig de la Bellacasa 2017; Stengers 2015).

One may cluster these terms under the umbrella of (re)assembling, not to privilege assembling as a general approach to the social (Latour 2005), but rather as a way of binding together three forms of agency central in this study. First, (re)assembling is a logical reaction to disintegration and dispersal and the forms of dispossession it implies. Where elements fall apart, they may be recombined and recomposed, and postsocialist contexts form an established site to study this. One may recall David Stark's (1996, 995) famous formulation of rebuilding organizations and institutions "with the ruins of communism." This book, too, investigates the relationship between ruination, recombination, and agency, which allows questions of agency to be linked to disruptive change while acknowledging that the context is no longer that of the post-Soviet phase. Second, assembling is as much about assemblages as it is about the agency that both underlies and emerges from it. Agency is conceptualized in a co-constitutive relationship to structures and infrastructures across a range of theoretical traditions and social-scientific studies.[23] In this study, we will see the important role of forms of agency that aim at creating better conditions for further agency by strengthening infrastructures and collectives. Creating "transitional infrastructure" (Berlant 2022, 24) responds to disintegration and crisis and helps to navigate and play an active role in ongoing transitions. Third, assemblies of people, in a more traditional sense of the social, play a constitutive role for collective agency in this study (chapters 2 and 5). As with other infrastructural work, assembling people requires *and* creates and strengthens a basis for collective agency.

Outline

While this introduction aims at presenting dispersed dispossession as a coherent concept, the chapters present partly contrasting insights that reflect complex realities, including local and regional differences. The idea of dispersed dispossession should help us to think across such differences. As the chapters build on one another, I recommend reading them in the given order.

The brief first chapter introduces the empirical cases and fieldwork sites along with the study's approach and methods, including reflections on multi-locality and multitemporality.

Chapter 2 explores the prevalence of large-scale farming and the persistence of certain Soviet-type arrangements from the viewpoint of current conflicts and organizing at the village level. It traces actors' creative and inventive ways to involve themselves in such changes and act toward them. This includes the revaluation and negotiation of institutions with a Soviet stamp—such as the *kolkhoz*, which I reconceptualize as a set of social relations enacted under conditions of fundamental change, reinvented rather than persisting. Empirically, the chapter mainly draws on a village community's mobilization against an attempted takeover of farmland by an investor. This case provided a rare opportunity to study contemporary *kolkhoz* relations as an object of dispute and adaptation, and the transformation of land entitlements (which have long been considered rather irrelevant) into crucial instruments to support the functioning of the local enterprise.

Chapter 3 shifts the focus to slow crisis and recursive rounds of dispossession over time, rooted, seemingly paradoxically, both in the Soviet agrarian system and its disintegration. It shows how historic disintegration and devaluation continue to matter. Rural dwellers refer to the ruins of built infrastructures and other constituents of place to make sense of and express drawn-out losses and constitutive absences. I argue that following such sense-making is a powerful way to better understand how dispersed dispossession unfolds on the ground and what was lost and by whom. It turns attention to context-specific forms of dispossession inscribed in prevailing conditions: production and social infrastructures disintegrated; agricultural assets and labor undervalued; agency limited; and futures uncertain.

Chapter 4 illustrates and contextualizes the renewed interest in farmland and agriculture in Russia from the early 2000s. It shows that much of the accumulation process is based on the massive devaluation and disintegration of the agricultural sector, which made assets cheap and available, and state policies that—by the turn of the century—shifted back to privileging large agricultural producers. It deconstructs the image of investors' omnipotence and their promises of investment in farmland being a safe bet and brings economic and managerial failure into the picture. The question of who wins and who loses should be seen in this context. Some managers and others draw benefits despite or because of enterprises' economic difficulties, as they promise solutions to fix and finally overcome them. For many rural residents, in contrast, the recurrent failures of agricultural projects stand in a long row of unfulfilled improvement promises.

Chapter 5 investigates local rearrangements after investing companies have entered the scene. It sets a particular focus on the occupation and reconfiguration of the historically established local monopoly status enjoyed by enterprises and the implied questions of power. Some investors have tried to disentangle themselves from social obligations but failed to do so if they could not fully disregard their workers' social needs and conditions of local compliance. Also, as agricultural operations remain insecure on their purely economic side, some companies take over responsibilities of rural development, which allows them to tap into state resources. Such conditions complicate class relations, and the chapter describes how they nurture specific forms of dependency but also how they compromise. It describes the tactics used by workers and rural residents on the one hand and enterprises and companies on the other.

Chapter 6 concludes by wrapping up the previous chapters' insights on a conceptual level. It reflects on relational goods, unequal capacities to navigate disruptive change, the perpetuation and exploitation of historical injustice, and the conditions for alternative visions, resistance, and agency in the context of dispersed dispossession—in Russia and elsewhere.

CHAPTER 1

Traces

I start from the assumption that we cannot know the problem of dispossession before the inquiry, and that it therefore deserves both close empirical attention and context-sensitive conceptualization. The idea of dispersed dispossession does not boil down to individual experiences of dispossession. Rather, in this study, I build on the exchange with my interlocutors about such experiences and the interpretations of them as a lens to investigate patterns of dispossession contingent on historical trajectories and political-economic structures and shifts. I understand such patterns as shared experiences under given historical circumstances, affecting larger numbers of people over extended periods. Hence this study starts from ethnographic situations, but it does not stop there. Rather, it makes sense of these situations through references to historical circumstances, agrarian political economy, and structural change. It is thus that patterns of dispossession come into view and situated accounts of historical change become possible.

To trace changing sets of relations within changing systemic circumstances, this study builds on a tradition of ethnographic research that aims at generating, questioning, and expanding concepts by bringing them into conversation with empirical inquiry and hence adapting them to the analytical and political pressures and requirements of historical circumstances and lived realities. It is a tradition that takes real-world complexity and puzzlement about the limits of familiar assumptions and categories as a starting point of study, reflection, and conceptualization.[1] Such intellectual work is not unique to ethnography, of course. We may understand it as a form of "mobile thought" that follows the idea to never cease to "think about the same things differently" (Foucault 1997, 136) and "opens to what concepts implicitly and often quietly *foreclose*, as well as what they encourage and condone" (Stoler 2016, 18–19). Ethnographies use mobile and "thick" inquiry (Rabinow and Marcus 2008, 81) as one way of achieving this. This chapter introduces the main sites of my inquiry and relates fieldwork and conceptual work.

Tracing Dispossession

Fieldwork does not lead ethnographers to tell authentic stories. At the very least, however, fieldwork urged me to let go of inadequate stories I might have told if relying only on written sources and interviews. I arrived in the field as a critic but found that I had to reimagine my own critical orientation to develop what I think is a more adequate account of dispossession, appropriation, and rural change. The unlearning of incorrect assumptions was a critical step in the process, enabled by long conversations with rural dwellers, enterprise workers, managers and directors, local politicians and bureaucrats, and Russian colleagues. Tania Li (2014a, 5) describes ethnography as a form of research that "disrupts the ethnographer's prior categories and assumptions, exposing uncharted territory where familiar categories don't hold (and thus) opens up the possibility of generating new knowledge and connections." The discordancy and disruption thus generated should spur inquiry and critical reflection, implying the question of what sort of translation between theoretical concepts and empirical encounters allows "for the process to be potentially heuristic" (Fassin 2014, 70). Such irritations inspired me to reformulate the problem of rural dispossession in a more complex and interesting way.

This is an ethnography of social and political-economic processes much more than of local cultural characteristics or research participants' lifeworlds. I understand my ethnographic interlocutors as their *"own ethnographer(s)"* (Mol 2002, 15)—not ethnographers of feelings, meanings, or perspectives, but of events, situations, and shifts, offering their interpretations and reflecting on the implications for someone in their position. Understanding interlocutors as their own ethnographers can be the basis for forms of epistemic partnership in which research participants offer their descriptions, interpretations, and theorizing (Biehl 2013a). In this sense, too, this is an ethnography of dispossession more than of "the dispossessed."

During fieldwork in villages, I lived in several homes with families or by myself, joined work, leisure activities, and events, immersed myself in various aspects of local life, engaged in long conversations, and conducted interviews. In parallel, I met with, interviewed, and accompanied company managers, enterprise directors, representatives of local or district administrations and regional ministries. That I was moving between these spheres was at times perceived as unusual but relevant. Many foreign company representatives are agricultural experts but sometimes not familiar with rural Russian settings or the Russian language. They found it curious that I was staying in villages for longer periods and were interested in what I had to say about interactions with village inhabitants and workers. Rural residents and workers were often interested in my experiences with managers of investment companies and also in villages in other parts of the country. My position was characterized by such forms of "betweenness" (England 1994; Katz 1994). My Eastern European family background and my proficiency in Russian helped me to be perceived as a partial insider in some ways, although many found my role as a Western European academic rather curious. I was crossing social boundaries constantly, finding myself lighting my way to some overflowing outdoor latrine through ankle-deep mud and chicken manure, and half a day later I was passing double security checks at a company entrance beside a manager. To some people I met, the distances and modes of my traveling appeared as an unaffordable luxury. Others thought I might wish to stay in hotels that would have consumed the three-year project budget within a week.

As mentioned in the introduction, the causes and courses of dispersed dispossession may seem hard to reconstruct and responsibilities hard to ascribe from a ground-level perspective, rooted as they are in complex and layered processes spanning several decades. It is often outside forces that are blamed. It may be obvious who took over an enterprise or farmland, but much less who or what contributed to a situation in which people saw no alternative to and became dependent on investment companies or state agencies to get things running again. What should be blamed: the failed models, projects and promises of state socialism, or market capitalism? Was the main problem with individuals who exploited uncertainty for fraud and individual gains, or with circumstances that may have forced many into illicit activities? Rural dwellers regularly discuss such questions, which mirrors some of the challenges in making sense of a condition perceived as obscured by historic events. Many of the more concrete forces shaping villages, such as agribusinesses and state authorities, can also appear relatively elusive. They may make concrete improvement promises about which villagers may be highly skeptical, and for good reason. They may also operate in relatively obscure networks of power and control with uncertain responsibilities (chapters 4 and 5). While foreign investing companies may seem alien with their attempts to implement new business rationalities, the deliberate obscurity and lack of transparency that characterize the operation of many Russian companies do not make the latter any more approachable. Local enterprise directors, bureaucrats, and politicians often appear to be more approachable. However, their agency or their ability to make a real difference are often called into question by rural residents, and by such actors themselves, who claim the decisions that really matter are made elsewhere.

In his reflections on multisited research, George Marcus (1997, 97) describes "the anxieties of knowing that one is somehow tied in to what is happening elsewhere" and suggests that they can result in particular forms of ethnographic complicity. Rural dwellers' sense of being affected by an "elsewhere" spurred many discussions—they were curious if my traveling and multisite research offered any insights relevant to making sense of their condition. A sense of depending on powers beyond individual reach runs through this study. It relates to a broad range of supports mentioned in the introduction and detailed in the following chapters. On a very general level, this reflects how "interdependency establishes our vulnerability to social forms of deprivation" (Butler and Athanasiou 2013, 5). On the level of empirical analysis, the idea that lives and livelihoods inevitably depend on relations that support and sustain them directs attention to how and how much such supports (or their relative absence) are unequally distributed across places and subject positions, and how dispossession is already part of the conditions that some inhabit.

Landscapes

This book is an inquiry into the changing relations and interactions between rural communities, companies, village administrations, and state representatives. These partly unfold in villages; however, villages are not bounded or isolated sites but rather nested within complex translocal relations. Established rural–urban ties include villagers' daily, weekly, or seasonal commuting, in- and outmigration, urbanites spending weekends and summer holidays at their dachas or visiting relatives in the countryside, or the trading of household agricultural produce at town and city markets. Certain villages have become more isolated over time through the diminishing of regional markets or the loss of public transport options while new connections may have emerged, for instance, by new companies entering the scene. In historical and structural terms, rural economies have long been, and remain, fundamentally shaped by regional, national, and transnational political-economic powers.

There is a long history of centralized control over the countryside and its inhabitants, as well as state-directed programs and experiments: (forced) resettlement schemes, the industrialization and collectivization of agriculture in the early Soviet period, the countless large-scale agronomic and technological experiments that followed, and state programs that reshaped many facets of rural life, from education and culture to family arrangements. The post-Soviet plans for the reorganization of agriculture were written in and implemented from the center, too. As the state withdrew control and resources in the process, resulting "voids" were partly filled by private companies that entered the village scene from "elsewhere," or remained unfilled. In any case, many rural dwellers recount this as a historical experience of increased dependency on decisions and powers far beyond them. This study, too, starts from specific places but follows problems that refer to other places, spheres, or times.

During extensive research trips, I conducted fieldwork in three villages affected by large investment projects. I also gained direct insights into the everyday operations of one of the largest Western-listed investment companies, Agrokultura, and an agricultural subsidiary operating within the web of power and capital of Russia's largest gas company, Gazprom. After exploratory visits in 2011, I kept revisiting these places from 2012 to 2014 and during brief follow-up research stays in 2017 and 2021. I conducted ten months of fieldwork, including longer stays in villages, several multiday excursions with company managers who took me along on visits to their enterprises, and interviews with enterprise representatives, officials and bureaucrats, trade unionists, and various "experts" in different places. After fieldwork, I could draw on rich insights gathered in hundreds of field notes pages and around seventy-five interviews with rural dwellers and administrations, enterprise and company representatives, different kinds of experts, and others. The names of most places and companies are anonymized. As an exception, I refrained from anonymizing Agrokultura, which was bought in 2014 by a Russian company. The operations of Agrokultura have been analyzed in various studies (see chapter 5), and readers should be able to compare them. The anonymization of persons is guaranteed, however.

The Russian Federation is a vast country spanning not only eleven time zones but also a large number of climatic and vegetation zones, highly differentiated settlement and infrastructural patterns, and eighty-two federal administrative units (not counting three federal cities) with partly differing agricultural regulations and policies. It has been emphasized that this spatial complexity corresponds with a highly variegated rural and agrarian landscape (Ioffe, Nefedova, and Zaslavsky 2006). This study cannot represent such regional diversity and does not intend to provide an encompassing picture. Rather, it draws on several contrasting cases in four main regions, plus scattered insights from several others (see figure 1.1). The regions of Rostov and Voronezh count among the country's most fertile; Lipetsk is part of the Central Black Earth region, just like Voronezh, but located farther north and not included in the country's top ten regions; and the region of Perm is less favorable in terms of agriculture.[2] Working on four cases in parallel allowed for fruitful contrasting and helped avoid inadequate generalizations based on a single case. What I learned from the trajectories and actors' interpretations in one case would often help me readjust my perspective or assumptions in another.

Setovka

Setovka is a village in the region of Perm where I was often reminded of stories that people elsewhere told about the past. It seemed that a particular mixture of relative remoteness, a solid agricultural enterprise, and an active and well-organized village administration have preserved some of the relations that people in other places were lamenting: For instance, an enterprise keeping people employed and sticking to *kolkhoz* obligations to care for the village infrastructure and household needs (chapter 2), and a village administration that also contributed to upholding social functions.

People in Setovka are no economically better off than those in many other rural places that I have visited. They, too, complain about poverty, a lack of prospects in the village for them and their children, the insecurity of rural life and the fragility of local institutions. In the recent past, the village community took an active stance in preserving relations and institutions that served it. It mobilized against and eventually turned down an attempted takeover of the village farmland and enterprise by an external investor. Business interest in agriculture was a relatively recent phenomenon in the region at that time, where more farmland was still becoming fallow than falling prey to any land grabs, so the attempted takeover came as a surprise. One of the things that makes this case so interesting is how the mobilization against the takeover—and for the preservation of the kolkhoz—articulated a vision of what rural life after the failure of many earlier promises and beyond investment should look like. It provided an opportunity to study the rearticulation and reinvention of kolkhoz relations as a contingent social contract, in and for the present. My research in Setovka provides the backbone of chapter 2 and informs other chapters to a lesser extent.

Letnevo

Letnevo is a village in the region of Lipetsk. With about three thousand inhabitants, it is one of the larger villages in the region and the largest in this sample.

It has shrunk since the end of the Soviet period, however, when the population of 4,500 inhabitants corresponded with the equally unusual number of four major agricultural enterprises. It offers important insights into the partial and gradual disentanglement of the agricultural and the rural, and into inhabitants' tactics in the face of changing circumstances. Mikhail,[3] for instance, my host in Letnevo, runs a small farming unit with some pigs and chickens, and a 0.4-hectare household plot on which he grows mainly potatoes and pumpkins. He owns a tractor and two smaller trucks with which he offers services to fellow villagers, filling gaps left by the vanished agricultural enterprises that previously provided machinery for private subsidiary agriculture. During labor-intensive times such as plowing and harvesting, Mikhail would leave on his tractor early in the morning and return late, after sunset. However, as subsidiary agriculture in the village gradually diminishes, he is now experimenting with new services beyond agriculture, such as baking bricks, which he offers in his own and surrounding villages.

Many villagers describe agriculture as fading away from the village scene. Two comparatively small private farmers work some one hundred hectares and employ a handful of workers each. Many households produce vegetables, fruit, eggs, milk, and meat for their own consumption, but increasingly less for sale. The village's farmland has been under cultivation by various larger holding companies for several years. During my fieldwork period, in 2013, the land and the remains of the local farm were taken over, again, by one of the largest Russian sugar-producing companies. People did not lament the withdrawal of the former operator that had gone into bankruptcy and not paid wages for months. The new company, however, abolished the local production base and shifted operations to a central base around thirty-five kilometers away, a move that further decoupled the village from commercial agriculture. This case study supports mainly chapters 3 and 5.

Lipenka

I visited Lipenka—a village of two thousand inhabitants in the Rostov region in the Southern Steppes—to speak to a private farmer who was in a dispute with a Rostov-based investment company over approximately 130 hectares of farmland. The latter controlled around 4,500 hectares in this village, which made it the largest but not the only agrarian producer: there were also around forty private farmers, the greatest number of all villages in this study's sample and one of the reasons, villagers told me, for relatively frequent conflicts. I interviewed villagers who were involved in the land dispute, as their land was under lease contracts with the company and they wanted to hand it over to the farmer. Two hours after I paid a surprise visit to the local farm director, I received an unexpected phone call from the regional capital and was invited to meet the company director.

I met the man in his office where one could see him—in a photograph— posing next to Alexey Miller, CEO of Gazprom, who had just made it to Forbes's list of the world's most powerful people that year. I left with a business card that displayed his former formal ties with the State Duma (the Russian parliament). His boss turned out to be the CEO of one of Gazprom's regional branches, deputy of the regional parliament, and holder of several central regional-level positions in the ruling party United Russia. With the director of the agricultural branch, I traveled, for several days, to the farms and other enterprises belonging to their complex and opaque company network. I also kept returning to the village of Lipenka for follow-up research and exchanges with villagers. The case mainly informs chapters 4 and 5.

Agrokultura

Agrokultura was a Swedish investment company that operated in four Russian regions and Ukraine. During fieldwork, I mostly engaged with some expat agricultural specialists who had left behind homes and families to become part of what they regarded as a grand and promising project. They would proudly show the farms and fields they operated here—the size of which was unknown in their countries of origin. They would also emphasize that they were confronted with an extraordinary task. In their eyes, the Russian agricultural system was inefficient, corrupt, run-down, and reliant on state support that certain companies would receive and others—such as theirs—did not. Many of them thus seemed to perceive themselves as part of a historic experiment to realize a new business model. Their job was to fundamentally reorganize production schemes on a scale unprecedented for a private company. To this aim, they brought different kinds of expertise, new machines and production technologies, and a degree of command over the company's financial means. While some of them lived in the villages where they worked, many traveled to farms from cities. Many relied on interpreters for their work and would hang out with fellow expats in their free time.

In 2014, the company's assets were bought up by a Russian competitor. For the operational managers I engaged with, it was no secret even years before that there was a substantial gap between the company's great plans and bright promises on the one hand, and the operational business on the other. They knew very well that profit and efficiency would not emerge solely from

FIGURE 1.1. Western part of the Russian Federation with research sites (in frames).

the availability of cheap, fertile farmland and rising demand on global food markets. Their stories and interactions with workers and farm directors documented here reveal much about the contradictions immanent to the investment project. At first sight, the company may have appeared as a typical land-grabber: foreign, stock-exchange listed, taking control of a quarter of a million hectares within a few years. Chapters 4 and 5 demonstrate the implications of large-scale operations and holdings, and that they do not necessarily result in sovereign strategies or stable operations.

Timescapes

Scholars have recurrently warned that the past is being overemphasized in post-Soviet research on the region. Todorova (2010a, 3) sees an "obsession over *Vergangenheitsbewältigung*"[4] in the transformation literature. Concepts of transition/transformation as well as those of the postsocialist/post-Soviet have been criticized for being teleological, outdated, and imposed by Western scholars (Buck-Morss 2006; Gille 2010; Humphrey 2007; M. Müller 2019; Stark 1996; Verdery 2007), or, again, for "defining the present in terms of its past" (Sakwa 1999, 3). The idea of postsocialism further privileges a certain rupture (the collapse of the Soviet system) and thus the formative power of actually existing socialism over other systems such as capitalism (M. Müller 2019).

Such concerns apply to studies of the Russian countryside. Much has changed there since the early post-Soviet years. In many places, and respects, the conditions for rural residents have improved. There has been a return of pension and unemployment transfer payments, and better conditions for rural entrepreneurship. New smaller and larger businesses in and beyond agriculture provide opportunities for some. And still, hardly anyone here seems to perceive the past as over and done with. Research participants in this study are most immediately concerned with the present and future, and yet many of them refer to memories and accounts of the past to make sense of the present, and they interpret their current situation as fundamentally shaped during past processes and events. The recurrent bankruptcies of agricultural enterprises, the many who have left, or the lasting disintegration of infrastructures and institutions have left their mark. They do not determine the future, but they have eroded the possibility of certain futures for certain persons. This is part of what makes dispersed dispossession a historically rooted experience.

This illustrates how we must move away from imaginaries that are stuck in the past but may not forget about the histories that shaped the present, and how various elements of the past are "out there" as parts of the world we encounter or inhabit (Gordon 2008, 166). Hence the importance of broadening the temporal scope and considering how Soviet and post-Soviet history is folded into present situations in often complex ways. Historical reverberations may continue to matter in more obvious ways in rural settings compared to urban ones. This study thus takes the Russian countryside as a privileged setting to theorize social and political-economic transformation within complex "timescapes" (Adam 2010). Building on analytical traditions that show how institutions with a Soviet legacy do not simply persist as a product of inertia (Dzenovska, Artiukh, and Martin 2023; Stark 1996; Todorova and Gille 2010), the study demonstrates how elements of "the past" are being reclaimed, reinvented, and enacted by both rural dwellers and enterprise managers in the face of fundamental change.

As Ann Stoler (2016, 352–53) puts it, notions of legacy or path dependence offer only vague orientation to distinguish "between what holds and what lies dormant, between residue and recomposition, between what is a holdover and what is reinvested, between a weak and a tenacious trace," and few conceptual tools to better understand why certain institutions remain important and how they prevail or change. Rather, we must show *how* histories matter in particular contexts and to particular people. This study does not refer to history as if it was merely context, or, even less so, destiny. History must make its way through the present to make a claim on the story: being narrated and reactivated in conversation and discourse, mobilized and redeployed in practice, or leaving a clear mark on material and institutional landscapes, or persons' agencies. In an ethnography attentive to complex timescapes, then, one task is to trace how the past is "reinvented and textualized through the discourses and practices of the present" (Britzman 1995, 234). Another is to go beyond past boundedness and the sense of a "futureless present" (Ringel 2018, 158), even if this mirrors local perceptions and narratives, and illuminate how actors actually remain agents under these circumstances and how they relate to the future.

Chapter 2

Kolkhoz

"There is no kolkhoz any longer." Such a statement would count as true in various senses and situations today. In its original meaning, the term kolkhoz refers to Soviet collective farms. As those were formally abolished shortly after the dissolution of the Soviet system, kolkhozes ceased to exist in a legal and formal sense. Market reformers envisioned peasant farms as taking their place. To a significant extent, however, they were replaced by large farming enterprises in a different formal guise, registered as joint-stock companies, private or state agricultural enterprises, cooperatives, or forming part of larger holding companies. So, while the kolkhoz may be dead, large-scale farming is alive and well in contemporary Russia. And this is only the formal side of things.

"There is no kolkhoz any longer. This isn't the Soviet Union anymore." I have repeatedly heard such statements in conversations and arguments during fieldwork. While in a literal sense they confirm a truism, in a more comprehensive sense they indicate that there is more to the story. More than the repetition of a known fact, these statements are mostly uttered in contested situations and respond to actual or alleged persistence of elements of the Soviet agrarian system. Large farms were reregistered and renamed, but they "never became what their new names implied" (Ioffe, Nefedova, and Zaslavsky 2006, 29). In this sense, continued kolkhoz talk also stands for attempts to make sense of hybrid forms that are neither a continuation of the old nor the realization of new models envisioned in reform policies (Pavlovskaya 2013). Furthermore, many references to the kolkhoz are framed in positive rather than negative terms. Many stories related by my interlocutors literally started from and ended with the kolkhoz, and I encountered what I shall call kolkhoz relations in all the villages covered in this study. They were present in the material texture and infrastructures, in organizational patterns, economic rationalities, and social expectations, or the claims and judgments of various actors, from

FIGURE 2.1. Kolkhoz base in Setovka. Author's photograph.

workers to bureaucrats. Hence the importance of understanding not only the persistence and dominance of industrialized large-scale agriculture as such but also the liveliness and contestations beneath its surface.

Stories of Soviet kolkhozes and their post-Soviet afterlives have been presented to an international readership early and prominently by Caroline Humphrey (1983, 1999), and the kolkhoz remained a central theme in post-Soviet rural studies (Allina-Pisano 2008; Nikulin 2003). So why do I revisit the kolkhoz theme in a book on rural dispossession? I will show how it points to institutionalized support, material infrastructures, collective arrangements, and entitlements as goods on which rural dwellers and livelihoods depend—often more than on land rights or property titles. I do not approach kolkhoz relations in terms of path dependence or legacy, however, since such framings provide few conceptual tools to better understand *why* some elements and relations remain important and *how* they prevail (Collier 2011; Humphrey 2002; Stoler 2016; Todorova 2010b). I start from situations characterized by change and uncertainty rather than continuity, and I trace actors' creative and inventive ways to involve themselves in such changes, including the revaluation, negotiation, and reenactment of elements with a socialist history. Contrary to images of rural stagnation, I argue that invoking the kolkhoz remains important because recurrent changes and reorganization generate ruptures and contradictions that open up situations for negotiation and criticism.

Past and present kolkhozes

The kolkhoz has been the primary organizational unit of Soviet agriculture at a local level. The term is a contraction of *kollektivnoe khoziaistvo*, a collective farm. Kolkhozes existed alongside state farms called *sovkhozes*. The historical origins of collective and state farms differ, as did certain formal characteristics. However, variation within both categories has been found to exceed variation between them, and attempts to unify working conditions across farm categories have led to a further blurring of strict differences over time (Ioffe, Nefedova, and Zaslavsky 2006, 21–22).[1] When people speak of Soviet collective and state farms today, they rarely differentiate between these two variants of the Soviet agrarian enterprise model, and the term kolkhoz is used as a shorthand for Soviet agrarian enterprises in general in the places covered in this study. Collective and state farms have been described as "a microcosm" or "extensions" of the Soviet state (Humphrey 1999, 3–4), but they are also shaped by a significant portion of local rationalities, dynamics, and requirements. This echoes the broader idea that the Soviet enterprise was not simply an economic institution but "the primary unit of soviet society" (Clarke 1992, 7). State guarantees and protections were mediated through collective farms, and so were many practical social services such as housing, heating and electricity, repairs of homes and roads, and even the support of medical services, schools and kindergartens, and local cultural activities.

Khoziaistvo—usually translated as "farm" in *kollektivnoe khoziaistvo* (collective farm)—reflects some of the ways in which it is more than a farm or an enterprise. The root *khoz* originally referred to the household and its organization and management. In recent and contemporary uses, it can refer to a range of different subjects like *sel'skoe* or *narodnoe khoziaistvo*: agriculture and national economy. Hence it refers to ways of managing the economy. Stephen Collier (2011, 81) argues that it originally referred to units at the nexus of production and need fulfillment, and hence a *substantive* understanding of the economy in a Polanyian sense,[2] in contrast to the liberal *formal* understanding. If we follow that logic, the idea of *khoziaistvo* would not apply to a farm managed by principles of the Western economic mainstream.[3] Actually existing kolkhozes did not fully comply with Soviet planning either. For instance, they failed to fully displace the household as the nexus of production and need fulfillment; rather, they became part of a complex of industrial and household farming that has been described as symbiotic (Humphrey 1999; Visser, Kurakin, and Nikulin 2019).

Yet the idea that a *khoziaistvo* is responsible for fulfilling a population's material needs, rather than merely providing jobs and paying taxes, remains prevalent, both regarding kolkhoz successor enterprises and agriculture more generally, which in Russian is *sel'skoe*—that is, rural—*khoziaistvo*. As one agricultural bureaucrat argues: "We are either *sel'skoe khoziaistvo*, which ensures the country's strategic food security, or we are business. Let's decide. If we are *sel'skoe khoziaistvo*, then you support us with subsidies, and we produce the products the country needs. Or we are business, but then we sell [our produce] to the state at the price we set. And the market will show" (Head of district agricultural department, Nizhniy Novgorod region, 2021).

While the idea of the *khoziaistvo* opens possibilities for criticizing the market economy, or its specific shortcomings, and arguing for economic alternatives, there is no point in romanticizing the historic kolkhoz. At its worst, the Soviet agrarian system was grounded in a totalitarian state project (Scott 1998, 217) that combined oppression, economic inefficiency, ecological devastation, and manifold gaps between policies and local realities. It is well documented that, unlike the name suggests, collective farms were hardly egalitarian and, in many respects, they were quite hierarchical organizations. Humphrey (1999, 435) found that "jobs in the farm [were] very unequal in pay and conditions of work" and that there was a distinct power hierarchy headed by the kolkhoz chairman and including a ladder of specialists, party representatives, and foremen "above" the kolkhoz workers. Also, while the general meeting of kolkhozniks was formally the highest authority, studies found that in practice it mostly affirmed decisions made by local authorities or higher-level officials (Humphrey 1999). Dependence on local authorities was, and in an altered form remains, particularly strong as villagers depend on the enterprise not only for jobs but also for a range of supports and services that are also governed within the kolkhoz microcosms. Furthermore, in many instances, rural dwellers depended on household food production "while toiling for a kolkhoz" (Ioffe, Nefedova, and Zaslavsky 2006, 25) and hence carried a double burden of fulfilling state-directed production plans and ensuring their own subsistence.

As collective and state farms became the dominant form of organizing Soviet agriculture during the collectivization (1928–1940) under Stalin, their history is further bound to what is remembered as a particularly grim chapter of Soviet history. Collectivization was a project based on ostensibly universal political-economic laws and principles that aimed at integrating a vast territory with a heterogeneous population into a centrally planned national political economy. It aimed at developing the countryside, overcoming what the Soviets perceived as painful backwardness. It also aimed at generating resources that could be used for the USSR's ambitious industrialization plans more broadly (Ioffe, Nefedova, and Zaslavsky 2006, 13).[4] While some promises of collectivization, such as the delivery of tractors and other machinery, were perceived positively among large parts of the rural population, and certain groups such as landless peasants benefited, the majority of the rural population generally opposed collectivization, partly through hidden or open resistance. Collectivization was "a massive economic and social experiment" (Humphrey 1999, 1), but the Russian peasantry had been subject to great—and often greatly failing—experiments before. Particularly in the Central Asian republics and "ethnic" territories of the vast Soviet empire, collectivization continued much older patterns of what has been called Russia's "internal colonization" (Ėtkind 2011). There, it was experienced as an attack by the center on locally distinct values and ways of organizing households, villages, agriculture, and local economies more broadly, which provoked particularly strong resistance in these territories (Humphrey 1999). But resistance occurred in other parts, too. The Soviets responded with force, and many deemed enemies of collectivization were resettled to places such as Siberia or Kazakhstan. Best known is the instance of the so-called *kulaks*, peasants who were wealthier than average and experienced high levels of expropriation and persecution, partly because of resistance to collectivization and partly because of their being labeled as class enemies within Soviet society. A combination of state-imposed punishment for peasant boycotts and other resistance strategies, mismanagement, and droughts resulted in famines that led to the starvation of millions over the first decade of collectivization. In the Ukrainian Soviet Socialist Republic, there was comparatively strong popular resistance to collectivization, and the effects of the Great Famine in 1932–34 were particularly grave, resulting in millions of deaths and still remembered as *Holodomor* across Ukraine.[5]

Despite its high degree of centralization, the Soviet agrarian system did not form or create a monolithic block (Shanin 1985). Policies were changing and some were ambiguous; gaps between what was written on paper and what occurred on the ground were prevalent. Many got by despite rather than because of the insufficient Soviet schemes, by inhabiting and altering them (Smith 2014; Wädekin 1973). Market reforms did not create a monolithic system either. Rather, they marked the beginning of a process that resulted in a spatially variegated and still shifting rural landscape (Ioffe, Nefedova, and Zaslavsky 2006). Many rural dwellers today are aware of the violent and dysfunctional sides of the Soviet agrarian system. At the same time, in retrospect, they still acknowledge the commitment to equalizing living conditions in the country-side alongside the provision of social services as a Soviet achievement. As inequalities between families, between different villages, as well as enterprises and regions, increased after the collapse of the Soviet system, the deterioration of these equalizing forces is often addressed as a loss.

The market-oriented agricultural reforms were carried out along several main lines: the reorganization of the kolkhozes and sovkhozes, the support of the emerging private agrarian sector, and land reforms (Kalugina 2014). They were directed mainly by the federal government toward the regions, *raiony* (districts), and villages where communities and officials had little direct influence.[6] Certain reforms were launched in the late Soviet Union after Gorbachev, but they were pushed much harder under Yeltsin. On December 27, 1991, one day after the dissolution of the Soviet Union, Yeltsin passed Presidential Decree No. 323, "On Urgent Measures for Implementing Land Reform in the Russian Federation," which required kolkhozes and sovkhozes to complete their reorganization by January 1, 1993. The majority of enterprises formally met the target of reorganization, but most enterprise authorities and assemblies chose to reorganize in ways that allowed for leaving the workers' collective and the organizational structure of the enterprise more or less intact (Lindner 2008).

This had much to do with the general political-economic condition at that time. Throughout the 1990s, many of the large farm enterprises were in a difficult economic situation, did not pay workers wages for months or even years, and often went bankrupt. Still, leaving the enterprise and starting their own seemed like a worse option for many workers. The entire agricultural sector was in a desperate situation at that time, drained by the withdrawal of state support, low prices on agricultural produce caused by the decline of domestic household purchasing power and cheap agricultural imports that came with trade liberation, and government strategies of keeping food prices deliberately low to ensure food supply in cities. Simultaneously, input prices for machinery, seeds, and fertilizers rose. Access to markets and state support was often difficult, especially for small producers,[7] and markets were volatile. In short, most rural dwellers had little opportunity to become peasants, and rather remained wage laborers (Kalugina 2012). The deterioration of the formal economy, including hyperinflation and chaotic, sometimes inaccessible, agricultural markets in many instances, *increased* local populations' dependence on large farms. As money became relatively worthless, or at least insufficient to keep up and organize the flow of materials, goods, and services, informal exchange and various forms of barter became crucial elements of local economies—and became reasons why, from the perspective of rural dwellers, collective farms had to continue. As Humphrey (1999, 461) puts it, "In these circumstances people are attached to collectives because they are the only thing that looks like a functioning intermediate institution and stand in for what is almost a nonfunctioning state at the village level."

What accounts for this failure of the goal to create peasant farms? Some ascribe it to the circumstances of implementation, such as farm directors and other local elites manipulating land distribution to defend their privilege and status (Allina-Pisano 2008). Others argue that the reform was not really designed to prevent large farms from keeping their land and remaining the main agricultural producers (Wegren 2009). Yet others emphasize that large farms did not persist because they were doing well, but because rural dwellers and state and local authorities all preferred to keep them running for the simple lack of other employment options in the villages (Ioffe, Nefedova, and Zaslavsky 2006, 92)—so they provided a "vehicle for collective survival" (Ioffe, Nefedova, and Zaslavsky 2006, 117). In terms of lasting effects, which interest us here, the important point is that most former collective and state farms were not split into smaller units but, as business interest in agriculture gradually emerged, incorporated into even larger agricultural companies.

State policies were oscillating between creating conditions for small private farms and benefiting large agribusinesses (Nefedova 2014, 78). State support for private farmers was relatively strong during a brief period from 1992 to 1994, when the number of registered private farms rose significantly. It never became a mass phenomenon, however, partly because starting a business was difficult enough to keep most of the less powerful rural dwellers out of business. After the turn of the century, the Putin government implemented an overall more supportive agricultural policy but dedicated most attention to the strengthening of large agricultural enterprises. At this time, the total number of private farms—which had been below initial expectations from the beginning—was already decreasing again (Wegren 2011, 219). Under the official category of private peasant farms, today one finds a wide range, from small units based on family labor to large enterprises that have outgrown former collective enterprises in size (Nefedova 2014, 118; Uzun 2012, 141–42).

The category of private farms, used in official statistics, is thus not an adequate indicator of the development of smallholder farming in Russia. While there are certain regions and places with a significant portion of smaller private farmers, the predominant form of household agriculture today is supplementary—that is, noncommercial or semicommercial—agriculture on household plots (Pallot and Nefedova 2007). Assessments of how much household farming continues to depend on large farms differ substantially. Some scholars report that surveyed households rely much more on the support of family members and relatives rather than on large farms (Wegren 2009, 122), while others emphasize that household farming still fundamentally depends on resources provided by large farms (Ioffe, Nefedova, and Zaslavsky 2006; Pallot and Nefedova 2007). Many of these studies are dated. In the current study, the importance of large farm support for household agriculture, and local communities more generally, varied across case studies, with the case discussed in this chapter being an instance of strong and complex interlinkages between kolkhoz and household economies.

Post-Soviet Land

During the Soviet period, all land belonged to the state, and individuals had certain use rights but no ownership of land. Land reform in Russia—in contrast to postsocialist Eastern and Central European states (Hann 2003; Verdery 2003)—was organized as a distribution rather than restitution. Land was not returned to families who had owned it before collectivization (which, due to prerevolutionary property structures, would have been difficult anyhow). Rather, the former kolkhoz workers and certain other professional groups received certificates for fractional ownership in the enterprise property such as buildings and machinery and agricultural land.[8] Still, the scale of this distribution was massive. Between 1992 and 1997, approximately 117.6 Mha were formally privatized, and 11.9 million land shares were allocated. By 2002, 7.7 million shares had been distributed to private owners (Wegren 2009, 16).

In Russian, land titles are mostly referred to as *pai* (shares). Much kolkhoz property was organized in *pai* in early socialist times, too, but these *pai* disappeared with the development of collective ownership on later Soviet farms in which the "direct participants in production and appropriation [were] big collectivities of people" (Humphrey 1999, 94). So *pai* played a transitional role on the way to Soviet agriculture as well as out of it. They certified a shareholder's right to land of a certain size within large land banks that now formally belonged to the collective of shareholders.[9] It has been argued that the persistence of large farms can be partly explained by the distribution of entitlements rather than real land during the post-Soviet reform (Wegren 2009, 6). It also created conditions for the distinct forms of rural dispossession in Russia over the last decades.

As mentioned, due to the dire circumstances very few rural dwellers could or wanted to start their own farming businesses and work the land themselves.

FIGURE 2.2. Three household plots. Author's photograph.

As Jessica Allina-Pisano (2008, 4–5) notes, "Economic constraints limited rural people's desire and capacity to convert paper rights into actual allocation
of land in the fields," as land acquisition to start a family farming business
was not a particularly attractive prospect for most (Humphrey 1999; Kalugina
2014; Ryzhova 2022). In many regions, the demand and price for land were
low. After the bankruptcy of agricultural enterprises, land documents sometimes lost their value completely or were sold for merely symbolic amounts.
Hence a land title's use *and* exchange value were limited for individual shareholders. Furthermore, given regularly changing legislation, landownership
seemed highly uncertain.

Differentiating between abstract land titles and "real land" is important to
understand not only the course of land reform but also rural dwellers' actual
attachments to land. Setovka's community, to which we turn shortly, is an agricultural one and people are living on and from the land in various respects:
They grow food on household plots, many work for the agricultural enterprise,
some work land as private farmers, and some keep livestock. For many, their
relations to the place, and the land, are a reason to stay and live in this remote
village. But the land that rural dwellers work on a household basis is different
from that which has been distributed through entitlements. In Soviet times,

FIGURE 2.3. Enterprise director Dmitry Ivanovich overseeing work on a commercial field. Author's photograph.

most rural households had access to land—usually around 0.4 hectares—often located around houses, which they could use for private subsidiary agriculture.[10] Food production on these plots remains important and sometimes constitutes a major source of family income (Pallot and Nefedova 2007). Kolkhoz fields reorganized during land reform, by contrast, sometimes reach sizes of several hundred hectares as they were designed for industrial agriculture (see figures 2.2 and 2.3) and can be located kilometers away from a village. Household farms can work parts of these fields, but this presupposes agreements with running large enterprises as well as machinery and infrastructure that many households could not afford. Large enterprises, in contrast, usually still command such machinery and infrastructure. Hence, for maintaining land relations through industrial agriculture, a working enterprise is much more important than individual land titles and property.

Land Sales

Setovka is a village in the Perm region. Around 900 inhabitants were registered here in 2013, out of which 190 were younger than 16, and 160 of pension

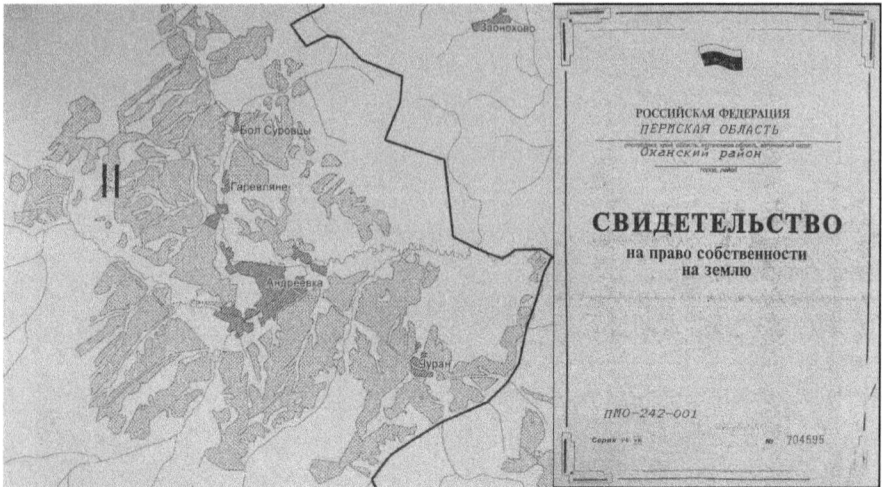

FIGURE 2.4. Map of settlement (dark) surrounded by fields (bright gray), and land document. Author's photograph.

age. The agricultural enterprise has changed its legal form and organizational structure several times over the last two decades, but it is commonly understood as the direct successor of the Soviet collective enterprise, still controlling around 4,500 hectares of farmland. With around 140 workers in 2014—a relatively large number due to keeping 550 dairy cows—the enterprise remains, by far, the village's biggest employer (followed by the local school and kindergarten with 32 employees). A significant portion of village inhabitants commute to work in towns and cities. The enterprise had been loss-making for some time but reached profitability in the early 2010s. The village administration's budget hinged (80 percent) on transfer payments from the regional and federal levels.

Conditions for agricultural production in the district are average, good for dairy farming or growing potatoes, but barely profitable for large-scale production of crops or most vegetables. Business interest in agriculture—beyond existing enterprises' attempts to carry on—was practically nonexistent over the last decades and remained relatively weak even during times of rising interest in agriculture since the late 2000s. This sets it apart from regions such as the Central Black Earth and the Southern Steppes, which have been dominated by large grain-producing companies for many years (see chapter 4).

The attempt by a neighboring enterprise to gain control over the village's farmland in 2007 thus took the village community and authorities by surprise. This takeover was ultimately prevented by a coalition of the village mayor, the enterprise director, and the assembly of owners of land shares. Instances of community-based resistance and collective action to prevent land sales are rare in rural Russia, according to both the literature (Mamonova 2016; Mamonova and Visser 2014; Visser et al. 2015) and my investigations. This is part of what makes this case so interesting. Also, this mobilization spurred a debate and reflection on the material basis as well as the social contract of communal living in Setovka. The inhabitants of the village have called the local enterprise "their kolkhoz" before, but during the controversy, the term has been given more explicit and to some extent new meaning. As the kolkhoz could no longer be taken for granted, stories about what it is and why it matters gained impact. This is not to say that an authentic kolkhoz has been preserved. The enterprise in question had been a private farm and not all villagers called it a kolkhoz all the time. Rather, we are dealing with a hybrid and contingent organizational form that is not only subject to continuous change but also stands at the fringe of quite contradictory organizing and guiding principles—not least between the private and the collective (Lindner 2013), which creates a tension that is navigated more than resolved. Such renegotiation of kolkhoz relations started with land sales.

For many years, I was told, there has been little concern about agricultural land in Setovka. After the formal dissolution of kolkhozes, the former kolkhoz workers received two kinds of documents entitling them to fractional ownership in the enterprise property: certifying property in buildings and machinery and in agricultural land. Titles in enterprise infrastructure and equipment were redeemed in exchange for enterprise services, raw material, natural produce, or housing property, and most of them were fully covered in 2013. But the documents certifying property in 7.5 hectares of farmland were mostly ignored by both their owners and the farm enterprise over the first fifteen years. As in other instances, only very few would work the land privately, and possibilities to sell titles were limited by the fact that only the local enterprise had an interest in it. The enterprise just carried on working the land as it had done before *without* buying land shares or paying rent. This also implied, however, that it worked this land without a legally binding contract. As the enterprise director reflects in retrospect, "It was our fault that we did not conduct the work of clarification in time. We thought: Who would ever care about this land?" (LFE director, Perm region, 2013).

This silence around supposedly useless land titles ended in 2007 when a businessman from the regional capital Perm, who thus far had made his money in industry, started buying land shares in Setovka and other villages. He had already taken over and restructured the entire enterprise in a neighboring village the year before, one year after its bankruptcy. Being also involved in regional politics, he further presented plans to develop the villages in which he operated. In Setovka, as in many other instances, the exact form of land title transactions remained somewhat foggy. A local middleman is said to have approached title-owning villagers individually and offered them 8,500 rubles (around $320 in early 2007) per land title certifying ownership of 7.5 hectares. The village's mayor found out about the land sales by chance from a regional land registry and informed the enterprise director. He could not at first believe that villagers were selling land entitlements; the mayor had to convince him. Land sales thus hit the village authorities by surprise; they appeared unexpected or even unthinkable. The mayor describes her reaction to the news as a shock that she felt bodily: "At that moment I went through this very horror, and I literally stopped moving—I had some terrible pain in my legs. Seeing that our people could behave this way came as a real shock for me. I could understand if they sold land lying fallow already, [land] of a nonexistent kolkhoz. But that of a working enterprise! It was the first time that I encountered such a thing, that the land of a working enterprise was bought up. And I was very worried" (Village mayor, Perm region, 2010).

The expanding enterprise had already bought seventy out of the 539 land titles of the enterprise's land bank. Most of these documents were not formalized as individual property: they entitled the holder to fractional ownership but without specifying any concrete parcel of land. Few shareholders had taken up the lengthy, complicated, and costly bureaucratic process of formalizing land titles. Thus, while property entitlements were owned individually, the land bank as such remained collectively managed.

The law[11] defines the collective of shareholders as the authority to decide on any changes to a land bank in which individuals own titles but no clearly defined physical parcel of land, including the process of formalizing ownership in such a piece of land (Shagaida 2010). As the "investor" had bought entitlements and not actual farmland, the assembly of shareholders had to approve the location of the land before he could legally work it. The assembly is not obliged to approve the location preferred by the party demanding the formalization, and thus has substantial power to block such requests. The investor thus aimed at acquiring most of the land shares, which would have brought him the majority of votes in the shareholder assembly, enabling him to outvote all other members on the formalization of land titles. Thus, stopping sales before this political tipping point and regaining control over the village farmland became an urgent task for the village authorities.

After the mayor had convinced the kolkhoz director that land sales had occurred, they jointly initiated a shareholder assembly. Until then, sales had been conducted privately, beyond public attention, and not articulated as a matter of collective concern. This changed with the assembly that brought together 241 shareholders, which made it the largest in decades. The matter of land sales was turned into a more-than-individual, collective issue potentially threatening the very fabric of common village life. The effects were immediate, as the village mayor recalls: "We really brought together a big, a very big number of inhabitants, living on our territory, explaining that their action creates the threat of liquidating a running enterprise. And then sales actually stopped" (Village mayor, Perm region, 2013).[12]

How could shareholders so quickly be convinced to stop selling their shares? The mayor describes the shift away from the indifferent attitude toward share ownership that had prevailed before the assembly:

> [People would think,] what's the use of this piece of paper lying around? It was, after all, issued in the year 1992, but the sales occurred in 2007. This is to say, the document is lying around for fifteen years, without movement, and . . . is of no use for you. "Will you work this land?"—"No, I won't."—"Well, so then sell it, there is an opportunity; there is someone who wants to buy it and will give you money. Why should it bother you?" I suppose that in most cases people did this either unconsciously or out of material necessity . . . because when they later came to us, and we told them: "Why do you give away land which [the enterprise] is working? . . . Your children are living here, work in this kolkhoz. You sold this land today, where will your son be working tomorrow?" They weren't aware of this issue. . . . When you start talking to them, they really begin to sweat instantly, they flush; "What, why did we do it like this?," but they have already done it. . . . Therefore, when during the meeting we explained to people what this might lead up to; to the abolishment of the jobs of their own children, relatives, and friends. . . . Then people began to realize (Village mayor, Perm region, 2010).

Land documents were perceived as useless paper lying around. A further reason for rural residents to consider selling land certificates was the perceived uncertainty of this ownership. One rural dweller explained her reasons for considering selling her share in 2013: "And maybe it will happen that, just as it came, it will be gone, this land. And that's it. Just as they gave us these certificates, they will take them from us. They will say: 'You used to have land, and now it is gone.' The government has its own policies, after all. . . . Who knows what turns policies will take. We cannot, so to say, foresee that. A bird in the hand is worth two in the bush. At least something, at least 15,000 [rubles]" (Rural dweller, Perm region, 2013).

These 15,000 rubles that shareholders could get for a share at this later point were roughly equivalent to $500, or an average monthly agricultural wage. This amount seems formidable if one understands it to be in exchange for a useless and worthless certificate. However, not everyone saw it that way. Some emphasized that shares in enterprises and land, besides becoming a political instrument to keep the local enterprise alive, were meant to reward workers for long years of labor on collective enterprises *and* should have allowed them to gain economic independence. To some degree, both claims correspond with the official reform logic. Seen this way, 15,000 rubles was no great sum at all.

Six years after the assembly, villagers remember the possibility that "the kolkhoz will be left without land" (Rural dweller, Perm region, 2013) as a critical turning point in the village and in local attitudes. The shareholder assembly turned land certificates into a contested and political issue as the realization that the kolkhoz could be lost in Setovka reshaped the kolkhoz and the village. Some villagers describe others' decision to sell land as irrational because at that time prices were so low and the benefits from selling a share were so limited that they could not possibly outweigh the risks caused by the damage done to the enterprise. Others emphasize that those who sold needed money urgently, even these "cheap, worthless eight thousand [rubles]" (Former village mayor, Perm region, 2013), for instance, for medicine or surgery. Further, since land titles brought so few benefits in the present and possibly also in the future, the decision to sell made sense from an individual viewpoint: "We understand what this land really gives, it will not give its gains immediately. . . . They sold, and they also understood. Say even some heavy drinker, he also understood that the situation will not change within the next ten years. . . . But money is needed today! And so, will he be a hero of the day or not, and so he didn't hang a care on this decision. . . . They announce it today, I will go, give it to them" (Former village mayor, Perm region, 2013).

Others similarly describe sales as quite understandable since people were offered "real money" or "living money" (*zhivye den'gi*) for "dead paper," as the land documents were often called. The investor's offer to buy shares created an opportunity that had not existed before to sell titles. Thus, seen from the angle of private property, the decision to sell land titles may seem perfectly rational: gaining no benefit from owning these titles, people realized some benefits by selling them. In this sense, the assembly was also mobilized against individualistic notions of freedom implicit in the concept of private property. Interestingly, I have not heard villagers complaining about a curtailment of their freedoms. Rather, the land entitlements were given new meaning and worth. Had they appeared as worthless to an individual, they now became meaningful and even vital for the functioning of a collective. While selling land appeared as a rational and legitimate decision at one point, it was turned into something to regret and be ashamed of in retrospect. Land titles have become a different thing in the process.

"We forgot about [the land titles], . . . and then when the law began to work, everyone took them out, remembered them," is how the enterprise director describes their life course in the village (LFE director, Perm region, 2013). To remember land titles, their owners had to be reminded of them. During the shareholder assembly in 2007, the mayor described the history, role, and current state of land titles: their number and size, who received them in 1992, shareholders' rights and options, and the current status of collective long-term leases.[13] Thereafter, many villagers began to sell their land documents to the local "kolkhoz." This implied investing labor. They had to search for their forgotten documents, these "pieces of paper." If they could not find them, they had to get them reissued. Lawyers and surveyors had to be involved, and someone had to pay for the procedure. Efforts and resources had to be invested to formalize property titles, and there had to be a reason for doing so. Therefore, the "law began to work" only after land titles had become subject to explicit interests. The "fuzziness" of post-Soviet property relations (Verdery 1999), and institutional constraints on the full formalization of land entitlements (Allina-Pisano 2008; Shagaida 2010), certainly had hindered formalization before, but more importantly, the formalization of land titles had to become meaningful for villagers and the local enterprise alike to be set in motion. The formalization of land titles promised to stabilize rather indeterminate land relations, but different parties followed different aims. The two enterprises struggled to consolidate their control over land banks, the local administration supported its enterprise to protect the village's economic basis, and shareholders were enrolled in the struggle as their individual decisions turned out to stabilize or destabilize some of the village's most fundamental arrangements. Land titles, long seen as dead paper, now became vital tools.

Kolkhoz Relations

Besides calling the enterprise their kolkhoz, villagers today refer to the enterprise as the *gradoobrazuiushchee predpriiatie*. The term refers to the monofunctional settlement model that dominated Soviet planning and effectively shaped most villages' economic structures. Here, enterprises are planned to be a settlement's single main economic base that results in the (often ongoing) dependence of whole villages' economies and wider social functions on single enterprises (Nefedova 2014, 74).[14] In a relatively isolated village such as Setovka, the impact of and dependence on such an enterprise is amplified, and even today the vanishing of an enterprise can appear as an existential threat to villagers: "How should we live without the kolkhoz? . . . So many people will be left even without work . . . but the kolkhoz won't be anymore, our school won't be anymore, nothing will remain then. People will go somewhere, will go to search . . . and the last children that remained here will leave us. . . . All the village lives around the kolkhoz" (Rural dweller, Perm region, 2013).

To better understand what brings people to the conclusion that "the village lives around the kolkhoz" and would be threatened in its entirety by its disappearance, it is important to understand these enterprises as more than agricultural producers and employers. To varying degrees, they continue to be units of production *and* need fulfillment in the sense of the *khoziaistvo*, even after kolkhozes and the underlying planning structures were formally abolished long ago. Setovka's inhabitants pointed to neighboring villages that had lost their local enterprises. The mayor of one such village describes the event as follows:

> When the kolkhoz ceased to exist, I was in shock. I said to myself, how shall we live at all? How? Here the kolkhoz, there the kolkhoz helped out. I knew that the [former] mayor, just after the roads were covered with snow, immediately would call the kolkhoz—"Help us immediately with the machinery." They come and do it. The water pipes are old. We need this dredger urgently. The kolkhoz would come and helped anyway. I was in such perplexity. I thought, oh my god, how shall we live, how shall we live at all? We won't be able to. Well, the devil is not as frightening as he is painted. So we, gradually, got over it by ourselves. But how, who helped? . . . Private tractor owners . . . and other kolkhozes [from neighboring villages]. . . . They didn't let us die. I would like to thank them. They helped (Village mayor, Perm region, 2014).

The event she describes is the complete sell-off and dismantling of the local agricultural infrastructure in 2004, after a change in enterprise ownership. She addresses the effects in existential terms, as in many other comparable instances: "How shall we live at all?" Part of the reason is that the enterprise is more than an agricultural producer; it "helps" the village in different ways by satisfying individual and collective material needs. The quote indicates that maintaining these functions is more important than preserving the organizational or legal form—if there are other units that can take over these functions, the collective farm enterprise can in principle be substituted. Kolkhoz relations as conceptualized here are hybrid and changing, and we will encounter them in different forms over the chapters.

Three different terms are commonly used for enterprise provision for rural dwellers, households, and village administrations. *Pomoshch'* translates as help, aid, assistance, or succor, and may imply dependence on authorities' goodwill. *Podderzhka* translates into support or maintenance and implies a stronger sense of obligation and necessity. If *pomoshch'* is based more on personal relations and friendship, *podderzhka* points to a form of responsibility that comes with authority. *Podderzhka* is what parents are obliged to provide for children, or what the state is obliged to provide for citizens. *Podderzhka* rests on a social contract and considers recipients' specific needs and vulnerabilities. *Usluga*, finally, translates as service or favor and bears a similar dual meaning to the English term. It may refer to a service offered for payment, but also to the act of serving (*sluzhit'*)—a person, a cause, or a god. These different meanings illustrate that kolkhoz relations of help and support are contingent and hybrid from the very beginning, related as they are to different rationalities and orders of worth. As we shall see, they may also be altered, employed, and redeployed by different actors for different ends.

The obligation to help is institutionalized and an object of negotiation between various authorities, from the local to the state level. But it also results from concrete needs. To sustain social life in a village, someone must clean the roads after heavy snowfall or repair them from time to time, someone has to take care of the school or cultural center buildings, someone has to take care of and repair local water systems, and someone has to remove the garbage from a village. Even private subsidiary agriculture often depends on machinery provided by a local enterprise. Obligations to provide such services are formalized to varying degrees, but formal responsibilities often do not match actual capacities or willingness. Enterprises with the technical and organizational capacity to do something about concrete needs that arise in their villages thus often substitute formal responsibilities of the state or of underfinanced and understaffed village administrations (Moser and Lindner 2011). They may have strategic reasons for doing so. At a basic level, they have an interest in keeping village life going because they depend on villagers as workers and landowners. An enterprise does not have to be in an economically stable or powerful position to provide support that appears vital from the perspective of villagers and the village administration. Even enterprises that struggle to be profitable can provide machinery, workers, know-how, and organizational capacities that can be vital for local communities. On a local scale, enterprises bundle a wide range of resources. As one farm director puts it: "Everything goes through the kolkhoz (*Vse idet cherez kolkhoz*)" (LFE director, Perm region, 2013). The enterprise constitutes an "obligatory passage point" (Callon 1986) that coordinates decision-making, capital and resources, instruments, infrastructures, and labor (see chapter 5).

Enterprises' support for workers or villagers is significant because wages may be high enough for workers to get by, but they are often insufficient to set aside money for extra expenses. Without the enterprises' support, for instance, a young specialist will often be unable to create a home and family. Private subsidiary agriculture, for example, gains significance for households that have to get by on low incomes. Enterprises' support in situations of special need, or by technical support for subsidiary farming, thus represent fixes that are also related to low incomes and poverty (Pallot and Nefedova 2007, 26).

As Setovka's kolkhoz came under threat, making an implicit "social contract"[15] explicit provided the basis for problematizing and criticizing individual decisions, navigating possible development pathways, and stabilizing social relations. That the kolkhoz was mobilized, and the kolkhoz contract rearticulated, rather than simply left unchanged, is important for two reasons: first, adapting and stabilizing these relations required action and justification. Second, it occurred under conditions of change rather than stagnation. Land sales catalyzed the use of land titles to ends very different from privatization, and these were bound to the articulation of the kolkhoz as a social contract. No longer taken for granted, the kolkhoz was turned into a shared matter of concern, an institution that had to be upheld collectively. As a private farmer in Setovka concludes: "The kolkhoz needs us, too."

Had individual land rights caused a threat to the enterprise before, now they were used to enroll shareholders in the project of preserving the kolkhoz. One shareholder describes this new engagement with land entitlements from his perspective:

> The fact that all stick to their kolkhoz is still present here, with . . . our collective, village collective. And that's why particularly the attitude to selling land away somewhere is seen as somewhat negative. . . . See, I am a shareholder myself. . . . Of course, I didn't hurry to give [the land to an external enterprise], but I also see that I will not work it myself either, I am not quite a *kolkhoznik*. Thus, I took it and gave it to [the local kolkhoz director]. Although a year has passed already since [then, he] didn't give me a penny yet. This shows that he isn't even able to pay for the land shares that we gave him, that is, his economic

condition is very weak, you see? But, knowing about this situation, we will still give him [our shares]. Let him work this land rather than some [neighboring enterprise] there. Even if I haven't received my money from [him], I know, that . . . the land will stay in place, the kolkhoz will keep on existing for some time on a legitimate basis, and people will be employed (Former village mayor, Perm region, 2013).

From the viewpoint of property ownership, giving your land titles to the local enterprise without being paid seems irrational. But we see a different kind of normative framework here. After the village assembly, property titles were used for stabilizing and recreating kolkhoz relations. Kolkhoz relations were politicized and turned explicit to be preserved. The land would "stay in place" for the kolkhoz, and the kolkhoz would keep the land available for villagers to work it, and allow the village to stay in place, too. This became the prevailing story about the village and the kolkhoz. It shows, among other things, the complexity of land relations.

Kolkhoz relations have been and are rearticulated in other places, too. In a village in the Central Black Earth region, Dmitry Ivanovich, a former kolkhoz agronomist, started a private farming enterprise in 2004. That same year, a regional company took over the former collective farm and land bank, promising fresh capital, new machinery, and an increase in production. The shareholder assembly agreed on a preliminary lease contract limited to eleven months. As in many other instances across rural Russia at that time, the investor did not revive production but sold off what they could (see chapter 3). As Dmitry Ivanovich describes in retrospect: "Within one year, practically nothing was left of the enterprise. All basic facilities, everything possible, all metal they carried away for sale, buildings . . . they even took out the doors. They dug up the irrigation, there had been ten kilometers of irrigation here, for around six hundred hectares. . . . They slaughtered all cattle, not even one pig, not one cow remained. These investors . . ." (LFE director, Lipetsk region, 2012).

Having witnessed this looting, local shareholders approached Dmitry Ivanovich with the request to take over what remained of the enterprise as the lease contract was about to expire—although the initial start-up of his private farm had not earned much local sympathy some months earlier, similar to many other private farmers at that time (Nefedova 2014). After the dismantling of the former kolkhoz, however, shareholders were ready to let him use all the village lands for free: people did not expect him to pay rent, but to revive the enterprise, employ villagers, and reestablish kolkhoz services, says the man who thus became an enterprise director. Only when the enterprise had been stabilized would land rents be reintroduced. He agreed and took over the enterprise along with the responsibility of sustaining the village. In 2014, ten years after having started his private farm on 160 hectares, the enterprise that Dmitry Ivanovich headed has grown beyond the former kolkhoz, comprising a land bank of about 7,000 hectares.

The enterprise is formally registered as a private farm, but kolkhoz relations are as strong there as they are in Setovka. To revive the enterprise and its collective functions was, after all, a central part of the agreement with the village collective from the beginning: "They gave us these papers, saying 'Here, yours'... We took them, people united, and the enterprise remained, as it had been before" (LFE director, Lipetsk region, 2012). The director lives in a house right opposite the farm enterprise's three-room central office, and the several hours we spent in conversation revealed what being a *khoziain*—the head of a *khoziaistvo*[16]—meant for him: people would approach him at home or in the office, look for him across the vast farm territory, and his two mobile phones would often ring simultaneously. Villagers' inquiries would concern employment or building materials, enterprise machinery for repairs or cultivation, and financial help in crisis situations. People asked for his advice on agronomic or market issues or approached him to sell him their land titles. He would never reject any request straight away, villagers told me, even if people approached him at home before he set off to work early in the morning.[17] He never even rejected any of my requests for meetings.

The director explains that his engagement also reflects the enterprises' founding agreement. People delegated power and responsibility to him to run the enterprise as a kolkhoz. This obliges him to provide support and services, but also to keep the enterprise intact and running: "People ... gave me their land shares. This is why they come to the enterprise as if it was their home. I take up all the questions and give them millet. And if I would sell, where would they turn to?... They would treat them like livestock, and in the end, you do not only sell the enterprise but your people. Your village" (LFE director, Lipetsk region, 2012).

Obligations to people's needs form part of agreements. For instance, even after villagers sell land titles to Dmitry Ivanovich, he will keep on cultivating their household plots and deliver them an as-if rent of two-hundred kilos of grain per share per annum. He thus upholds kolkhoz-like forms of support even after the formal privatization of the enterprise and land.

Sticking to kolkhoz obligations does not necessarily contradict economic rationality. For instance, villagers, workers, and district authorities repeatedly told me that Dmitry Ivanovich is managing with only a few guards keeping an eye on machinery, products, and workers. "Why should people steal," one man commented, "when they are getting what they demand, and it is the enterprise that is keeping up the entire village?" This is remarkable, given that in many other enterprises, guards outnumber agricultural workers—to prevent theft, but also to control labor discipline. Foreign company representatives blamed up to 50 percent of losses of operational profits, or an equivalent of 25 percent additional "taxes," on theft and its indirect consequences (Lander and Kuns 2021, 23). This echoes results from other studies that found that "some instrumental reasons for social support have partly remained in place" (Visser, Kurakin, and Nikulin 2019, 582). At a more general level, it has been argued that *khoziaistvo* can be understood as a form of governance at different scales, from the biopolitics of managing national populations (Collier 2011) to the networks of rights and obligations that the *khoziains* of agricultural enterprises create and steer as a basis of their own power and authority, which, to comply with local moral economies, implies social obligations (Rogers 2006).

Back in Setovka, one manager in the investor's enterprise tells a similar story about the kolkhoz that he describes as puzzling in comparison to his own experience: "I asked [the kolkhoz director], how do you work? 'But [our workers] work themselves, they work with me,' he said, 'get ready themselves. Although their wages are much lower than with us. We [in contrast] must chase them, unfortunately'" (LFE director Perm region, 2014). In the investor's enterprise, another interlocutor explains, people would perceive themselves as working for a master, in contrast to Setovka, where they perceive themselves as working for themselves.

Kolkhoz relations can be translated into economic strategies. I witnessed how directors and managers calculated that by investing in support and thus building loyalty, they would save more on security measures. Only one step further, managers' strategic use of support associated with the kolkhoz can help them "to persuade people to work for them for the miserly money wages they can pay" (Pallot and Nefedova 2007, 26; Rogers 2006) or want to pay. We will return to related issues in chapter 5. There are further downsides to such forms of authority. Patronage is part of what is expected from a *khoziain*, but it is largely informal and can be quite arbitrary. Paternalism is part of what constitutes their power and authority, and we will encounter different examples of how old and new "masters" used and misused such power for their benefit.

Enacting the Kolkhoz

In Setovka, we see that, among other things, kolkhoz relations can also both reflect and ground rural residents' agency and their ways of navigating present conditions. When villagers started to mobilize to preserve their "kolkhoz"

FIGURE 2.5. Dmitry Ivanovich and a worker on his enterprise investigating machinery. Author's photograph.

in 2007, they fought for an institution that had been formally abolished fifteen years before. And yet this is not a story of stagnation. The concerns that I encountered in Setovka and other villages were not that kolkhoz relations might change; they were constantly changing anyhow. Rather, concerns were that they may break down and leave a void that would not be filled. Even in Setovka, where the sense of kolkhoz was described as particularly strong, it was not perceived as intact or stable even before the 2007 local crisis. For instance, when land sales occurred, some villagers were angered by a form of betrayal against the "kolkhozness" of their enterprise, including one villager who actively agitated for and helped to mediate land sales. The mayor recalls: "There was an ongoing reorganization of the enterprise from one form to another. There was a sort of anger. A kolkhoz is a collective enterprise, and thus when it was transformed into a private one, sensible people did not understand how it was that they found themselves in a private one . . . Kolia was angry, and offended, that wages were not paid out, and the enterprise was made a private one at the same time" (Village mayor, Perm region, 2010).

Frustration among rural dwellers about the simultaneous nonpayment of wages and actual loss of enterprise shares—and hence the devaluation of both current and past labor—are not unique to Setovka. The enterprise here, just as many others, had gone through various collective and cooperative organizational and ownership formats[18] before it became a private limited liability company in 2008.[19] Shareholders' titles have evaporated in the process and been transformed into the informal right to benefit from kolkhoz services.

The 2007 land sales were followed by the formalization of land relations and the accumulation of land property in the hands of the "old" kolkhoz director. The number of land shares he owned increased from insignificant in 2007 to 87 in 2011, and 270 in 2013, which made him the majority owner. He states that he had not expected "that people would bring their shares so actively" (LFE director, Perm region, 2012). The increase in sales was not only the effect of local dynamics but also of a growing fear that state authorities were becoming more serious about requiring the formalization of land titles and nationalizing non-formalized land shares sooner or later. Three years after the assembly, the two enterprise directors met in person, and "the investor" proposed to incorporate the Setovka farm into the structure of his enterprise. The old "kolkhoz director" turned down the proposal. However, now the single owner of the enterprise and majority owner of the land bank, it was up to him to decide, and he could have sold the enterprise without any assembly having a say.

An enterprise task force initiated the formalization process for more than 325 land titles.[20] The leasing contracts between shareholders and the farm enterprise were renewed, and for the first time they implied something akin to rent: the shareholders were assigned the right to kolkhoz services equaling 500 rubles.[21] This introduced a new distinction among village inhabitants, as before the assembly the only effective differentiation concerning enterprise services was whether people were enterprise employees or not. But now, those without land titles had to pay higher prices for kolkhoz services. Furthermore, a gradual monetization of leases followed.[22]

To think of the kolkhoz as relations being *enacted*, rather than being the product of institutional inertia or structural persistence, allows us to acknowledge the agency of those who actively uphold or reinvent kolkhoz relations, but it is also important because this kind of continuity is far from guaranteed under given political-economic circumstances. Kolkhoz relations are not a mere legacy but constitute goods that have to be defended as some agricultural enterprises struggle for economic survival or actively try to get rid of them. As Setovka's former mayor puts it: "Today a kolkhoz stands as an ordinary businessman. That is, if it exists or not doesn't concern anyone . . . If it crashes today, well, that's it, sorry, the businessman didn't make it, the business collapsed. That's it!" (Former village mayor, Perm region, 2013).

Seen from this angle, claiming the kolkhoz means laying claim to a form of organizing the economy that stands against its time, defending a substantive approach to the economy against a formal one. Claims to the kolkhoz are employed against economic models that would lead to the abandonment of workers, farms, land, machinery, or cattle. Many thus look at the kolkhoz as something that exists despite rather than because of current political-economic conditions. When such claims are enacted, they bring into being new and hybrid arrangements. Villagers often emphasize that things would be organized differently if market principles were fully applied and that this would not only affect the formal economy of the agricultural enterprise but also household production, which relies heavily on kolkhoz support: "Without the kolkhoz, we will be lost. . . . If private [entrepreneurs] will cultivate [our household plots], prices will rise. Private is private, in the end. Demand creates supply. . . . We will turn to him, he will charge an exorbitant price, and that will be the end of the story. And we will be left with our plots and with a shovel [laughs], digging" (Rural dweller, Perm region, 2013).

The kind of agency described in this chapter, mobilized against such prospects of losing formal and informal arrangements that uphold livelihoods, does not quite match most established images of rural resistance and radical politics. We don't see a grassroots movement defending smallholder farming, no opposition against industrialized agriculture, and no well-coordinated rural movement. What we see is a struggle for the maintenance of social contracts and obligations, the preservation of infrastructures and institutions, agricultural enterprises that produce goods but also provide various supports. Underlying such strategies may be the sense that preserving what still works is more realistic than setting up or waiting for alternatives. This is how a farmer in another region puts it: "The entire infrastructure in agriculture was built under the USSR It is rarely built today. It persists. But someday it will fall into disrepair" (Private farmer, Nizhniy Novgorod region, 2021).

Such strategies may seem somewhat conservative. But they can also be understood as a reasonable form of situated agency, which I framed in the introduction as (re)assembling: bringing or holding together people; maintaining social relations and material infrastructures underlying individual and collective agency; and becoming even more important under conditions of much uncertainty and fundamental change.

Situating Present Kolkhoz Relations Historically

The prevailing relevance of kolkhoz relations speaks to the limits of post-Soviet agrarian reforms, including the land reform that failed to fill many of the gaps created by the dismantling of the previous system. To some degree, kolkhoz relations persisted because they were not substituted, for example, through working schemes based on land rights and family farm agriculture. The hybrid formations that resulted from this differ substantially from rural economic patterns in other parts of the world (Averkieva 2017), and this matters greatly for a context-specific understanding of rural dispossession in Russia. In the introduction, I defined dispersed dispossession as a drawn-out and recursive process that implies the deterioration, separation, and rearrangement of webs of relations. We can now see kolkhoz relations as among the goods at stake.

Addressing kolkhoz relations as being enacted and reinvented in correspondence with distinct historical-geographic situations helps free them from the "sovietness" sometimes ascribed to them, and to disqualify related claims; it allows them to be rehabilitated as legitimate claims to organizing economic relations in specific ways. Rural dwellers do not romanticize the Soviet past by referring to the kolkhoz, although memories may appear a bit too rosy in some accounts when contrasting the relatively robust social policies during the late Soviet period with the harsh post-Soviet crisis. But people disagree and argue about what has changed for better or worse over the past decades: memories and opinions expressed by some are criticized as overoptimistic or nostalgic by others. Some emphasize how village life has *always* been comparatively hard; others talk about family members' deportation during "dekulakization" or the supply shortages during the Soviet period. People may stress they liked Soviet-era employment security but appreciate the relative freedom of choice of employment now. Some say they were better off during the early transformation period, when no wages were paid and workers were allowed to use kolkhoz produce, materials, and machinery for private purposes (such as building or renovating houses, or private subsidiary agriculture) than after the return of monetary wages that did not cover basic needs. They may acknowledge that nowadays many more people own private cars than ever before, but also that the deterioration of public transport in rural areas poses problems for many who do not. People may appreciate the current influx of urban capital—people from the cities buying land, hiring villagers for constructing dachas, and spending on their weekend trips and summer holidays (Caldwell 2010)—but at the same time they see the rural–urban divide growing. They may lament the ongoing decrease of agricultural jobs but acknowledge the rise in pensions or government support for entrepreneurial activities.

Many rural dwellers' narratives on the changes over the last years very much consider and are even built on ambivalence. This is different from being nostalgic about the Soviet system. Through their stories on how systemic changes translated into place-specific trajectories, they demonstrate that "lamenting the losses that came with the collapse of state socialism does not imply wishing it back" (Gille 2010, 286). Rather, paying attention to how the past is selectively mobilized and reconstructed in contemporary social practices (Hörschelmann and Stenning 2008) allows one to grasp how it is invoked "to contrast it with, and thereby criticize, the present" (Pine 2007, 111), to draw clearer contours of a present that often seems unfavorable, uncertain, and somewhat elusive. Hence many such references have "no more to do with the desire to return to a re-membered or idealized past than with the project of defining and claiming au-tonomy in the present" (Boyer 2010, 25) and to lay claim to goods that remain unrecognized within the now-dominant orders of worth.

It has been shown in many studies and is widely recognized that many of the ways in which the past is being evoked and reinvented in contemporary Russia are regressive or otherwise politically problematic. It is not always pos-sible to draw a clear line between past-bound political propaganda and pop-ulism and what I described in this chapter as understandable and often le-gitimate claims. One of the tasks, then, is to recognize ambivalence both of historic conditions and claims made on this basis.

Chapter 3

Ruins

The following words, uttered in 2014 by the mayor of a small village in the Perm region, recall how the local farm enterprise was taken apart in 2004. The event marked the end of a local agricultural enterprise in the village.

> There was a war going on here. They took away, seized, drove away . . . this was a terrifying moment. There was a tractor standing in our village administration. . . . They even stole that one, took it. . . . In such an instance today, I would understand that they . . . [lack] the documents for the tractor . . . it would be possible to hide it somewhere. . . . Such big guys came, really took everything, and drove off. Such excitement. It carried on, it was really terrible. Day and night the screech of nails. They completely took everything apart. Made off with everything that remained. Because, they said, "we worked in the kolkhoz for all of our lives, and they take away everything; so we take home at least something, a nail, a plank." Such was people's attitude. It was impossible to stop them from taking apart all these. . . . There was such a nice garage here, our man said: "Come on, guys, we will not take it apart. We will use it for our machinery." But they could not stop them, they could not. Just day and night screeching of nails, planks, iron . . . only some were able to hide something. What belonged to others, they just took away. . . . See, one of our [men], drove on a tractor. They took him off the tractor. Gave him a thick ear. Got on the tractor, drove away, cut it up, that's it. He even howled. A man howled, with pity for his tractor, on which he worked. It was a new tractor. They took it and drove it away (Village mayor, Perm region, 2014).

This narrative is dramatic. The event fundamentally changed village life. It occurred suddenly, it seemed to come from the outside, and it took villagers by surprise. The mayor's description makes tangible the process of destruction: sounds, materials, actors, feelings, and interactions. But however vivid the description, a closer reading reveals that what happened was far from straight-forward or obvious. The mayor describes her puzzlement in this situation in which she simply did not know what to do. It is only in retrospect that she identifies some agency she may have had, but which she did not realize at the time. Agency seemed to be on the side of those who caused the destruction, but even here the picture becomes blurry. Who were they? On the one hand, there were the "big guys" who "came" to the village as strangers. They had been hired for taking apart the enterprise infrastructure. But then there were also the villagers themselves. As the "outsiders" took apart the farm, some of the locals began to appropriate parts of the formerly collective infrastructure, tak-ing home bricks, iron, and planks. It became hard to distinguish who did the looting and who was affected by it.

Responsibility for the event is ascribed to the farm owner who had taken over the enterprise from his father. He never explained his decision publicly, but apparently he decided to get rid of the nonlucrative farm and squeeze out whatever money he could get. He quickly sold off a nonprofitable asset. But the enterprise closure reflects a more complex temporal structure. The breakup of the farm goes on for days, and even ten years later it is remembered vividly as an event with fundamental and lasting effects. Villagers justify their appro-priation of material by claiming their part in building up the enterprise. To them, the ruination of the enterprise means the devaluation of both past la-bor and future possibility, as for the man who will not be able to work on "his" new tractor in future. There is no agricultural enterprise left in the village, only some of the land is worked by neighboring farms.

This description is among the more spectacular ones, but it is not unusual. The agrarian and rural crisis that set in with the collapse of the Soviet sys-tem became manifest in the breakdown of organizational, subsidiary, and dis-tributional structures from the national to the local level. Among the effects were the bankruptcy of many enterprises, the reduction of labor-intensive pro-duction and mass dismissal of workers, and the deterioration of material in-frastructure and institutionalized support of the kind described in the previ-ous chapter. To address such forms of loss, concepts of dispossession must go beyond individual property, rights, or access and include the decay and dis-mantling of webs of relations that (used to) support various aspects of collec-tive and individual life. Dispossession occurs not only in but through crises (Dudley 2000; Harvey 2003), and it results not merely in individual but in col-lective loss.

Actors on the ground refer to ruins as heuristic tools to make sense of com-plex processes of dispersed dispossession as an iterative process drawn out over time that spans a range of scales and in which individual stories and world history are intermingled. The reflection on ruins and ruination, as I shall argue, helps to address representational challenges that have to do with the dispersed character of the forms of dispossession discussed here. As reported in earlier studies (Paxson 2005; Rogers 2006), during fieldwork I often heard rural dwellers summing up experiences over the past few decades with the statement *vse razvalili*: "They ruined/broke down/messed up everything." So if creative destruction, or dismantling an existing system to pave the way for installing a new one, is among the core aims of "shock therapy," the destructive part has clearly left a lasting impression. Building a new system turned out to be more complicated, however. Many rural dwellers still describe their situation as unstable and unpredictable. I will argue that their references to the ruins of a more stable and comprehensible past can be understood in this specific context of a precarious present. References to ruins illustrate what exactly has been lost, but also indicate that things have been, and could become, otherwise: they "denaturalize the present" (Gordillo 2014, 14) and (re)orient it toward the past and future. While the previous chapter focused on kolkhoz relations being enacted in and for the present, this chapter looks at the post-Soviet agrarian crisis and investigates its implications for/in the present, as part of the history that shaped it and as part of how actors make sense of it.

The perception of ruination goes beyond the built environment. Millions of hectares of overgrown fields spread across Russia became a symbol of agrarian decline. In this respect, they came to be regarded as ruined landscapes.[1] The scope of farmland abandonment is at times interpreted as an immense loss of agricultural productivity on a national scale. Indeed, much agricultural land fell fallow during and after the collapse of the Soviet agricultural system (Prishchepov et al. 2013), and researchers described the abandonment of millions of hectares of agricultural land in the former Soviet republics—with Russia having the lion's share—as the most abrupt and widespread land-use change in the twentieth century in the northern hemisphere (Kurganova et al. 2014). Although most farmland abandonment occurred in cold northern or dry southeastern parts of the country and areas remote from larger cities and villages, it created fine-grained and dynamic patchworks. Scholars have described the resulting spatial pattern as "fragmented space" or an "archipelago" of productive farms amid deteriorating and abandoned "black holes" (Ioffe, Nefedova, and Zaslavsky 2004).[2]

Dwelling on ruination, I am aware of the risk of reproducing stereotypes of the Russian countryside as generally "ruined." This would be politically problematic but also counterfactual. People find ways to get by, and new opportunities emerge. Just like other places, Russian villages are home to people who appear to be optimistic, happy about what they have, and curious about what the future will bring. Many give explicit reasons why they prefer to live in the countryside: a calm and green environment rather than urban chaos and noise, or the possibility to live in a house, grow one's food, and get by with occasional jobs rather than stronger dependence on waged income, rental housing, and commodified food supply. In more productive agricultural regions, there are economic opportunities for skilled workers or drivers, and some private farmers have improved greatly over recent years. There are also possibilities beyond agriculture. In the village described in the opening quote, for instance, the regional government opened a psychiatric hospital; a rich businessman registered in the municipality and pays taxes there; and some new entrepreneurial projects have emerged. A growing number of *dachniki*—urban dwellers setting up huts and houses for weekend trips and summer holidays—generate demand for local produce and bring jobs in construction and maintenance. Some village inhabitants commute to other villages, towns, or cities for work. To what extent people kept or lost jobs, found acceptable income alternatives, and find it easy or hard to adapt to changing circumstances varies across places and subject positions. And yet what I describe as ruination here is part of the picture, and ignoring that would risk leaving both harsh material realities and misrepresentations unaddressed. I shall continue this venture into ruination by giving some background on the post-Soviet agrarian crisis, and from there move on to problems and challenges of representation, and the ethnographic present of this study.

Systemic Crisis

Many analysts, commentators, and persons with firsthand experience point to the downsides of post-Soviet disintegration and market reforms when addressing the dire conditions for rural communities in that period. They do not always agree on its causes, extent, and durability, however. More optimistic commentators interpret the post-Soviet agrarian crisis as an interlude between more stable and prosperous periods. For them, it is finally modernized production infrastructure, a consolidated state budget allowing for expanded spending on agrarian subsidies, rural development, and social services, and the closure of infrastructure and provision gaps concerning roads, products, and services providing a basis for relatively optimistic foresight (Izryadnova et al. 2015). More pessimistic interpretations by rural actors and analysts see permanent damage rather than temporary reshuffling. For agrarian sociologist Zemfira Kalugina (2014, 118), for instance, "the reforms have not only failed to achieve what they intended, but have in some sense 'turned back the clock,'" throwing many households back to reliance on informal income and household farming, and dependence on manual family labor. Many analyses lie between such poles and differentiate upsides and downsides. They may acknowledge the lasting increase of inequalities among regions, enterprises, and households, but also point to economic recovery, new social policies, or models of sustainable production (Wegren, Nikulin, and Trotsuk 2023, 2018; Nefedova 2014). There is indeed a need for a nuanced view. The emergence of new forms of rural life, economy, and livelihoods, improvements to the overall economic situation in the countryside, and social provision should be acknowledged. It seems equally important, however, not to overlook the sectors that did not recover and the wounds that would not heal.

The question of how far the agricultural crisis was a direct consequence of the reform as it was designed, or rather resulted from a failure to implement it properly and fix underlying issues remains contested. The question of state withdrawal is a case in point here and complicates the picture (Wegren 2000). As Ioffe and colleagues (2006, 29) reflect, the "most significant change in agricultural production was never legislated, yet it had a more immediate and far-reaching impact on productivity than any law passed by the Duma. This far-reaching change came from the collapse of the state-run procurement and output distribution system and the removal of government price controls. In other words, collective and state farms . . . suddenly were largely left to their own devices."

One may object that state withdrawal was very much part of a political agenda to dismantle an existing agrarian system and replace it with a new one. In a decisive period, the push in this direction came less from the legislative State Duma and more from then-president Yeltsin and his administration, and was propagated by influential Western politicians, technocrats, and institutions such as the IMF. The question of whether the "collapse" of the state-run system was an integral part of a deliberately imposed shock therapy (Klein 2007), or rather resulted from a cascade of crisis dynamics, remains important in terms of historic assessment (Matveev 2019b) but goes beyond the scope of this book, which is more concerned with the structured and structuring effects of agrarian dispossession and crisis as opposed to the drivers behind those effects.

In any case, the gap between optimistic reform talk and the actual withdrawal of resources and breakdown of agricultural production and rural livelihoods was obvious in the 1990s. Agriculture was certainly not on top of policymakers' and businesspersons' interests at that time, and some of them openly labeled Russian agriculture as a rather hopeless sector. State investments and subsidies in agriculture were severely curtailed or cut (Nefedova 2014, 78; We-gren et al. 2014, 382). State policies had an "urban bias" (Wegren 2014, 82) and favored industrial over agrarian production and urban over rural develop-ment. While prices for industrial products and agricultural inputs increased, the government did little to support agricultural wholesale prices but rather kept them low to support food availability in the cities. If the entire Russian economy was deeply affected by instability and a massive devaluation of assets and commodities, the agricultural sector was hit particularly hard. In a con-tracting economy, agriculture lost volume and productivity relative to other economic sectors, and its contribution to the national GDP halved during the 1990s. Food production fell about 50 percent in this decade (Wegren 2014, 83), and agricultural enterprises' output decreased by over 60 percent (Rosstat 2002a, 205). While agricultural wholesale prices were kept low by consumers' limited purchasing power, government food-price regulation, and cheap im-ports, the prices for agricultural inputs, machinery, fuel, energy, and chemi-cals increased and resulted in a steadily growing gap between input costs and output prices. In contrast to Soviet policies that benefited the farms (Nefedova 2014, 75), agrarian producers became strongly disadvantaged in comparison to other sectors along the food chain, with profit margins shifting dramatically to food processing and retail (Zinchenko 2002, 69). During the first three years of market reforms, consumer food prices rose 4.5 times more than wholesale prices (Nefedova 2014, 79–80). State subsidies also plummeted. While agricul-ture was receiving 28 percent of the total investment in the Russian economy from 1965 to 1985, in 2001 agriculture got just 2.7 percent of "the vastly dimin-ished total investment" (Ioffe, Nefedova, and Zaslavsky 2006, 28).

The majority of large farms fell into debt after 1991, and the share of non-profitable enterprises reached 84 percent in 1998 (Rosstat 2002b, 30). The amount had decreased to 28 percent by 2011 (Rosstat 2015a, 48) but this, to a large degree, was due to changes in state legislation and accounting that spurred the liquidation of nonprofitable enterprises (Uzun, Shagaida, and Sa-rajkin 2012, 5–6): the total number of agrarian enterprises decreased from nearly twenty-seven thousand in 1995 to around sixteen thousand in 2007 and less than seven thousand in 2011 (Rosstat 2002b, 2011, 2013). Many of the surviving enterprises radically cut back the former kolkhozes' wide range of products and shut down facilities for vegetable and fruit production, milk and meat processing, and local bakeries. Crop production—which is seasonal and less labor- and capital-intensive—became predominant. The number of agricultural workers declined from more than 9.7 million in 1990 to 7.3 million in 2007 and 4.6 million in 2020 (Rosstat n.d.; Wegren 2014, 100).

Rural inhabitants were greatly affected. Alternative local jobs were limited, as were options to find work elsewhere. From 1991 onward, the deterioration of rural living conditions can be seen along with several indicators such as income, material consumption, housing, infrastructure, and access to and quality of services (Wegren 2014, 50).[3] The result was a "ruralization of poverty" (Gerry, Nivorozhkin, and Rigg 2008). Agricultural workers faced the double burden of falling real incomes across the national economy and "a drastic divergence" (Wegren 2014, 50) in average income compared to other sectors of the economy. This was the reversal of an earlier trend. From the 1950s onward, Soviet state policies led to an improvement of rural populations' living standards in comparison to other areas. According to official statistics, a farmworker in the RSFSR received 81 percent of the monthly monetary income of an industrial worker in 1975 and 102 percent in 1990. The figure declined to 32 percent in the RF around the year 2000. Agricultural wages were lower but also more uncertain than those in other economic sectors. Throughout the 1990s, higher percentages of rural workers did not receive their salaries, and higher percentages of rural pensioners did not receive pensions (or salaries) (Wegren 2014, 51). The percentage of the agricultural workforce with a nominal salary at or below the subsistence minimum declined from a staggering 80.2 in 2000 to 67.8 in 2004 (Rosstat 2005, 162). It was down to 3.7 percent in 2019 (Rosstat 2019, 127). At a household level, however, 53.4 percent of rural households are reported to have had monetary incomes below the subsistence minimum in 2019 compared to 46.6 percent of urban households (Rosstat 2021, 76).[4]

During the height of the agrarian crisis in the 1990s, feedback loops led to downward spirals. Managers' confidence in the largely unprofitable agricultural sector was so low that they shied away from any investment (Nefedova 2014, 81). Farm enterprises, in their struggle for economic survival, often avoided taxation, which affected village administrations' budgets for maintaining social infrastructure (Kalugina 2014, 120). The collapse of safety nets at different scales further increased poverty rates. Even though inequality *within* the rural sphere remained far below urban levels (Wegren 2014, 52–53), the Russian government estimated that 27 percent of rural dwellers were "extremely poor" based on monetary income (and 15 percent based on total income) (Wegren 2014, 79). The fall in rural life-expectancy by almost six years between 1986 and 1994, according to official statistics, cannot be fully explained by poverty, but it is certainly related to the political-economic crisis in the country and particularly the countryside (Eberstadt 2010, 72–74; Rosstat 2010, 101).[5]

Rural households continued to depend on crisis-ridden large farms as the single main employers in villages, the main providers of social functions, and as technical support for household production (chapter 2). In effect, the restructuring or vanishing of large farms in some instances also caused trouble for private subsidiary agriculture (Pallot and Nefedova 2007), which became increasingly important during this period. In the late 1990s, according to some sources, the total labor hours spent in personal subsidiary farming exceeded those in formal agriculture, and a significant part of rural populations reported it was their main food source (Pallot and Nefedova 2007, 19–21). The share of household production of potatoes, vegetables, and livestock increased. For instance, while the number of cattle and pigs held on large farms decreased massively in the early 1990s and steadily thereafter, numbers remained relatively stable and partly increased for personal subsidiary farming. If households already produced a large share of milk and beef during the Soviet period, the share increased in post-Soviet times and stood at 57 percent for beef and 42 percent for milk in 2017 (Uzun, Shagaida, and Lerman 2019). While subsidiary household farming thus helped rural households avoid starvation even in the most severe periods of crisis, the downside is being thrown back to an economy of survival with very limited economic benefits and heavy reliance on burdensome manual labor. Instead of peasant self-sufficiency, rural dwellers kept depending on large farms (as suppliers of fodder and machinery) and on unstable agrarian markets.

Different social groups were affected differently by the crisis, and stark differences remain. In agricultural enterprises, women provide most of the seasonal labor and temporary employment, as well as ill-paid and exhausting jobs in animal husbandry, cleaning, or maintenance (Wegren et al. 2014). Better-paying jobs such as tractor drivers, engineers, or mechanics are male-dominated, and female agronomists, economists, or farm managers are comparatively rare (Wegren et al. 2014, 375). Outside agriculture, women are predominantly employed in rural economies' worst-paid sectors: retail, culture (such as the local cultural centers called *doma kul'tury*), village administration, or as cooks in schools, farms, and kindergartens. And, as elsewhere, women do much more unpaid work in households and personal subsidiary farming (Pallot and Nefedova 2007). As mentioned, stark differences between agrarian workers and rural elites (such as farm directors, specialists, and party officials) were characteristic of Soviet agrarian communities. Such class differences turned out to be more persistent than the political-economic system. For instance, rural elites did much better during restructuring and were more likely to benefit from land reforms by acquiring or renting more land (Wegren 2009). The agrarian crisis also meant different things for different generations.

Older generations saw the devaluation and deterioration of the products of their lifelong labor, ranging from the abolishment of farms they helped build to the plummeting of pensions. For the working generation, the crisis brought a long phase of extreme uncertainty with very different outcomes for individuals. And rural youths left the countryside at very high rates in historical or international comparison.

When an overall economic upturn occurred around the turn of the century, its benefits were distributed unequally across the rural–urban divide: urban poverty declined at twice the rate of rural poverty, and so the latter became predominant by 2004 (Gerry, Nivorozhkin, and Rigg 2008, 599). This trend continues. In a 2009 survey among rural households in twenty-nine regions, low income/rural poverty was named as the number one problem (65 percent of respondents) confronting the countryside (Wegren 2014, 77–78). The 2013 average nominal monthly income in agriculture, hunting, and forestry (the statistics aggregate these three sectors) was 14,129 rubles (around $460), which was 53 percent of that year's national average (Rosstat 2014, 435–40). In 2019, it had increased to 31,728 rubles (still around the same U.S. dollar equivalent by the exchange rate at that time), which was 66 percent of that year's national average (Rosstat 2019, 150–53). Rural unemployment, too, remained significantly higher than in the overall economy (Kalugina 2014, 125).

National food production has increased remarkably over recent years. During the first two decades of the twenty-first century, Russian agriculture grew steadily (Uzun, Shagaida, and Lerman 2019), and the nominal ruble value of agricultural production has increased more than fivefold. Pre-tax profits in agriculture have risen from 11.8 billion to 160.3 billion rubles, and average annual grain harvests have increased substantially (Wegren, Nikulin, and Trotsuk 2023, 3). The recent production volume of several field crops was increased by factors of two to six compared to the late Soviet period (Uzun, Shagaida, and Lerman 2019), a trend that reflects increased productivity and specialization, and global demand. The growth in gross product from agriculture has exceeded the growth rate in national GDP in six of eight years, from 2013 to 2020 (based on ruble value), and Russian wheat exports ranked either first or second globally by volume in every agricultural year since 2014/2015 (Uzun, Shagaida, and Lerman 2019).[6] However, the recovery of agriculture is concentrated in a few regions and agrarian sectors. Out of Russia's eighty-five federal subjects, food production is strongly concentrated in the top five and top ten regions (Wegren, Nikulin, and Trotsuk 2023). This confirms the older hypothesis of spatial fragmentation of the post-Soviet countryside (Ioffe, Nefedova, and Zaslavsky 2004, 2006). Parts of the labor- and resource-intensive livestock sector, notably beef and milk, either contracted further or did not grow significantly (Uzun, Shagaida, and Lerman 2019) as domestic demand partly decreased with diminishing purchasing power, and remains covered mainly through imports.

Hence the effects of some recent national-level agricultural revivals are highly unequally distributed among regions, places, sectors, and households. Primary agriculture remains risky and often hardly profitable for family farmers and some larger farms struggling with unfavorable prices and costs; high interest on loans for seeds, chemical, machinery, and further investments; or crop failure. In consequence, many rural dwellers see themselves, enterprises that employ them, and even large agricultural investors as structurally disadvantaged by the fact that they work in agriculture.

Crises on Top of Preceding Ones

As is well known, the reforms of the late Soviet and early post-Soviet periods were framed and justified as a necessary fix to an inefficient and run-down agrarian system. While some were promoting targeted measures to deal with flaws, others claimed it was necessary to fundamentally dismantle the old system and replace it. In the end, the reform was a mixture of both. Analysts and actors on the ground energetically discussed the question of how flawed the Soviet agrarian system was. It is still relevant, not least for judgments on whether post-Soviet reforms caused the crisis or failed to fully fix a previous one.

The late Soviet phase is described by rural dwellers and historians as one of relative stability and prosperity, especially in contrast to the economic hardships and state repression during collectivization and the postwar period on the one hand and the 1990s' agrarian crisis on the other. The agrarian sector gained attention and some priority in the Brezhnev era. From the 1960s to the 1980s, state expenditures on agriculture increased to 20–28 percent of the overall state budget in contrast to 7 percent in the postwar era. The effects on rural development (including rural housing, social and medical provision, schools, and culture) were significant, and agrarian jobs became relatively well paid. However, the effects on productivity levels were rather modest, and consequently the attempt to intensify agricultural production went along with an excess of expenditures over results. In the late Soviet period, agricultural subsidies accounted for more than 80 percent of the sector's gross output, which made them the highest in the world (Nefedova 2014, 61–65). Therefore, under its relatively stable surface, late Soviet agriculture was strongly dependent on state support and thus relatively prone to crises even before market reforms, such as when, around 1990, decreasing state income from oil and gas exports had a direct impact on the agricultural system. Yields per hectare, milk yields per cow, and other indicators of farm productivity had increased up to the 1970s but remained rather stagnant thereafter while state subsidies increased substantially (Nefedova 2014, 76). The crisis of late Soviet agriculture was a silent one—silenced in official accounts, not always tangible on the ground—but the perceived stability was far from sustainable economically, politically, or environmentally.

The downsides of the Soviet agrarian system are well documented. The plummeting of agrarian productivity over the first years of collectivization resulted in famines. Agricultural expansionism, including the infamous so-called Virgin Lands campaign, was overall ecologically devastating, drew on involuntary resettlement, wiped out other land-use forms such as grazing, and drained resources from core agricultural regions. Ecosystems, landscapes, and rivers were sacrificed for agrarian industrialization. Soil erosion and salination became serious problems overall and degraded some areas to the extent that agriculture became impossible there. The intensification of fertilizer and machinery use without much worker protection had serious health impacts. And pouring incomes from oil and gas exports into agriculture was part of what stabilized an inefficient system for quite some time.[7] Besides cutting subsidies, with some devastating effects, market reforms offered little to fix many of these problems. During the early years, they rather stimulated withdrawal from agriculture. More recent agrarian recovery raised the level of outputs and monetary wages, but many of the problems inherited from the Soviet or early reform phase remain unresolved.

Overall, authors have drawn different conclusions from the Soviet agrarian system. Historian Jenny Leigh Smith (2014, 6) argues that because many of the studies about Soviet agriculture were written by Cold War–era researchers with anti-Soviet biases, the tendency to describe Soviet agriculture as a complete failure still unduly dominates its perception in the West. She concludes that "Soviet agriculture had much in common with its counterparts in capitalist countries around the world" (Smith 2014, 20). It was functional but "inefficient, vulnerable, chaotic, and frustratingly reliant on the natural environment" (Smith 2014, 20). Such a framing allows for acknowledging the dysfunctionalities of and damage caused by the Soviet agrarian system without turning that into a general justification for the "shock therapy" that followed. Many Russia-based researchers abstain from taking a general pro- or anti-Soviet stance when judging the merits and downsides of the Soviet agrarian system (Nikulin 2014; Shanin 1990), and, as this study shows, rural residents often do so as well.

This study follows that path, putting forward the argument that dispersed dispossession is inherent to rounds of succeeding policies and projects, their intended and unintended consequences, and failures. All are part of a history of dispossession in this specific context, and dispossession is part of this context's history. However, as mentioned, it is only a part of it, and the (hi)story of dispossession is one among many stories.

Spectacular Despair: Clichés of the Russian Countryside

Most Western audiences are provided only little insight into rural Russia. The general decrease of attention and spending directed to the country by Western news outlets over recent years and decades went in parallel with a strong (some claim nearly exclusive) focus on geopolitics, Moscow, and the Kremlin. The Russian "provinces" are hardly covered at all (Gathmann and Scholl 2011; Neef 2012). Amid this relative silence, however, one finds striking stereotypes of the Russian countryside, with portrayals of it as desperate and in constant decline. One finds comparable stereotypes in discourses within Russia, too, even though there are surely more alternative stories available. I dwell on such representations here to address and deconstruct stereotypes, but also because they are pointing to actual representational and analytical challenges that should be addressed and not simply avoided.

"Vodka and isolation: welcome to rural Russia" is how a 2007 Reuters article introduces rural Russia to its readers, and it goes on in this spirit: "Alcoholism, devout religious faith and a sense of scratching a living on the fringes of civilization—the hallmarks of the Russian countryside down the ages—linger, sometimes just below the surface" (Kilner 2007). Describing the Russian countryside as a place where nothing will be accomplished, and not much ever was, is a common representational pattern. Another author describes her first impressions of a village called Paradise: "A few slow hours on a wildly bumpy, muddy road, and here we were in the half-abandoned village of Paradise, with black, crooked houses, a heavy-drinking population, and everybody depressed and angry with [the district center] and Moscow authorities. Paradise seemed forgotten among the fields covered in wild grass" (Nemtsova 2015). How do people get by in such places? Hardly at all, such articles often seem to suggest. One article published in the German *Der Spiegel* starts its exploration of a village called "Future," stating that "the struggle for survival begins right at the place name sign" (Schepp 2010, February 7). The story evokes the impression that there was little to say about the village's population besides its drinking or dying. Decay seems omnipresent; even the village shop had to close because "the old were too old, too ill or too drunk, [and] the young moved away, or were too dumb, too apathetic or too drunk" (Schepp 2010, February 7). A dying village with a dying population. "Mother I have some news for you; I will die now" are said to be the last words of a man who drank himself to death. These words are the caption to a photograph showing his mother drinking the same kind of schnapps in the company of neighbors (Schepp 2010, February 7). The article emphasizes that the scene was not unusual, but that what it describes for the village "Future" holds true for rural Russia more generally: "'Future' is everywhere, and in vast Siberia and Central Russia, except some booming cities, its plagues are omnipresent: the backwardness, the decrease in population, and alcoholism" (Schepp 2010, February 7, all translations mine).

To display "dying villages" as exemplary for (rural) Russia as a whole is an established representational pattern. In an article titled "Rural Russia Is Dying of Poverty, Neglect," the author states: "The area around this rural enclave is in steep decline; once-thriving fields are empty and the population is in free fall. Along with many other towns and villages in vast rural Russia, it's a microcosm for a country that, according to recent studies, is withering away. . . . Today, the hamlets dot a forsaken land of rampant poverty where men drink from morning to night. The interconnected crises of low fertility, high death rates and ragged infrastructure have left much of the nation barren" (Lasseter 2009, August 5).

Such diagnoses are generalized for "myriad villages dying a slow death in Russia's provinces" (Khazov-Cassia 2015) and without "much hope left for revival" (Nemtsova 2015). One report concludes that "the lifeblood of Russia's vast and fertile countryside appears to be draining away forever" (Shapovalova 2011, August 30).[8]

Deterioration, a dead end, despair. These are descriptions of the more drastic kind. But they are not exceptional either in their content or in the use of figurative language and photographs creating vivid images of decline and despair, particularly in Western media representation where they exist in a broader context of stereotypes about Russia.[9] Rural residents are othered twofold: as postsocialist and rural (Kay, Shubin, and Thelen 2012). Readers familiar with the post-Soviet context may be reminded of post-Soviet ruin-gazing as a more general pattern of perception, beyond villages. Rebecca Litchfield's 2014 photobook *Soviet Ghosts: A Communist Empire in Decay*, filled with crumbling buildings and infrastructure, illustrates what can be described as a broader tendency by Western journalists, photographers, bloggers, or scholars to fetishize "the infrastructural ruination of places" across the former Soviet Union (Bennett 2021, 332) as traces of "a past civilization" (Bennett 2021, 336). The display of postindustrial decay in the West has been criticized as "ruin porn," with the city of Detroit being the most prominent example (Pohl 2021), and we see that much of this critique holds true concerning descriptions of the Russian countryside: a voyeuristic and potentially obsessive focus on decay and negativity projected onto such places, and a tendency to turn invisible or misrepresent those inhabiting "ruined" spaces. Stereotypes are not necessarily absolutely "wrong" but—as Stuart Hall (1997) reminds us—are situated within "regimes of representation" that generate reductionist, binary, essentializing, and naturalizing truths about groups of people, places, or other entities.[10] Hence the need for a different politics of representation that will address disintegration, loss, and suffering as part but not the essence of these rural realities.

Misrepresentation and projection are by no means new phenomena when it comes to the Russian countryside. Bolsheviks, including Lenin and Trotsky, had lamented peasant conservatism and remained ambivalent about their role in the Soviet project (Shanin 1985). Later Soviet state discourses, however, cherished agricultural workers' vital role in feeding the Soviet nation, celebrated the productivity of the scientific industrialized agrarian system and its workers, and romanticized the harmony and pleasure of collective labor in the kolkhoz (Buck-Morss 2000; P. R. Josephson et al. 2013).[11] In the 1990s, Russian and foreign market reformers problematized rural communities' ostensible conservatism and reluctance to change and ascribed it to collectivism and egalitarianism, which they saw as rooted in the prerevolutionary *obchshina*,[12] Soviet collectivization, or both (Lindner 2008). Different political camps within Russia recurrently mobilize ideas of villagers' ostensible backwardness. The oppositional former Duma deputy Vladimir Ryzhkov, for instance, blamed national stagnation on a rural Russia dissociated from modern urbanites:

> There are, indeed, two Russias. The first Russia consists of about fifteen million "modernist and European" citizens . . . who live mostly in large- and medium-sized cities, have a higher education, and are employed in the private sector . . . they are the foundation of the opposition movement. The second Russia consists of about forty million conservative citizens . . . they are nostalgic about the Soviet period, support Putin, and believe the country as a whole is moving in the right direction. They are mainly residents of outlying provinces, small- and medium-sized cities, and rural areas. Their distinguishing feature is their dependence on government support in the form of sala-

ries, pensions, social benefits, and subsidies from the federal budget (Ruzhkov 2012, September 18).

Around the same time, Putin in his electoral campaign declared demographic decline—symbolized by "ghost villages"—as the "most acute problem of contemporary Russia" (True 2012). Projections and problematizations of the countryside in their various forms are often employed for the sake of intervention and programs of reconfiguration, as will be discussed in the following chapters. The remainder of this chapter is concerned with the continuation and aftermath of the agrarian crisis.

Silent Violence

I get involved in a random chat with two elderly ladies sitting on a bench on a small side street in Letnevo. It is one of the first sunny and mild days after a cold winter, and coming together on the street, picking up some sun, and chatting with whoever happens to be out there seems quite natural. The two women continue with their talk and seem to accept me as an interlocutor who happens to be there, not evoking much surprise, and quickly a sense of familiarity emerges. They speak about things that happened in the village, something that Putin said on television, and about their families. This is where their narratives take a sad turn.

One woman's son died in a Moscow hospital three weeks earlier. She says it was murder, or maybe an accident. In any case, she thinks it was related to his job there, and it was the search for a job that had taken him to Moscow several years before. She has not seen her daughter for ten years since she left for Austria and has not been back to Russia since then. Her mother says it is because she fears that she may not be allowed to return once she leaves the country where life is easier. The other woman begins to talk about her son who died in Moscow twelve years ago, stating that he had been killed but not knowing much about the details of his death. She has a second, younger son who stayed in the village and, as she says, spends his days hanging around and drinking in the village center. Her daughter, who holds a college degree, had been working at the local branch of a bank for eight years, earning 7,000 rubles (around $250) a month. Recently she found a job with an agri-company, which comes with several hours of commuting every day, but also with 22,000-ruble monthly wage. A third woman joins in. She mentions how her son died in a car accident some time ago, probably drunk.

The three continue to talk about sons and grandsons who had been working as guards in a city for some time, spending a good part of their modest income on transport or a city apartment. Some of them quit these jobs and went back to informal or irregular employment in the village, often accompanied by heavy drinking. The women do not seem to blame these young men for how they live, although it makes them suffer, too. Rather, they seem angry about the violent conditions that foreclose options and choices for a good and safe life. It strikes me how they seem to perceive the choice to drink one's life away as not being of less legitimacy or dignity than life-threatening, underpaid, or otherwise humiliating labor for someone else's profit.

All of this does not appear as spectacular or even unusual in the women's narratives—they speak of these things as if they were rather *normal*. Nor am I surprised, as these stories remind me of many others that I have heard over several months during fieldwork: about untimely deaths related to hard and dangerous work, heavy drinking, or suicides, and the sorrow of those (mostly women) outliving their (mostly male) children and spouses. They also remind me of a half-eaten potato that I saw lying on a table at the construction site of a *bania* some days ago. A friend who was showing me the place remarked that the man who had left it there died the next day, unexpectedly, at the age of twenty-four. But the half-eaten potato still lying on this table, while the person who had left it there died two weeks before, did not seem out of place as it would have in many other sites. (Why would a young man die so suddenly? Why would the potato he started to eat transcend his own presence on that scene?)

Such encounters remained disturbing, but they were not unusual. They reminded me of zones of latent warfare that I have visited. Rural dwellers, too, sometimes compared post-Soviet transformation to war. I conducted one period of fieldwork some weeks after the Russian army annexed Crimea. Fighting in Eastern Ukraine intensified and became a constant topic on Russian television. I found the propagandistic coverage in Russian state media hardly bearable and was shocked how many, though certainly not all, of the people I talked to seemed to believe it, or at least not actively question it. But other reactions were remarkable, too. In response to images and stories of people losing relatives, property, places to live, and livelihoods in the Donbas—much emphasized in state media coverage—my interlocutors would express their compassion and often also relate to these images by describing how what they saw reminded them of their own experiences: for many, the most severe parts of the reform period had occurred alongside the loss of family members, savings, jobs, perspectives, and homes. Others have experienced and still remember the war brought upon them by Nazi Germany. Some of them would compare the taking apart of enterprise infrastructures—such as the one described in the opening quote of this chapter—to the looting by German troops or the hardships caused by the breakdown of monetary wages, state support, and supply structures during market reforms with the situation after World War II.[13] Even though most remember the 1990s as the most severe phase and point out that many things have improved substantially since then, many still seem to consider the present condition as substantially shaped by crisis, not full recovery.

This does not bring us back to images of the desperate Russian village. It rather points to the subtle ways in which violent and traumatic pasts can be woven into the present (Das 2007) and become part of an "uneventful violence" (Nixon 2011, 8) and "dispersed suffering" (Povinelli 2011, 4) that require analytical, societal, and political attention even if "there is nothing spectacular to report" as "nothing happens that rises to the level of an event let alone crisis" (Povinelli 2011, 4). We see analytical and representational challenges here. The potato would not have made its way into my field notes had my friend not told me the story behind it. The three women would have remained within what I perceived as a peaceful normalcy of sitting in the spring sun had our conversation not shifted to the "normalcy" of their sons' untimely deaths. In representational terms, such conditions may be said to "suffer from a drama deficit" (Nixon 2011, 52) that may be substituted through dramatization as a means to turn the normalized and dispersed visible. One is thus confronted with a representational landscape in which poverty and distress usually remain normalized and of little interest to the public and gain attention mostly through dramatization, adding urgency to drawn-out calamities that easily elude event-centered patterns of representation and perception. Both options seem wanting.

Speaking through Ruins

Abandoned factories, mines, military bases, and towns may come to mind as among the better-known visual symbols of post-Soviet disintegration. Their appearance is often more spectacular than that of crumbling agricultural infrastructure or bushes growing over fields. Still, the remains of former agricultural facilities and abandoned houses, as well as abandoned fields, seem omnipresent across rural Russia, both visually and in people's narratives. Often, such "ruins" are part of inhabited places—and not abandoned ghost villages—with people living beside and among them. Even as they became dysfunctional, they did not become meaningless. References to ruins and voids are frequent in rural dwellers' narratives. They are referred to and can be read as signifiers of complex processes and symbols of changes often difficult to grasp but still impactful.

I encountered the abandoned remains of former production bases, stables,

FIGURE 3.1. Abandoned stables surrounded by abandoned farmland. Author's photograph.

offices, irrigation systems, dormitories, canteens, and installations in every village that I visited (figures 3.3–3.5). These ruins have different histories: sometimes their disintegration evolved around clear-cut events such as the one described in the opening quote of this chapter; sometimes they fell out of use and slowly into decay. Traces such as building skeletons usually remain, and even if they disappear completely, there remains a spot to point to and recall what used to occupy it. In an often stunningly detailed manner, rural dwellers recall the names of farm directors and specialists in succession over decades; the number of workers, specialists, brigades, cows, or sheep that their farms used to consist of; and how many tons of wheat, potatoes, or other field crops they used to produce. They also emphasize that from today's perspective, it seems as if they had been living in another world. Some people I spoke to seemed able to reproduce a more detailed picture of the state of the village decades ago than of the present one, which I understand as an effect of estrangement and the simple fact that they no longer worked for a local kolkhoz.

Many rural dwellers say they still find it hard to understand or describe *how* things have changed so fundamentally over the years: how enterprises were reorganized, and property relations reconfigured, how some enterprises got by while others failed, how production breakdowns, dismissals, and bankruptcies

FIGURE 3.2. Abandoned kolkhoz base. Author's photograph.

came so suddenly, and how villagers themselves made ends meet under harsh conditions. In this light, their frequent references to ruins can be understood as pointing to a past that remains relevant. "Have you seen the remains of these buildings standing on the left when you enter the village? These used to be stables with five thousand goats. Have you seen how solid these walls were? They would have served their purpose for decades to come." "There used to be a machinery base between the main road and the graveyard. I used to work there. All the kolkhoz machinery was repaired there." Or: "All these buildings were built by the kolkhoz, the kolkhoz built houses and apartments for its many workers. Have you seen in what state they are now? They are run down, and half of them are empty." Ruins point to a vanished past that remains relevant—allowing for comparison over time and allowing sense to be made of what seems like a "displacement without moving" that "leaves communities stranded in a place stripped of the very characteristics that made it inhabitable" (Nixon 2011, 19). Given the broad consensus among both rural dwellers and many commentators that the post-Soviet collapse and restructuring had particularly painful effects on rural sites, one may understand references to ruins as among the ways to express *how in particular* they were painful. Rural dwellers in this study thus were not interested in ruins as mere leftovers, but as symbols for connectivities to histories that "bear on the present [but] can escape scrutiny" (Stoler 2016, 5).

FIGURE 3.3. Abandoned stable complex. Author's photograph.

Villagers hence draw on the "pluritemporality of the ruin" (DeSilvey and Edensor 2013, 471) as it resonates with the pluritemporality of the changes they witnessed. They employ ruins as "trans-temporal hinges" (Pedersen and Niel-sen 2013); as heuristic devices that allow connecting phenomena across time, create links to a vanished past that remains relevant, map complex timescapes, and depict particular absences. One rural dweller describes security men guarding abandoned stables as the sign of an absurd situation: "They all left, all. They left from here and now four people are watching over the farm build-ing. What are they guarding there? There's nothing left, only bricks" (Rural dweller, Lipetsk region, 2012). These ruins are understood as signs of both rup-ture and continuity, and a vanished and devalued past, troubling those who have decided to stay on. They point to what actors are "left with" (Stoler 2013, 9), to "the uneven pace with which people can extricate themselves from the structures and signs by which remains take hold" (Stoler 2013, 7–8), and to a perceived gap between what is and what could be (chapter 4).

How exactly people are "compelled to live amongst the ruins of their former lives" (Butler 2013) is distributed unequally across different subject positions. Elderly people often describe how the crumbling infrastructures surrounding them are more than dead substance to them since they represent their own past labor, their own "sweat and blood" that they invested in the kolkhoz, as an elderly former worker puts it (Rural dweller, Rostov region, 2012). The tragedy they express is not what Alexander Herzen called "chronological unfairness, since late-comers are able to profit by the labors of their predecessors without paying the same price" (quoted from Arendt 1970, 27), or Immanuel Kant when he wrote that "the earlier generations seem to carry on their burdensome business only for the sake of the latter [who] . . . should have the good fortune to dwell in the [completed] building" (quoted from Arendt 1970, 27). For many former kolkhoz workers, however, the *promise* of building up something that would benefit their children is among the many promises that were not realized. It turns out that progressivism's failure annihilated their efforts to build a house that later generations could dwell in, and that many of their children today must pay a different price.

The ruins of buildings and infrastructure point beyond themselves. To some extent, they are interpreted as signifiers for decay and disintegration of entire villages. Recall how rural actors refer to kolkhozes and their successor enterprises as *mestoobrazuiushchee* or *gradoobrazuiushchee predpriiatie* (chapter 2): enterprises that were designed to be villages' single main economic bases and employers and effectively came to uphold large parts of villages' economic and social life. The term is suggestive. *Predpriiatie* translates as enterprise, *grad* (or *gorod*) as town, and *obrazuiushchee* links the two. *Obrazovat'* is to found, to establish, or to form, and it is attributed to the enterprise: it is the enterprise that founds, establishes, and forms, and it is the village that is being founded, established, and formed by the enterprise. When villagers speak of the *gradoobrazuiushchee predpriiatie* nowadays, they often address the implications of its disappearance. What happens when the enterprise vanishes but the village remains? What will reproduce life in the village in the future? What is left of this intrinsically relational formation when one part crumbles? What will become of the village without this foundation? We are reminded of the kolkhoz, and encounter it again, in "ruins."

Rural dwellers' references to ruins often point to the very *specific* changes, voids, and losses that occurred over recent decades. They are employed to make specific points even if general judgments about the course of history remain disputed or are seen as pointless. They point to how systemic collapse became concrete. As scholars of ruination point out, ruins allow for telling contingent stories that "emerge at the interface between personal and collective memory, as material remains mediate between history and individual experience" (DeSilvey and Edensor 2013, 472). Rural dwellers refer to ruins to point to the shared loss of places built and inhabited collectively through systemic change and collapse, thereby connecting the locally specific and the historical. Because kolkhoz infrastructures, similar to factories, were bound to Soviet modernization ideologies, ruins here stand "as stark reminders of a vision of the future—a mode of relating the present to a possible future—that [are] now past" (Collier 2011, 6). Similar to developmental projects in other contexts (Anand, Gupta, and Appel 2018), infrastructure promised development in Soviet modernity, too, and the disintegration of infrastructures was seen as a sign of shattered future promises (Buck-Morss 2000; Humphrey 2005).[14]

How rural residents point to abandoned farmland is often similar to how they point to crumbling built infrastructure. Ioffe and colleagues (2006, 222) offer a vivid description of deteriorating or abandoned landscapes and built infrastructure that reflects some of the more pessimistic descriptions from rural residents I encountered: "Pervasive signs of regress include abandoned villages, spontaneous reforestation of previously cultivated fields, rapacious timber cutting in forests, lack of social services, and the profound decay of the communication infrastructure." From rural dwellers' perspective, the abandonment of production facilities and farmland can be understood as symptoms of the same underlying problems, the loss of productive capacity and the withering of diverse relations that, in combination, used to be generative of agricultural produce, income, and meaning. It has been suggested that soil can be understood as infrastructure (Puig de la Bellacasa 2017). Rural residents in this study, too, point to a breakdown of infrastructure that includes built environments, land, and soil.

Devaluation by Disintegration: Instruments, Infrastructure, and Income

Let us return to this chapter's opening quote, the village mayor's description of how the local farm enterprise was being taken apart. Recall how she describes a tractor driver's reaction to losing his tractor: "He even howled. A man howled, with pity for his tractor, on which he worked. It was a new tractor. They took it and drove it away" (Village mayor, Perm region, 2014). One may ask: What is it that made this man so desperate? The tractor driver's relation to his tractor seems substantially different from, say, that of an imagined prototype worker to a means of production that belonged to someone else and from which that worker is therefore already alienated.[15] So, what *kind of thing* may the tractor be to the driver, and how does it matter to him?

Context-specific meanings offer a partial explanation. One may point out that in Soviet times, drivers would often take tractors home after work and park them in front of their houses as if they owned them, and some do so even today. On past and current large farms, two drivers will continuously work on and care for one specific tractor for many years and perceive any commands to change this as an open assault. Beyond historical and habitual reasons, however, the tractor establishes a certain *relation* between the driver and the world he inhabits and thus can be seen as actually becoming a part of an extension of this subject. Without his tractor, one may say, in analogy to John Law (1992, 383–84), that the driver would be "something quite other." It is not only the tractor that constitutes his worker personality, of course, but also experience gathered and competence gained in this role, maybe the reputation earned of being a good driver, and so on. The loss of the tractor may thus mean the devaluation of both past and future labor, as the labor invested in creating skills and competencies is made worthless and decoupled from future employment and income options, and livelihood options are made uncertain. When the interviewee emphasizes that "it was a *new* tractor," she indicates that it could have fulfilled this function for years to come. This is the kind of loss that redefines futures. The tractor is thus part of a bundle of relations that constitutes the driver in the world he inhabits, linked to a place in society, a productive capacity, and prospects for the future, and thus losing it bears aspects of "desubjectivation" (Butler and Athanasiou 2013).

Hannah Arendt's reflections on the role of *instruments* in the labor process are instructive in making explicit the relationship between such desubjectivation and livelihood. For Arendt ([1958] 1998), labor—in contrast to work that creates specific things—is an ongoing activity that sustains and reproduces life itself in a repetitive process. Instruments are an integral part of the labor process, in which "the tools lose their instrumental character, and the clear distinction between man and his implements, as well as his ends, becomes blurred" (Arendt [(1958) 1998], 166). To refer to the tractor driver for the last time: the distinction between agricultural laborers and their implements becomes blurred, as does the clear distinction between means and ends and the labor process itself. Losing a tractor is not merely losing some abstract job. Rather, the loss of the tractor decouples the driver from an ongoing productive and value-creating process, from a labor collective, exchange loops and markets, a national economy, as well as the ideology of feeding the nation. In this sense, the loss directly relates to different levels of desubjectivation.

This argument can be "upscaled" from machines to infrastructure. Akin to this chapter's opening quote, former kolkhoz workers vividly describe how irrigation systems, stables, and machinery in their home villages were taken apart and sold off for scrap metal, and how remaining buildings fell out of use, underlining the relationship between infrastructure and people's capacities. A former mayor states that "they broke the kolkhozes and broke the occupation at the same time. Within one, two years . . . it is a different story when they take apart some . . . factory where you can take it apart . . . and nothing around really changes. Within a year another factory will have emerged somewhere . . . but we peasants have to live somewhere, for us, this is a *gradoobrazuiushchee predpriiatie*, we have to exist somewhere. Here, they destroyed it all at once" (Former village mayor, Perm region, 2013).

Here, we reencounter the *gradoobrazuiushchee predpriiatie* (an enterprise that grounds and shapes a village) as providing the material and organizational basis for production. At stake are not just jobs but agriculture as an occupation—an occupation that many villagers are not only used to but also trained and qualified for. In a sense, the enterprise plays a similar role for the village community that the tractor plays for the driver: enterprises with vehicles, machinery, irrigation systems, stables, bakeries, and functioning farm management constitute a productive relationship between a village population and its agricultural potential, and so the collective productive *capacity* and the potential to generate future income are at stake here. Infrastructures here are among the *conditions* of productivity, value creation, and employment. They are not stable once they are set up; they require maintenance (Gupta 2018) or can be actively dismantled. The role and value of land, if understood as a "*medium* of expression" (Nichols 2020, 74) rather than naturally given, is fundamentally entangled with these infrastructures.

Many rural dwellers today emphasize the painful divergence between local agricultural potential on the one hand, and local productive capacity on the other: fields lying fallow, meadows and stables remaining empty, and people with the power and skills to turn this potential into productivity remain unemployed. For them, there is an obvious gap between what could be and what is, between a given resource potential and the means to realize it. The agricultural potential is still there, every day, just in front of their eyes, but as they do not benefit from it, it rather appears as a reminder of lost possibilities.

A Ruin and a Gap: Dispossession in Transformation

Ruination has been a prominent theme in representations and reflections of the crumbling Soviet empire. David Stark (1996) prominently proposed a different reading of ruins that emphasizes not so much decay but making and becoming in complex, contingent, and contested processes of "recombination."[16] Stark conceptualizes post-Soviet societal change as "rearrangements in the patterns of how multiple orders are interwoven" and undertakes the analytical task to "examine how actors in the postsocialist context are rebuilding organizations and institutions *not on the ruins but with the ruins of communism* as they redeploy available resources in response to their immediate practical dilemmas" (Stark 1996, 995). The idea of "building with the ruins of communism" has become one leitmotif for understanding postsocialist transformation in the Western social sciences. It underscores actors' agency in rebuilding and hence directs attention to the future. But what about the ruins?

In Stark's writings, ruins are turned into building material in transformative processes of rebuilding. Ann Stoler's (2013, 2016) reading of the ruins of colonialism, imperialism, and slavery offers a fruitful contrast. Stoler does not start from a set distinction between ruins and a generative activity of rebuilding. She suggests shifting the focus away from "ruins" as a noun and on "ruination" as "an active, ongoing process" and on the verb "to ruin" (Stoler 2016, 346). The focus is "not on inert remains but on the histories they recruit and on their vital reconfigurations" (Stoler 2016, 348). This helps to understand how ruination yields new damage and renewed disparities, not so much what is "'left' but what people are 'left with': what remains that blocks livelihoods and health . . . the social afterlife of degraded infrastructures; distressed sensibilities," etc. (Stoler 2016, 348). Following Stoler, we may say that one should not *replace* a focus on the past with a focus on emergence that turns a blind eye to history. Rather, the task is to deal with the different temporalities of ruination, how historical formations leave their marks through "uneven temporal sedimentations," and how their "ruins contour and carve through the psychic and material space in which people live" (Stoler 2013, 2). Ruination, then, not only leaves actors with material to recombine and reconstruct, but with "leftovers" that may stick to them in unwelcome ways and become part of the structural circumstances that limit their agency.

Importantly, capacities to disentangle from or redeploy ruins and recombine their pieces are distributed unequally among actors. This does not mean that only elites retained agency during the disintegration. In the context of this study, some villagers have gained advantage from appropriating materials and resources from disintegrating collective enterprises, as indicated in the chapter's opening quote. Some private farmers, as well as households, appropriated collective enterprises' resources for their family farming. Some who played an active role in the reorganization of enterprises reportedly sacrificed the village community's interest for their personal advantage. Some enterprise directors gradually transferred collective farms into private property. While some would argue they were forced into such tactics as the only available option to get by, others obviously used them to enhance their wealth.

The scenario of gaps that could not be filled was little accounted for in optimistic visions for post-Soviet transition, which saw private family farms filling the space hitherto occupied by state and collective enterprises (Spoor 2012). It seems more consistent with interpretations of market reforms as neoliberal "shock therapy" that deprived populations of hitherto state-controlled goods and made them available to domestic elites and international capital (Harvey 2003; Kagarlicky 2002; Klein 2007). It remains contested to what extent Western states and capitalist interests contributed to bringing down the Soviet system, which is a historical argument for caution regarding the implicit or explicit functionalism in such arguments. In any case, it is well documented how the post-Soviet disintegration provided the basis for large-scale appropriation of assets and accumulation of wealth and control by domestic elites, who came to be known as business oligarchs, and international businesses that came to penetrate vast "new" markets (Barnes 2006). Disintegration here is not a mere function of capitalist accumulation, but it can be exploited for its sake.

I do not suggest that we should return to the debate on post-Soviet disintegration, but that thinking along the lines of ruination and disintegration can help prevent an "inclusionary bias" (Bair and Werner 2011, 989) through a narrow focus on the expansion of capitalist relations and the incorporation of people, places, and assets into capitalist circuits.[17] This is not to disregard appropriation but to ask how it builds on the disintegration and devaluation without reducing the latter to a function of the former. Besides the need to acknowledge that there is a history to current forms of dispossession (such as the land grab's colonial predecessors), we need to understand how history can be a constitutive part of dispossession: how support, infrastructure, guarantees, and securities eroded over time; how the failure of one scheme or project prepared the ground for the following one; and how gradual devaluation and disintegration resulted in states of uncertainty and abandonment in which people felt caught between the "no more" and the "not yet." We are then reminded that dispersed dispossession is drawn out over time, not only in the sense that it unfolds slowly but also as it sticks. It cannot be reversed and fixed by simply reestablishing the connection, or by recognition of historical injustice (Coulthard 2014) as it created a new condition and restructured future options. Even the partial recovery of the Russian agrarian sector (Wegren, Nikulin, and Trotsuk 2018; Wengle 2018, 2019) has not solved issues of rural disadvantage and dispossession. At the same time, to return to two images from the introduction, it was not that a "black hole" was turned into an "investors' nirvana." The appropriation of devalued assets was not sudden, and it was rarely straightforward. The following chapter explores how companies navigate and try to capitalize on devaluation, suspension, and indeterminacy.

Chapter 4

Potential

Large enterprises, land banks, and transactions are no rarity in current Russian agriculture. They reflect a rapid and ongoing process of concentration. In late 2009, twenty-two companies each controlled land banks of more than one hundred thousand hectares—around twice the size of Andorra. This number increased to around forty companies in 2015, and further to seventy-one in 2022 (BEFL; BEFL 2015a; BEFL 2022). According to official statistics, commercial farming enterprises controlled roughly one-third of Russia's agricultural land. Out of these, the seventy-one giants with land banks of one hundred thousand hectares or more controlled roughly 9 percent. In 2019, the Russian meat producer Miratorg became the first company in Russia to control a million hectares (BEFL 2019) which is more than the territory of Cyprus, the Mediterranean island home to more than one million people which also happens to be the financial center through which a substantial part of Russian agribusinesses' financial flows are being channeled (Lander and Kuns 2021).[1]

While the concentration of agricultural assets is massive, it usually does not look very spectacular on the ground. In many cases, no particular signs visibly distinguish enterprises that now belong to agricultural holding or foreign investment companies from the successors of Soviet collective farm enterprises that people still call "kolkhoz." Further, rural residents and smaller agricultural producers describe how the land "went away quietly" (Private farmer, Nizhniy Novgorod region, 2021) and gradually, as they could no longer afford to rent or work it.

Over recent years, one could observe numerous large-scale bankruptcies and investment withdrawals that illustrate how the concentration process is less straightforward and stable than one may assume. These include the larger part of the most ambitious Western investment projects, including

Agrokultura. The challenges for foreign agrarian investors in Russia have been described in detail elsewhere with a focus on company performances, management, and investment rationalities and decisions (Kuns, Visser, and Wästfelt 2016; Lander and Kuns 2021; Luyt, Santos, and Carita 2013). This study combines company insights with insights from some villages in which they operate to shed light on the relationship between investment projects and rural populations' losses and benefits. I conceptualize investments as steps in longer processes of reordering, which allows for a more thorough investigation of the relationship between appropriation and dispossession than by focusing on the land deals. It reveals how companies, more than simply profiting from buying cheap assets, navigate and, if they can, exploit processes of de- and revaluation, both drawing on and accumulating different forms of capital: profit but also rent, and political and social capital.

I start with some vignettes that exemplify such maneuvering by managers and directors involved in large-scale agricultural deals and operations. I invite the reader on a trip through various scenes across western Russia and argue that many of these investments are a quite bumpy trip.

Investment Detours

We are on one of several long car rides to one of Agrokultura's farms with one of its expat production managers. I ask him about the company's recent purchase of several farms and around eighty thousand hectares of farmland. The contrast to the enthusiasm voiced in his company's announcements and press releases could hardly be starker. He complains how investment promises have been exaggerated from the very beginning. Estimates on the state of the farms, infrastructure, and machinery turned out to be inaccurate after the purchase, so the company faced much higher expenses than expected. He concludes that it had been a bad deal and that the financial difficulties that followed also had an impact on the company's other farms. The company had struggled to achieve net profitability for years now, and the badly planned purchase seemed to frustrate the manager. I ask him if he did not see the promised great potential in the expansion. Without any hesitation, he replies: "There is potential in everything, but in this case, it will be difficult to realize it."

We spend most of the day driving around the two-hundred-square-kilometer farm, checking field operations or searching for people and tractors scattered on the territory. It was an illuminating demonstration of things that can go wrong with operations at such a large scale: people, machinery, and spare parts getting lost, operators in various functions losing oversight over commands and duties, the smaller and larger leakages in long chains of command. It seems perfectly plausible that those who experience such un-solved "friction" (Tsing 2005) in finance-driven operations on the ground are highly skeptical about plans to expand operations further. Late at night, I travel back to town with the more senior production director. He calls the deal a "di-saster" and explains that the acquired production facilities and land bank are too large for the company to handle. He describes the purchase as a typical at-tempt to create shareholder value and speculates that what it took to convince shareholders and the board to get into it was probably some "beautiful Power-Point presentation." In fact, he says, the company was lacking ideas on how to manage the acquired farms profitably—yet another gap between investment discourse and local operations, as the company built much of its promises of profitable investment on the notion that the application of international best practices will uplift farming operations to international standards.

Traveling seven hundred kilometers south on a four-day farm-to-farm trip with the managing director of a Russian agricultural company, I learn that the fifty-thousand-hectare farm that we just visited has changed tremendously since Soviet times, when it had been a sovkhoz supplying the Soviet army. It has lost this function, and the number of goats held on the territory has dimin-ished from fifty-five thousand to three thousand. Attempts to revive grain pro-duction have been frustrated by unfavorable climatic conditions and soils sali-nized by one of the large and disastrous Soviet irrigation projects. The director doubts that the farm will ever be profitable in the foreseeable future and says it is not the sort of enterprise anybody would readily choose to invest in. He shares his assumption that his boss—one of the region's most successful busi-nessmen and a member of the regional parliament—was obliged by the gov-ernor to take over the farm, probably in exchange for access to more favorable farms and assets and other privileges. Similar deals between state representa-tives interested in preventing the total degeneration of enterprises and affili-ated villages and businessmen with an interest in state resources are common in other economic spheres in Russia, too (Wengle 2018). This manager believes that several farms and enterprises in their company network were taken over in a similar, not quite voluntary, way and complains that this greatly compli-cates his own obligation to run a profitable business.

On another farm the next day, a man approaches the director with an of-fer to sell a well-equipped agricultural enterprise with a two-thousand-hectare land bank for 70 million rubles (around $2.2 million at the time), but the di-rector turns down the offer and explains: "My boss is interested in land. Farms are like appendages for him, he calculates through land." He later explains this investment strategy to me: Suppose you have millions of rubles at your disposal, what will you do with that money? And at a time of falling gold prices and shortly after the 2012–13 Cypriot financial crisis, which led to the flight or loss of several billions of dollars of Russian state and private capital? Unlike Russian banks and Russian industry, land seems like a stable asset to pour in surplus millions. After having complained about hopeless investments yesterday, he now seems to be carried away by the prospect of investing in an asset that soon will "rule the world": grain. In short, we see a remarkable combination of heterogeneous rationalities in a single company: on the one hand, what seems like land-grab rationality in a pure form—spare capital betting on agriculture as a future market—and on the other a state-bound development agenda to uphold nonprofitable enterprises.

Two thousand kilometers northwest, a Russian businessman explains how the potential he sensed when comparing agricultural enterprises in Western countries with those in Russia—together with some spare millions in his pocket—motivated him to start an agricultural investment project. A biologist by training, he seized the opportunity to buy land with soil favorable for growing potatoes, believing that agriculture was the last undervalued asset in the Russian economy. He describes how disillusionment came to spoil his initial enthusiasm: "Our ideas of the business were very wrong when we entered it. This is to say, our evaluation of the business potential, returns, expenses, and the business in general corresponded with reality only to around 50 percent. It all turned out to be more difficult, more expensive, slower, and harder. I understand that the engineering company . . . that we first cooperated with . . . needs to sell its machinery. This is why they say that [this] is like Klondike, a gold mine! You just have to dig, and then dollars will pour down on you in a stream of gold, you will be rolling in money! And so we got into this affair, into this project. All turned out to be difficult" (Businessman, Perm region, 2011).

He admits he had missed that profitability had shifted from primary agriculture to other parts of the food production chain: processing and retail. Now he believes that "working land became unprofitable" and "you won't make any money on farmland" (Businessman, Perm region, 2011). Being an urbanite who has made his money in industry, agriculture has caught his attention only recently—which he notes is part of the problem.

Taking investment detours and failures into analytical account is important as the realization of projects on the ground turns out to differ remarkably from polished company representations, to which we now turn. At the same time—and this will be the topic of this chapter's second part—the partial "vulnerability" of agribusinesses should not distract from who profits and who loses, and that they are closely related to longer spirals of devaluation and dispossession.

A Promise and a Lack: Investment Imaginaries

Many Russian companies started to accumulate land from the late 1990s or early 2000s (Barnes 2006). Most of the foreign investment companies joined what in the beginning looked like a rush on Russian farmland from the year 2005. Companies listed and raising money on stock markets began with making spectacular promises and fostering high expectations, claiming both exceptional returns and high levels of security.

The three largest Western private investment companies—Black Earth Farming, Agrokultura, and Trigon Agri—all originating in Nordic countries and listed on the Stockholm stock exchange, were founded between 2005 and 2006. All of them started as "pure play" companies growing solely cereals and oil-seed crops, and all of them quickly took over vast areas of farmland from the start of their operations (Kuns, Visser, and Wästfelt 2016). Their predominant sense at this point was to seize the moment and bet on rising land prices. Brian Kuns and colleagues (2016, 205) cite one early investor in Agrokultura as saying, in 2008: "I believe it will be a fantastic trip. . . . The big thing is not cereals, but the growth in land prices," presenting a calculation according to which land prices in Russia are merely 5–6 percent of those in Sweden. Around this time, another manager in Agrokultura described how investors and hedge funds were pouring in millions of U.S. dollars, "ridiculous money," with the expectation to "buy land, buy land always" (Kuns, Visser, and Wästfelt 2016, 205). At that point, such promises and expectations were well in line with official company policies. In a public letter to investors on April 25, 2007, the Alpcot Russian Land Fund (later renamed Agrokultura) summarizes the start-up period as follows: "We are optimistic about the future prospects, and our main focus at the moment is to acquire arable land before prices rise too much. Our estimate is that prices for arable land will increase in the future and approach the price levels now prevailing in, for example, Central European countries such as Poland. In addition, our investment case is supported by increasing prices for agricultural commodities. . . . Global trends . . . should also lead to increased demand for agricultural commodities in the future."

Similarly, when EkoSem Agrar—by then the third-largest Russian milk producer—was listed on the stock exchange in Stuttgart in March 2012, it published leaflets that announced "two megatrends in one investment: the sunrise sector agriculture and a fast-growing threshold country"; an investment that

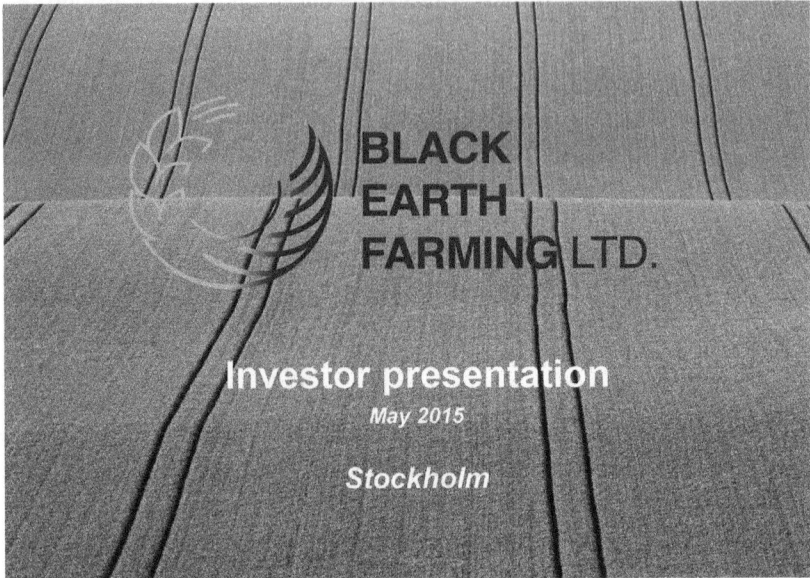

FIGURE 4.1. Promising fields. Source: Black Earth Farming website (inactive)

"profits from globally rising demand for agricultural commodities and dairy products." It declares its ambitions to expand the land bank further, as "the global run for agricultural land has begun."

Black Earth Farming (BEF), the largest foreign investment company by land bank and capital flows around that time, uses visualization of large land banks as a marketing strategy. A photograph of a vast field has been the cover image of its annual reports and investor presentations for years (figure 4.1), and an advertising information sheet graphically compares the area of the company's fully owned landholdings (232,000 hectares) with Central Park, New York (917 times), the special administrative region of Hong Kong (2.1 times), or the state of Luxembourg (90 percent). The message is obvious: a company controlling fields that could contain nearly one thousand Central Parks, and reaches the size of state territories, must be powerful.[2]

Investors expected land prices to rise due to market fundamentals and growing global demand for agricultural produce and farmland, but also by increasing farmland productivity and identifying "yield gaps" that they assumed could be closed. Accordingly, companies created images of great local potential waiting to be realized. BEF (2015) described the Central Black Earth Region where it operates as "endowed with some of the most fertile soils in the world" and in parallel emphasizes the company's "large state of the art machinery fleet." The combination of natural potential and technological and financial potency promised a smooth realization of lingering agricultural and economic potential.

Similar representational patterns can be observed across various companies: high-tech machinery smoothly operating on vast and fertile fields, and the reduction of operations to elements of technology, horsepower, wide fields, and yields. The implication is that machines and capital were necessary but also sufficient to realize the potential at hand, a powerful reduction that makes the conditions for profit appear self-evident and secure. One finds such patterns on company websites and investor presentations—and I suspect they were part of the "beautiful PowerPoint presentation" that convinced Agrokultura's shareholders of the deal that its production manager later described as a "disaster." More generally, around that time, investors did not hold back on promises to "revolutionize" or "unlock the potential of" agriculture in this region (Lundin 2008 and BEF 2008, cited in Kuns, Visser, and Wästfelt 2016, 200). Bracketing both people on the land and prior agrarian history, representations by investors and Western media often created the impression that the land was a tabula rasa. This led some investors to the assumption that average wheat yields on Russian farms could be doubled by relatively moderate investment and predictable amortization rates, and that the increase in demand and prices would do the rest.[3]

However, the grounds on which such expectations were built turned out to be shaky. Several local operators were aware of this gap between investors' expectations and the material conditions in which they operate, such as this production director for Agrokultura:

> Production director: I think the optimism in some of the people who are investing was always probably a little bit too high . . . some people were . . . suggesting it is easier than it actually is . . . the worldwide shortage of food, [the belief] that the commodity boom will go on for ever and ever.
>
> Alexander: You have to show people why to invest?
>
> Production director: Why to invest, yes. And a lot of people have been let down by the promises (Production director, Lipetsk region, 2014)

Similar to the above-cited millionaire who complains about the gold mine failing to materialize, this director describes how not only international investors but also Russian consultants and state agents compared investing in agriculture with harvesting "gold-bearing fields." But he concludes, after having worked such fields for years: "Boy, they are not. You can make money here, but it is bloody hard work." In contrast to gold-rush promises, many foreign companies constantly struggled to reach net profitability.

Even though investment promises were to some degree simply "spectacles designed to attract investors" (Li 2014b, 596), they were not entirely baseless. A variety of sources agree that in 2010–15 Russian farmland was and remained undervalued relative to its production potential and in global comparison (Luyt, Santos, and Carita 2013; Oliver and Horne 2013; Shirley 2011). Several high-profile reports around that time emphasized prevailing yield gaps in Russia (often along with Ukraine and Kazakhstan) and predicted substantial increases, particularly in grain productivity and exports (Deininger and Byerlee 2011; Luyt, Santos, and Carita 2013). At a national level, some of these predictions turned out to be relatively accurate (Uzun, Shagaida, and Lerman 2019; Wegren, Nikulin, and Trotsuk 2023). But profits were realized only for certain companies, and investing big money into farmland brought no guarantee for getting there. One reason is that in contrast to investors' early confidence in agricultural products' ever-rising demand and prices, agricultural commodity markets remained relatively unstable. In several regions over the study period, price volatilities and drops depressed results, and years with bad weather conditions did the rest. Experts confirm that price developments are "absolutely unpredictable" for agricultural producers (Academic Moscow 2014). State regulations at that time were aimed less at stabilizing commodity prices than at stabilizing output levels, or even keeping domestic grain prices low, which of course increases risks for producers.

On the operational level, optimistic expectations were grounded in "givens" such as large fields, large-scale production facilities and infrastructure, and workers trained for industrialized agriculture already in place. If infused with fresh capital, technology, and expertise, this potential could be brought to fruition, as even some expat agricultural specialists working for these companies expected. Some vividly described their excitement when getting out on the vast fields for the first time and realizing the scale of operations that would be possible. They would proudly post photographs of large fields and farms on social media or show them to visiting friends. And they identified with the mission to overcome yield and profitability gaps, as one Western specialist states: "Of course, it's not a boring atmosphere. And that made me decide to . . . go to Eastern Europe. Because . . . in Western Europe, everything is organized, pretty well managed, and it's only to improve the margins. . . . But here, with a lot of good common sense, you can make big steps forward. And then, of course, the scale of operations here is big. You will never find these large areas in Western Europe" (Production manager, Voronezh, 2012).

Realization: Mind the Gap

Part of what makes farmland attractive for investors at a global scale is the expectation that it could "store *and* produce capital" (Ouma 2014, 163)—if they are good investments.[4] In Russia, in regions with average conditions for agricultural production, storing capital in land without immediate plans to work it was not uncommon in previous decades, and the practice is still commonly criticized by rural residents. They emphasize that investors stored capital "cheaply," at a time when "money was still unstable" (Rural resident, Nizhniy Novgorod region, 2021), but never intended to produce anything, and this strategy contributed to driving weaker producers out of business. Such business practices have become less common, and they do not work for everyone. Western investment companies, in particular, had to learn that unless they produce capital quickly, their projects will count as bad investments. Managers describe how their initial enthusiasm began to crumble not only due to endless hurdles such as technical defects, spare parts never arriving, organizational difficulties, workers unwilling to be disciplined, or inflexible state authorities. Such friction contradicts images of straightforward operations. However, those familiar with large-scale farming, or farming in Russia, would expect difficulties to some degree and not see it as a general threat to planned operations. But sometimes such difficulties pile up. Expenses for infrastructure repairs, the modernization of machinery, and bringing production facilities and farmland that may have been abandoned for years back into production may increase costs far beyond expectations. In other instances, the production infrastructure has to be completely rebuilt, as this farm director puts it: "Particularly when a company goes through a bankruptcy procedure . . . all that remains is the bare place and the soil, because you can't take that in your pocket" (LFE director, Lipetsk region, 2013). Others describe how they found out about pending debts and unforeseen expenditures after the takeover and only then realized that they "have not bought enterprises cheaply at all" (Journalist, Rostov, 2012). Cost for land registration and the consolidation of the land bank, too, often turned out to relativize its low purchase price. This Russian director sums up the long road from a promising purchase to reasonable profits: "The business will enter the agricultural sphere, because [land] is very much an undervalued resource in Russia. This is the last undervalued resource in Russia. If you are buying land for some two or three thousand rubles per hectare, and its real worth is one thousand dollars, even two thousand, or even maybe three thousand dollars, you will increase your capitalization thirty times. . . . But land, agricultural land in the Russian understanding, isn't worth anything. And you have to convert agricultural land into land in a European understanding. And this will cost money. There has to be an enterprise on it, with a good turnover and a good high-quality agrarian production" (Businessman, Perm region, 2011).[5]

I doubt that agricultural land is "the last undervalued resource in Russia," but the quote illustrates the sense of a "first mover advantage" to invest in a resource with a "newly enhanced value, and the spectacular riches it promises to investors who get into the business early" (Li 2014b, 595). The chairman of the BEF board in 2007 expressed a similar expectation when he told a Swedish newspaper: "The possibilities for Russian agricultural land are now. That is why we want to be able to finance investments now and not in a half-year or a year" (cited in Kuns, Visser, and Wästfelt 2016, 207). However, when it comes to the level of "operations" (Ouma 2016), it turns out that you will not have realized an opportunity by acting at the right time, and things are far from settled once the deal is concluded. Production managers rather emphasized that land deals were only the beginning of a lengthy, slow, and risky process. This should not come as a surprise. If yield and profitability gaps were overcome easily, why would not others have done that before?

Managers and directors of different companies described how their strategies shifted, at least partly, from acquiring large land banks and betting on increasing land prices to focusing more on agricultural production and making it predictable and profitable. Kuns and colleagues (2016) suggest that, in the case of the "big three" Scandinavian investors, this reorientation from "asset play" to focusing on production started in 2008 when, after the previous peak, global grain prices started to fall, the financial crisis hit, and share prices collapsed. For instance, BEF shares lost around 75 percent of their value within ten months in 2008. By 2012, the share prices of all three companies stood below 50 percent of the price at which they had been issued.[6] All three companies also showed negative (at times two-digit) average returns on investment (ROIC) and returns on equity (ROE) for the period 2007–11 (Luyt, Santos, and Carita 2013, xxvi).

In reaction to business outcomes, and as reaching net profitability became the main goal, company strategies to control as much land as possible were partly reversed. One study even found a negative correlation between land bank size and economic success, as the two Western companies "with the weakest performance to date control the largest land banks, each with over

250,000 hectares" (Luyt, Santos, and Carita 2013, XXV).[7] So while the opportunity to run large-scale operations was often cited as a motivation for entering Russian agriculture in the first place, it was later addressed as among the
biggest problems: "Most people agree [that] even in Russia it is fairly easy to
turn a profit on five thousand, ten thousand hectares if you put in sufficient
investment. . . . Now the problem comes in when you try to scale up, from
ten thousand hectares to thirty, forty, fifty . . . [some companies operate] over
two hundred thousand hectares, that is where the problems came in. . . . It becomes much harder to manage, first because of the complexity of operations,
or because some of the farms are very scattered, the fields are literally fifty kilometers apart in some cases. . . . It just becomes more difficult to do what you
need to do at an optimum time. Things start slipping, costs go up and yields go
down" (Production director, Lipetsk region, 2014).

Managers would admit that their organizational capacities lag behind the
scale and complexity of operations. Miscommunication and delays in chains
of information and command were among the frequent examples. Size became
problematic, especially when things did not work as expected, and hours were
often spent searching for defective machinery or essential personnel. Some of
the investing companies achieved profitability on a farm and operational level,
but these profits were not enough to sustain an expensive superstructure of
central offices, higher management, and a board of directors. Some companies
substantially cut down on this superstructure, albeit relatively late.

Cost-cutting strategies imply deciding not to work parts of the land banks
(and if they were free to decide, enterprises would often work even less if they
were not bound to conditions and government policies), saving on wages, fertilizers, pesticides, seeds, and machinery. In the words of one Agrokultura
manager, a strategy of aiming for profit "that can be done by going for less than
optimum yields, but . . . running a much lower cost structure" (Production director, Lipetsk region, 2014). Even though net profitability and positive results
for the shareholders remain the element "that never changes," as one production manager describes it, "what might change is how the companies decide
to go about that" (Production manager, Lipetsk region, 2014). Many managers I interviewed between 2012 and 2014 described how they try to bridge the
gap between expectations and performance under such circumstances: "Unfortunately . . . all these [foreign investment] companies have not made any
profit since they started. . . . I really hope that . . . we can at least make a profitable farming business here in Russia. Because I'm 100 percent sure that it is
possible . . . that the potential is there to make a profit" (Production manager,
Voronezh, 2012).

By that time, however, vanishing optimism on the investment side also made itself felt on the ground as Agrokultura became less liquid and cut expenditures on machinery, seeds, and fertilizers and also investments in social services and infrastructure. One manager criticized those in the company leadership who "don't think about what they want to look like in ten years from now and how they want the countryside to look like in the long run" and explains this, partly, by the fact that none of the foreign crop-producing companies have " been profitable in the last six years. Which forces them to . . . be shortsighted actually. Just how are we going to survive another year?" (Production director, Voronezh, 2014). Such insights confirm findings by Kuns and colleagues (2016, 208), who argued that the time necessary to build up a successful farming company at the attempted scale takes considerably more time than expected by investors. They emphasize the tension between "investor short-termism" (Kuns, Visser, and Wästfelt 2016, 208) and the much longer operational time spans. Young, fast-growing, and foreign companies have been identified as particularly prone to economic troubles (Lander and Kuns 2021; Luyt, Santos, and Carita 2013) but others face similar risks. A study found that in 2014, half of the twenty-five largest agribusinesses in Russia (by land bank sizes) either run on huge debts or were unprofitable, and a quarter of them went bankrupt or were sold (Visser, Spoor, and Mamonova 2014).

In 2014, Agrokultura was bought out by Prodimex, a Russian sugar refiner that in 2015 became the largest landholder in Russia, even without taking into account the land of former Agrokultura (BEFL 2015a). The largest foreign investment company by the land bank, BEF, was bought in 2017 by a Russian company linked to the oil and gas industry via family ties. The takeover resulted in the creation of a new entity, Volga-Don Agroinvest (Lander and Kuns 2021, 3). Trigon Agri still operates under the name Agomino, but it sold off large parts of the business and was delisted from the Stockholm stock exchange in late 2020 (Nasdaq Stockholm 2020). In light of such developments, Kuns and colleagues (2016, 203) conclude that Russian investment-driven agriculture is "a dynamic sector with companies regularly appearing, merging and disappearing." I shall now turn to some implications of such dynamics with regard to appropriation and the relationship between companies and rural populations.

Concentration: Big Fish Eat Little Fish

We have seen that while the concentration of farmland and other agricultural assets has become a defining characteristic of the Russian agrarian landscape, the process of accumulation has often not been straightforward. Indeed, numerous investments in Russian agriculture turned into rather unfortunate ventures. So what to make of this concurrence of extreme concentration of power and assets on the one hand, and failing giants on the other?

It is important to understand this accumulation not as resulting from single investment projects, or a post-2007 global land rush, but as part of a longer process implying rounds of bankruptcies, disintegration, devaluation, revaluation, and dispossession. It is a historic process that started long before consulting companies and publicly listed companies drafted their presentations and created the image of an undervalued asset class, and it continued after they left the game. Foreign-led investment has overall not been a strong driver of the overall accumulation tendency; it has been small relative to the country's agricultural potential (Luyt, Santos, and Carita 2013, XIX). Foreign companies' land acquisition may have been most visible in parts of the media, and through their PR campaigns, but most of the giants in the sector are not foreign investment companies, and their operations go far beyond the production of field crops.[8]

Capital's resurgent interest in Russian agriculture represents a remarkable, though not sudden, reorientation after the state and private disinvestment from the sector during the 1990s. While the concentration of former state assets in a few private hands in the post-Soviet period is well known and documented (Barnes 2006), except for a few extraordinarily favorable regions, oligarchs entered or grew from the agricultural sector much later than industries or the energy sector. As Alexander Nikulin (2011, 56) summarizes: "The post-Soviet oligarchism emerged and rose up in Russian megalopolises and large industrial centers, and during the first post-Soviet decade it generally disdained to appear in the countryside, which was considered to be a depressed and unprofitable sphere." How, then, did agriculture become a field for economic opportunity seekers?

Major problems for the domestic agrarian sector in the 1990s were the concurrence of the failing and taking apart of the agrarian system while the domestic market was flooded with cheap imports. This began to change when the 1998 Russian financial crisis became a stimulus for domestic agrarian production. The deflation of the Russian ruble[9] improved the competitiveness of domestic agricultural goods in relation to imports, and sale prices for output increased more than input prices, which improved agriculture's terms of trade (W. Liefert and O. Liefert 1999). As Andrew Barnes (2006, 197) puts it: "The financial crash of 1998 did something extraordinary to Russian agriculture: it made it profitable, or at least solvent. Agriculture was the first sector in which the import-substitution effect of a fourfold currency devaluation took hold, as citizens switched from hopelessly expensive imported foods to acceptable Russian substitutes. The shift significantly increased the number of profitable farms in the country, and the output of Russian agriculture as a whole rose every year from 1999 to 2001." He identifies a group of primary beneficiaries of this renewed interest in agriculture—and these were not primary producers that were "simply too numerous, too debt-ridden, and too cash-poor" to compete. Rather, "the agrarian groups that fared best after the crash were those that had built up control over food-processing or commodities-trading bottlenecks earlier" (Barnes 2006, 199).

Many of the largest agricultural companies today started as Russian food-processing or commodity-trading companies that deepened their vertical integration and successively bought up their supply base. The aim of avoiding taxation was a further incentive for engaging in production.[10] Already around the turn of the century, the number of such "backwardly integrating food-processing companies" (Atkin 2009, 111) expanded remarkably (Nikulin 2011, 56–57). But also large players from the industry and energy sectors entered the game during this period. Lukoil leased about one hundred thousand hectares in 1998, and Metalloinvest acquired sixty-four farms, fifteen processors, six grain elevators, over three hundred thousand hectares of agricultural land, and other agricultural assets plus trade enterprises around the year 2000 (Barnes 2006, 202–3). Processor-led integration of agricultural producers into larger company networks and even investment by finance and industry had occurred already in the 1990s (Barnes 2006, 155–63), but the post-1998 partial readjustment of agricultural markets spurred company growth and more systematic integration of producers (Uzun, Shagaida, and Sarajkin 2012, 5).

Buying up farms and land at large scale became possible due to a massive devaluation and mass enterprise bankruptcies that freed assets. The portion of nonprofitable agricultural enterprises reached 88 percent in 1998, and the official total number of enterprises decreased from 26,900 in 1995 to 19,800 in 2005, and 5,900 in 2014 (Rosstat 2015a, 124; Rosstat 2002b, 109). In 2002, the legislature passed the federal law "On the financial recovery of agrarian commodity producers"[11] that enabled state-backed restructuring of enterprise debts. To benefit from this measure, enterprises had to "prove" their capacity to operate profitably in the future. Bankruptcy procedures were initiated for enterprises that were failing. As a result, devalued farms and land were put up for sale on a massive scale (Uzun, Shagaida, and Sarajkin 2012, 5–6). New land legislation that came into force in 2003 lifted most earlier restrictions on private land purchase and ownership (Lerman and Shagaida 2007, 16). Foreign companies, banks, and funds remain excluded but can acquire farmland through often fully owned daughter companies. Daughter companies also allow bypassing of regulations that limit the portion of a district's farmland that can be controlled by any single company—often 10 percent (Uzun, Shagaida, and Sarajkin 2012, 6). As state subsidies at this time shifted toward privileging large enterprises, they found favorable conditions for expanding further.

Also, state policies' return to privileging large farms was in part a reaction to the 1990s agricultural crisis, during which many enterprises were kept alive by administrative measures to prevent a collapse of the sector and job losses, and the administration was searching for more effective ways to organize subsidies (Uzun, Shagaida, and Sarajkin 2012, 4). A strong bias in state subsidies toward the largest farm enterprises has been observed and criticized since the early 2000s (Uzun 2005, 2012). The so-called agroholdings are often condemned for securing immoderate shares of government subsidies and profiting from corruption (Academic, Moscow, 2014).[12] Smaller agricultural producers are often not eligible to apply or lack juridical and economic expertise to produce a business plan for a successful application. One smallholder, echoing many, explains: "I am a real farmer. During harvesting or sowing, I have no time to sleep, let alone write any grants" (Private farmer, Nizhniy Novgorod region, 2021).

The shift toward large agricultural companies has been fundamental: "One of the most dramatic changes has been the emergence of exceptionally large, and in most cases externally owned and managed, commercial farming operations. . . . [Their] emergence and growth . . . offers a stark contrast to earlier expectations of the transformation of Russian agriculture. Rather than create a family farming sector, Russia may reestablish latifundia owned, not by the nobility, but by corporations that may not have a direct relationship to food and fibre production" (Rylko and Jolly 2005, 116).

This concentration goes beyond private and publicly listed companies entering agriculture. State-owned companies, many dating back to the 1990s, comprised the largest share of agricultural holding companies by the mid-2000s (Rylko and Jolly 2005; Uzun 2012). Also, some successor enterprises of the former collective and state farms have expanded, for instance, by taking over assets from (bankrupt) neighbor enterprises. So have "private farms," the average size of which is growing, with some of them "essentially run as integrated agribusinesses" (Wegren 2011, 219).

Managers explain that, operational difficulties notwithstanding, economies of scale have become a precondition for running a successful farm enterprise in Russia. A certain scale of operations is required for efficient usage of machinery and inputs. Many of the successful larger enterprises either comprise or are well connected to processing or sales, which is crucial given the distribution of profit margins along the food chain. In often relatively fluid agricultural commodity markets, large producers benefit from the negotiating power that comes with buying (of machinery, seeds, fertilizers, or fuel) and selling (to processors or exporters) large quantities (Production manager, Voronezh, 2012). Larger enterprises also can afford to hire lawyers, and sales specialists, or to outsource certain services. Such capacities are particularly relevant in a context where, unlike in many Western countries, there are few organizations and agencies that support farmers with issues around sales, bookkeeping, or legal tasks, and also uncertainties in property and market relations, rapidly changing subsidy schemes, etc., that require and will benefit players with more than agricultural expertise. As we will see in the next chapter, larger companies also often benefit from more powerful ties with state authorities.

If one were to search for a more context-sensitive alternative to the land-grabbing trope, it could be the proverbial image of "big fish eat little fish."[13] I would imagine a Russian agribusiness as a wels catfish. The wels is native to the region. It is the largest freshwater fish in Europe. It is not picky when it comes to its food, which can be small animals, fish, insects, but also occasionally frogs, snakes, rats, or ducks, which it usually swallows whole. While it is not fussy when it comes to the size of its prey, sometimes welses die attempting to swallow prey that is too large. The wels has been observed feeding on dead animals. Its feeding patterns are highly opportunistic and adaptive to its environment. When hunting, it relies on hearing and smell more than vision and can trace prey in muddy water. It can use its fins to create eddies to disorient its victim. The more successful agribusinesses, too, seem to be masters in navigating muddy waters and doing quite well by swallowing farms of various sizes and other opportunities that come their way. In effect, the "strong ones become stronger, and the rest become weaker" (Academic, Nizhniy Novgorod region, 2021)—or eaten.

Whose Potential?

Farms and farmland are often passed on over several rounds of sales and acquisition rather than seized once and for all. This is relevant concerning the question of who wins and who loses in the process. While hopes for investors to revive production to the benefit of local populations are often disappointed, takeovers are rarely judged as the appropriation of goods that should belong to the "locals," simply because local producers often are seen as unable to run stable and profitable businesses. Companies are criticized for closing meat, milk, or vegetable production, for paying low wages and providing little informal support, or for ultimately failing to set up a profitable business—but not for investing. Even though the redistribution of goods and gains does not follow a simple resource-grab pattern in this instance, the question of who wins and who loses in these turbulent takeovers remains relevant.

This chapter has focused on Western investing companies that were betting on rising land prices but withdrew after successive operational losses, plummeting company values, and the "value erosion" (Visser 2017) of Russian farmland. As company shares lost value almost constantly over the years, this meant losses for shareholders, including Western pension funds (Luyt, Santos, and Carita 2013). Companies tried to attain profitability by cutting costs, including those for personnel and management. In the process, they cut back the number of farmworkers, managers, and specialists in urban offices as well as board members. Payments to board members were cut during companies' late periods. And still, the wages, fees, and bonuses paid to expat managers and specialists, consultants, top management, and boards were substantial compared to the modest income of hundreds of farmworkers.[14] I will not discuss the fate of managers and investors here. Rather, I will stick to the operational side and ask how the gap between investment expectations and the partial failure of such expectations plays out at a farm and village level.

Did the owners of land entitlements eventually benefit from rising land prices? Price levels and increases vary greatly across regions and even places. In Letnevo (northern Black Earth region, Lipetsk region), for instance, land share prices (4.2 hectares) rose from 18,000 rubles in 2002 ($570) to 50,000 rubles in 2012 ($1,700). This price increase is considerable, but it will not make a fortune: 18,000 rubles is roughly what might be earned from two potato harvests on a subsidiary household farm, and 50,000 rubles is what a highly trained and well-paid tractor driver could earn in a month at that time. In Lipenka, located in the Rostov region's Southern Steppes, where earlier and steeper price increases occurred, share prices rose from 3,000 rubles in 2000 to 300,000 rubles in 2013. A man who had moved to the village around the turn of the century told me how, if he had sold his house in Ingushetia at that time and invested this money in land, he could have bought sixty-six land titles that would have brought him monthly leases of eighty thousand rubles, more than five times the official average agricultural wage. But, just as most others, he had not expected the return of interest and profitability in land-ownership. Across different regions, many told me that they regret having sold land shares early and below value. But many have effectively sold their titles—because gaining even a modest sum may have been crucial at the time, or because they thought there was no point in keeping the title (see chapter 2). Hence many of those who do profit from rising rents today are not ordinary villagers. Already in 2006, 33 percent of the acreage was leased to agricultural producers, not by individual shareholders but by commercial organizations—usually controlled by one or two people, but with an average of 2,500 hectares at their disposal—or new "landlords," as Uzun calls them (2012, 141–42).

Did agrarian workers benefit from investments in production? When managers and farm directors speak about profits failing to materialize, many of them, in particular those with a nonagricultural or non-Russian background, will emphasize inefficiency they see as rooted in the legacy of a Soviet agrarian system, which was not designed to be efficient (but rather output-driven) or resulted in an "overstaffing" of farms that they find hard to reverse (chapter 5). What many of them claim to be most needed are "modern" farming and management methods and schemes, technologies, and expertise. They often speak of themselves as modernizers who, with their expertise, will restructure farming operations to achieve higher efficiency. This implies differentiation between the "new" specialists and managers and "old" workers who become part of everyday interactions on a farm level. The former claim to push productivity to new levels; the latter are ascribed the role of running and maintaining production as is. New specialists claim to engage in bringing home the harvest and also in redefining and optimizing operations for the future. Such a division of roles is in line with investment as well as "modernizing" logics in which the closing of gaps between actual and potential levels of output and efficiency counts more than maintaining the status quo. The "modernizers"—managers, farm directors, and specialists—earn much higher wages, hold central decision-making competencies, and are higher up in the enterprise hierarchy. Crucially, they hold such privileges not despite companies' nonprofitability but due to it. Their job is to close the gap between the given and the possible, from an investor's perspective, and they embody the promise of future profits and yields. Workers, in contrast, are often presented as obstructing modernization by sticking to "Soviet" production principles and mindsets.[15]

Such divisions do not remain uncontested. In one instance, we visited a driver and the tractor-seeder unit he operated with an expat production manager and his interpreter. The driver explained how, with a self-made bolt, he fixed a fault that caused the seeder to lose oil. He concluded: "Here is the patent, would you give me five hundred dollars?" He repeated the question several times and stuck out his hand for the reward. What kind of a claim is this?

FIGURE 4.2. Expat production managers overseeing work on their company's field. Author's photograph.

Relative to other jobs on the farm, that of a tractor driver is stable and well paid. Still, the market price of the tractor-seeder combination exceeded the lifetime wages of both drivers working on it in shifts. And certainly, any expat working in the company, having been attracted to Russia not least by attractive wages, earns several times more than a tractor driver. One can thus understand the claim for a reward for fixing a crucial machine as a claim to be recognized: the driver is doing skilled and nonsubstitutable work, contributing to maintaining and improving operations, and wants to be rewarded accordingly: with five hundred dollars, not rubles.

In some respects, there seems to be more, rather than less, demand for such skills on farms that higher-level management seeks to quickly "modernize," and some recognize that drivers and "old" engineers contribute a lot to fixing technical problems before they become problematic for the company. An Agrokultura production director admits that they are "always experimenting" (Production director, Lipetsk region, 2014) with the organizational and agronomic changes they are trying to implement. As one of them puts it, speaking in the eight years after the company started its operations in Russia: "It is still very much a work in progress. There is not one, I don't think there can be any one template that would work. It may not even work within our company and certainly would not work overall" (Production director, Lipetsk region, 2014). Another manager describes foreign specialists as knowing very well how to count tons and hectares and how to handle high-tech machinery. However, when it comes to reorganizing farms that also consist of humans and social relations, the company appears remarkably clueless: "There is absolutely no company policy on how that could be done. There is an ideal of, say: we're looking to become more efficient, but there is no overall strategy" (Production manager, Lipetsk region, 2014).

This mode of running and reforming agribusiness clearly diverges from the images of smooth operations based on the implementation of technology, available (Western) know-how, and best practices described above—which all suggest that companies had all means and knowledge at their disposal already. When production managers admit that they do not have any ready-made templates but are in a constant process of experimentation—or trial and error, as others put it—they also reveal that their actual role in both running and reshaping operations is not so different from that of workers. What sets them apart is more a division of recognition and reward than a division of labor. Their experimental schemes very much hinge on workers', drivers', or specialists' skills and capacities to learn from gathered experience, figure out what to do when things do not work out as expected, and develop solutions. This kind of experimentation is a collaborative process more than the mere application of technology and expertise.

Blaming difficulties in reorganizing operations on workers, or solely on operational difficulties in Russia, further hides obstacles and limitations within company structures and asset-driven investment schemes. In the first years the boards of the "big three" foreign investment companies were staffed by members lacking experience in agriculture (Kuns, Visser, and Wästfelt 2016, 208), which was a common point of criticism by Agrokultura's operational managers. Russian businesspeople included in this study, too, had made the money they invested in agriculture in industry or fossil fuel extraction. If many of them had not expected the amount of follow-up investment, effort, and time required to develop functioning and profitable operations at the required scale, this also has to do with ignorance stemming from such lack of relevant experience. Many of my interlocutors agreed that the investment side had expected quick and easy profits or, in some cases, easy and safe money storage. Yet the capitalist company hands investment risks and misjudgments down to farm workers. As one Agrokultura production manager, whose role is between investors and workers, explained: "I also found that sometimes the people at the farm level actually forget who the ultimate owners of the company are [laughs], and . . . they forget who is providing investments . . . and sometimes they have to be reminded, that, no, we are not just farming here . . . Obviously, we have some local social responsibilities. We have to look after and pay our workers. But at the end of the day, we are, I personally, I am responsible to the shareholders of the company, who have employed me, and that's it . . . we have to deliver a positive result to the shareholders" (Production manager, Lipetsk region, 2014).

As investing companies saw nonprofitability last well beyond the expected initial restructuring phase of two to three years, the pressure on the operational side to demonstrate profitability came to override plans of longer-term restructuring. This study thus confirms the tension "between investor short-termism and the longer-term perspective" (Kuns, Visser, and Wästfelt 2016, 208) necessary to implement effective midterm changes. It finds such short-termism not only with listed companies, however, but with different investors, including Russian ones, that entered agriculture in expectation of safe and easy profits. Unlike foreign investors, however, some of the companies more embedded in regional and national networks play on multiple assets and forms of capital and thus are more likely to gain benefits even if initial investment expectations don't materialize. The following chapter describes such strategies in more detail.

Chapter 5

Tactics

With the directors of the local agricultural enterprise and stud farm, we arrive at a building site close to the farm's main base in the village of Lipenka. A dozen workers on tractors, bulldozers, and trucks are busy tearing down what was left of former kolkhoz stables. The massive brick buildings must have been solid in former days, still obvious nearly two decades after their abandonment. As the foreman approaches us, the director of the stables introduces the farm director with the words: "This is the director of Lipenka." Formally, one may object that the mayor is the head of the village while the man called "director of Lipenka" is the director of an agricultural enterprise called Traktor. One may also wonder why the director of the much more profitable stables ascribes this honor to a man constantly complaining about the economic performance of his enterprise. Furthermore, both men work for the same, not very transparent, company structure, headed by a powerful regional businessman and politician. Although they are directors on a local level, villagers will often speak of them as subordinates with limited competencies in their companies. Despite this, the "director of Lipenka" is widely considered to be the most powerful person in the village. As the conversation on how to transform this part of the village continues, they begin to call the place "Lipen*grad*," with the new ending upscaling the village into a *gorod*—a city or town. It is a joke or a fantasy. Beyond wealthy urbanites visiting the stables, there is not much of an urban feel to the village, and many young people keep leaving for the "real" cities. At the same time, the village receives some funds from the regional and federal budget, mediated through the company leadership's political ties. In this respect, the company does at least connect the village to flows of state resources.

I am reminded of another instance with a wealthy businessman from the nearby regional capital choosing to register some of his enterprises in the small village of Zhary, and his taxes suddenly came to make up the largest portion of the village administration's budget. He runs his own glossy magazine that published a report on the village titled "Republic of Zhary." With the businessman's portrait on the issue's cover, it is not hard to guess who the imagined sovereign would be. Again, what seems to be rather grotesque fantasies of sovereignty, on the one hand, correspond, on the other hand, with the opinion widely held by locals and village mayors that—given the breakdown of the local agricultural enterprise some years before—the village largely depends on the businessman's capital and influence. In this regard, he may be seen as the village's informal ruler.

Some business actors imagine themselves as equipped not only with the power to make live, but also to make die. I ask an expat production manager how they dealt with a driver who drove his tractor into a tree when drunk. "We fired him, but we should have shot him" was his prompt answer, probably intended to be funny, but it echoed much of the authoritarian tone in his and his colleagues' usual speech, how they justified poor wages and working conditions by workers' deviance, and portraying themselves as those who would bring order. I frequently encountered similar instances, somewhere between megalomaniac power fantasies and substantial authority. This chapter investigates what underlies such "fantasies" and the implications in terms of workers', villagers', and companies' power and agency.

Monopoly, Power, Interdependence

The "director of Lipenka" hosted me during most of my time in the village, and I gained insights into the workings of his authority. His patronage opened many doors for me. His support would enable and facilitate my efforts to meet enterprise employees or administrative personnel. But he could also block my efforts. He would often know what I was doing and pull his strings. My interlocutor's moderate criticism of the enterprise would suddenly turn into appraisal after a phone call during which I heard the director's deep and husky voice at the other end of the line. The enterprise canteen, preparing mainly the farm's own produce, would feed me for free. I had no vehicle in the village, but the director's brief phone calls would suffice to find a car or truck heading wherever I had to go or to reschedule a ride in that direction. His overview and command of machinery, vehicles, and workers enabled him to arrange various support for workers, villagers, the village administration, or, in this instance, for me. Just like directors of other farms, he was in a position to direct and redirect resources and operations that were useful for a variety of purposes, including but not limited to agricultural production: machines that could work kolkhoz fields but also private plots, carry agricultural produce but also building materials, specialists who could fix defects on the farm or in a household, workers who could run field operations but also maintain public infrastructure, or materials no longer needed for the agricultural enterprise but useful on a private building site. Requesting bank loans, villagers may depend on their director's guarantee of creditworthiness, and the latter's local authority may get them out of trouble with the police or juridical organs.

Even though the "director of Lipenka" works for a company investing fossil fuel capital, this is not where such monopoly power is primarily nested. Similar patterns can be found across enterprises with a strong kolkhoz lineage, private farming enterprises grown large, and investment projects. Many of the houses people live in were built and occasionally are still owned by the agricultural enterprise, which may also be the source of the sugar, butter, bread, or oil on kitchen tables, distributed to households as rent for land shares. Farm enterprises may provide food for the local kindergarten and school, sponsor the local football team and provide the van that will take them to matches on weekends. Some organize activities for local pensioners and provide a tribute to war veterans. They contribute to festivities and cultural events. At cost price, they provide technical resources or fodder for villagers' subsidiary production, or lay water or gas pipes to workers' houses. After heavy snowfall they have tractors and bulldozers to clean streets in the villages and the roads that connect them to highways and towns. In exceptional situations such as marriages, births, or family members' illnesses or deaths, workers and villagers may borrow money from enterprise directors. The enterprise will often provide a car to carry the dead and a tractor to dig out a grave; in some sense, it thus quite literally accompanies villagers from cradle to grave. We are hence revisiting the theme of the *khoziaistvo* introduced in chapter 2 and will investigate more deeply how it relates to questions of power at different scales. We will see how the "new masters" who came with outside investment navigate and reconfigure kolkhoz arrangements and how they exploit but also are obliged to them.

Investors build on local monopoly patterns rather than install them from scratch. And although some aspects of monopoly power work in their favor, it also demands responsibilities that they may not have chosen freely. In Lipenka, the businessman who owns the farm enterprise, stables, and a majority of land shares, and employs the directors, is also an elected member of the regional parliament, holds various ministerial posts, and is the chief regional manager of the company that runs the village gas supply. He usually travels to the village by helicopter; hardly anyone has ever seen him, and no one on the ground seems to have insight into the workings of the political-economic web he directs. And still, he is connected to the village in so many ways: sitting in parliament "for them," owning land that surrounds them, owning the gas pipes that run into their homes, employing large parts of the village population but also seeing a part of their earnings flow back to his enterprises when they pay for gas and other services.

The "director of Lipenka" often underlines his responsibility for the village, pointing out that he runs and creates structures that will provide jobs and income, sustain and stimulate the village economy, and eventually keep the village alive. "This is all for the people," he claims. "People want jobs, and how will they get them? And who will create them?" Even though such narratives of "good farm enterprises" are contested, they resonate with the widely held view that villages with no running enterprise are usually worse off and that if the "old" enterprises did not manage to survive under the new, tough economic conditions, it is up to new agricultural companies strong enough to resurrect production to sustain villages in future. Hope rests on the ostensibly powerful and stable investment companies that often promise to take care of village populations' needs.

The self-declared "new sovereign" has more in common with the *khoziain* from chapter 2—the enterprise director taking care of the enterprise, village, and workers—than one might expect (how far either of them meet expectations is a different question). Both hold much local authority. Formally, they decide whether to support individuals and the village at large in a particular way or not, to further downscale or rebuild an enterprise, to fire workers or employ them. This corresponds with frequent statements by rural dwellers and authorities such as, "Village X is governed by investor Y," or "they really established a government of their own here."

At the same time, the dependencies—in more "traditional" kolkhoz-like enterprises and incoming investors—covered in this study are not merely one-sided. In tiny villages often surrounded by dozens of square kilometers of fields, enterprises often depend on village populations' labor force to keep going. Rural residents today are free to leave a village and settle elsewhere. This is different from historical phases when agricultural labor was disciplined and organized through direct coercion, such as during the Soviet kolkhoz regime until 1969, when membership was inherited and members were not free to leave their enterprise or occupation, or during times of serfdom in imperial Russia. Thus, somewhat in contrast to the sovereignty fantasies that opened this chapter, my emphasis here is also on how different sides navigate and negotiate the circumstances they find themselves in. I argue that managers and directors often employ tactics that cannot but engage with the various necessities they encounter, including economic but also social circumstances in the places where they operate.

Fostering informal ties with villages may seem unexpected for investors. Following notions of economization, privatization, marketization, or commercialization, we may assume that takeovers by large companies would result in a streamlining of operations according to clear economic rationalities and a disembedding of economic operations. Profit-seeking agricultural companies would then reorganize "kolkhoz webs" according to purer economic principles, try to offload social responsibilities, and separate the economic from the social and political. I did encounter such attempts. For instance, one village mayor described the arrival of an investment project as follows: "Still in the process of arriving at our territory, they said right away that 'this social burden, we won't take it on ourselves' . . . [They] addressed the village population and said right away that 'we will not come forward with . . . organizing events and investing in social and cultural infrastructure. We will allot you taxes, they will go into the local budget, and you will be fine'" (Village mayor, Perm region, 2013).

But things did not work out that way for the company. "They kept on participating, even though they said we will not help, but they did" (Village mayor, Perm region, 2013). The enterprise did not become very profitable, the amount of taxes they paid were low, and the village administration remained dependent on informal help. Workers and villagers, too, remained dependent on informal support from the enterprise—and the enterprise remained dependent on workers. For the enterprise director, the urge to engage with the social sphere mirrored the simple fact that nobody else would and that dropping it would harm the enterprise—as he illustrates with this episode: "The governor arrived by helicopter and told me: 'If you want your school to be closed, leave everything as it is. But if you don't want it to be closed, reduce the expenses per pupil by 30 percent.' But how will you reduce expenses per pupil in a village school? Producing new children . . . is not realistic" (Businessman, Perm region, 2010).

The school was eventually preserved without spurring births for that purpose—which would mean a reversal of the tendency of shrinking classes, which increases the costs per pupil. Instead, the renovation of the school building allowed for sharp cuts in energy costs. The investor admits he was easily convinced by the governor to take over the task: for an enterprise that depends heavily on young specialists, the prospect of losing the local school—with the closest substitute twenty kilometers away on gravel road—could pose an existential risk. As state authorities were reluctant to take action to preserve the school, it was up to the enterprise to do so. While the governor had little stakes in a small village that he could forget about after leaving on his helicopter, the businessman had become invested in the village by choosing to take over its farm enterprise.

That the businessman had to adapt to the circumstances had much to do with the distinct operational environment. In contrast to his urban factory, which he says can be managed "without taking into account the social structure of the city at all" (Businessman, Perm region, 2010), his role in the village is "completely different." Here, "it turns out that the social infrastructure rests upon the enterprise anyway. There is no other variant. . . . For us, this is bad" (Businessman, Perm region, 2010). He is explicit that it is not enthusiasm for rural development or benevolence, but rather a necessity that urges him into this role: "I'm urged [to take up such responsibilities]. I'm still one of those who count money. You have to understand clearly that I'm not some, so to say, a socially oriented person. That's not true" (Businessman, Perm region, 2011). He makes explicit what other directors and managers rather formulate between the lines when he admits how much he adopts his tactics to the circumstances he encounters in a specific location. He had arrived with a tight business plan and management principles but then saw himself confronted with entanglements he may have wished to avoid but could not ignore or reject—as he describes in another illustrative example:

> The less private subsidiary agriculture there will be in this village, the better for me. The more people will work in the enterprise, the more attractive for me. The greater their devotion to their work, the easier for me to take them to work, even during their days off, during harvest time. Take them for twelve-hour working days, when they go home only to sleep and then back to work, sleep and back to work. Because the cycles of the highest workload coincide. I need them in August to September, but then they also need themselves on their household plots. Last year we gave them potatoes, said "Take as much as you want," to prevent them from planting and digging their own potatoes with a shovel on their plots. . . . But then, when people keep cows, I cannot go and tell them: you have to slaughter this cow; otherwise, I won't give you a job. . . . I have two options: either I will start fighting with their cow or make arrangements for this cow to consume as little time as possible. Thus I say: keep your cow, but don't mow your hay. When we have done ours, we will bring you two bales . . . and you can feed your cow all winter long. For me . . . the costs are minimal, but he will do his job as a tractor driver and not walk around with his scythe (Businessman, Perm region, 2010).

Here is our urban dollar-millionaire competing with villagers' potatoes and cows. Many of the "new" agricultural actors articulated similar surprise or frustration. I remember how shocked one expat production manager was when we arrived on one of their farms and learned that their half-million-dollar tractors were standing idle during a crucial harvest day because the drivers were busy digging potatoes on their household plots. Their large-scale operations were meant to run smoothly based on expensive technology, but molding workers' living realities into these schemes turned out to be more complex than expected. This stands in stark contrast to the image of smooth operations created by companies (chapter 4). While abstracting from social embeddedness in a shareholder presentation is easy, doing so on a farm level may be impossible—the increased employment of modern machinery and technologies notwithstanding.

Managers are hence urged to adapt to local demands to some extent. A representative of a foreign investor remarked:

> On the one hand, you can call it . . . trying to work responsibly. . . . This is one side of the story. On the other hand, you very much depend on the local people. Because they are your workers. In the end, it's the local Russian people who really have to execute the jobs. . . . In the end, it's in collaboration with the locals . . . so, you also try to keep the good relationships between them and you . . . provide them with either financial aid, but also sometimes to keep roads clean. . . . All publicly listed companies . . . need to have a chapter in their annual report about sustainable business, about responsible operations, so . . . of course, if you do things like that . . . you can write a chapter in your annual report [that is] always good for investors. . . . But . . . the main thing is that we want to keep a good relationship between the locals and you as a farming company (Production manager, Voronezh, 2012).

> One thing we have to be very careful about obviously is that we have some of the local people who [are owners of land shares] and we still need some of them, we still need their local support for us to carry on, on a long-term legal basis. That's important, we can't ignore that. And at the same time . . . you can't get away from the fact that there is a certain amount of social responsibility attached to being the only employer in most of the villages that we work. But at the same time, if we are not a profitable employer, there will be no one either. . . . I need to be able to pay the key personnel more than we're paying now, to keep them working on the farm . . . because they are the ones, these tractor drivers, sprayer operators, without them everything stops. So we have

to work on a system that keeps them motivated, happy, and working (Production manager, Lipetsk region, 2014).

Such interdependencies are context-specific and change over time. Some enterprises pursue strategies of cutting back on various aspects of local social embeddedness or refrain from rebuilding them in places where bankruptcies have erased previous relations and commitments. Where proximity allows enterprises to recruit workers from other towns or villages, they seem more likely to free themselves from responsibilities and less hesitant to close down local production bases, as they can continue working land banks from elsewhere. In other instances, companies split their operations in a single village into agricultural enterprises, which employ village populations on minimum wages and providing village services, and some more profitable businesses such as the abovementioned horse farm or a recreational center. The former keeps a village alive at a minimum, the latter has freed itself from the responsibilities that come with enterprises' local authority (Village mayor, Rostov region, 2013). Changes in farming technologies and organizational patterns reduce the number of workers needed, and many enterprises are in a process of shrinking their workforce. Managers describe that they are in a position to care less about villagers' and administrations' needs and demands as soon as they bring a majority of land shares under their control, so they no longer depend on shareholder assemblies. "People become insignificant" then, one journalist commented, since it becomes the investor "alone who constitutes any assembly" (Journalist, Rostov, 2012). In that regard, this study's findings are in line with others on changing formal and informal, or explicit and implicit "corporate social responsibility" in Russian large farm enterprises (Visser, Kurakin, and Nikulin 2019). It also indicates, however, that rather than straightforward uprooting, we should expect gradual reconfiguration of entanglements, not so much oriented to a pure market model but something more hybrid.

What I described as monopoly power is not beyond such hybridity. Large farm enterprises are pivotal nodes in local power relations and resource flows and often central in upholding various aspects of life in a village. At the same time, companies' dispersed control—and management structures—imply that the more fundamental decisions are often made elsewhere, by people and in spheres relatively distant from these enterprises. This dispersion of local control can lead to a "thinning" (Appel 2019, 51) of formal responsibility, liability and accountability, and weak predictability and reliability for rural residents.

In the cases discussed here, interdependence between enterprises and villagers does mean that the former cannot fully ignore the latter's needs and interests. Yet it also became clear that this interdependence is not stable but contingent on changing circumstances.

Tactics, Nonsovereign Power, and the State

When I approached huge farming companies in Russia, controlling hundreds of thousands of hectares and employing hundreds of workers, I expected them to implement their schemes straightforwardly. At a closer look, it turned out that even huge investors' projects remained prone to failure and bound to context-specific demands and necessities much more than even company directors and managers would have expected. The instances described in the previous paragraphs thus remind us that we should not reach conclusions on investors' capacities to implement business plans and models from their sovereignty fantasies, the goals they declare, and the sizes of their operations. Making business plans and acting in a social world are different, and market rationalities are not the only ones that matter, as I shall argue.

One may conclude that, somewhat against the grain of this chapter's opening passages, company leaders rarely act as omnipotent sovereigns; rather, they navigate tricky circumstances. The difference can be described as one between tactics and strategies. A strategy anticipates the desired result and for this purpose partly abstracts from concrete circumstances that it aims to transgress and transform: it forms realities according to a plan. Michel de Certeau ([1984] 2004, xix) calls strategy "the calculus of force-relationships which becomes possible when a subject of will and power . . . can be isolated from an 'environment.'" In contrast, he defines tactic as a calculus that cannot count on such a privileged position: "A tactic insinuates itself into the other's place, fragmentarily, without taking it over in its entirety, without being able to keep it at a distance" (De Certeau ([1984] 2004, xix). With this differentiation, one could say that enterprises are thrown back to tactic maneuvering when they would prefer to implement a strategy. One production manager states: "You can have the best strategy in the world, but unless you can successfully implement it, it is just a piece of paper" (Production manager, Lipetsk region, 2014).

Should we be surprised to see the evolution of tactics rather than an implementation of strategies? What may lead to surprise on the side of social scientists is that much social theory is biased to see strategies, the implementation of schemes and plans, and knowledgeable actors where there may be more open search, adaptation, trial and error, and ignorance (McGoey 2012; Stark

2009). We find a bias of that kind in many classical works and among some of the most brilliant and influential thinkers. Think of Karl Marx, for whom the capacity to *anticipate* results defines human action and the labor process[1]; of Hannah Arendt's emphasis on the models that will *guide* the work of the laboring subject[2]; or Max Weber's category of instrumental (*zweckrational*) action—an action that pursues ends that are defined beforehand (Weber 1922, 27).

A variety of approaches aims to include the unplanned, of course. In the terms of performativity-thinking, one can say that performative action rarely produces realities in the sense of bringing into being directly what it declares. A "weaker" (Christophers 2014, 18) version of performativity—a perlocution in J. L. Austin's terminology[3]—depends on an "external reality that does not immediately or necessarily yield to the efficacy of sovereign authority" and thus "operates on the conditions of non-sovereign power" (Butler 2010, 151). Such acts do not "produce realities" but rather "depend upon them to be successful" and thereby "alter an ongoing situation" (Butler 2010, 151). Hence the "assumption of a 'sovereign' speaker is lost, and whatever conception of agency takes its place presumes that agency is itself dispersed" (Butler 2010, 151).

Attendance to such nonsovereign performativity brings to light the interplay between economic ambitions and rationalities on the one hand, and circumstances that actors did not choose but cannot avoid on the other. It helps to unmask sovereignty fantasies for what they are and to better understand how even powerful companies must navigate complex webs of relations in their attempts to remold villages and enterprises. Companies may find local entanglements constraining or find ways to adapt their tactics and exploit them. For instance, they can try to exploit social and political entanglements to stabilize operations that would be rather fragile on their "pure" economic side.

Many agricultural enterprises in Russia continue to fulfill functions that overlap with state responsibilities (Lindner 2008). The picture has changed since the late Soviet period, when one-quarter of enterprise expenditures went into social infrastructure (Nefedova 2014, 76).[4] But especially in villages where an enterprise is not merely the only significant employer but also a money-lender, supplier of machinery, raw materials, and agricultural produce—the boundary between economic operations and social functions tends to be blurred. In Lipenka, the executive agricultural manager describes how he frequently explains to his boss why the company should invest in the village social sphere at all. The farm is not profitable, support is quite costly, and still, the enterprise has an interest in keeping the village alive and workers content enough to remain in their jobs. The slow decay of village social facilities, outmigration, villagers' discontent or even active opposition could all become problematic for the enterprise in the midterm. What is more, as local disputes have shown, "disorder" in the village can cause inconveniences to this boss whose involvement in the regional government makes him accountable, to some degree, to other regional elites who prefer calm over scandals (see also Mamonova 2016).

The pattern is not unique to this village. Enterprise representatives often complain about being forced to take on responsibilities that they say should belong to the state. When they "solve certain social problems . . . on their territories" (District administration employee, Lipetsk region, 2014), this can be motivated by vital self-interest in maintaining some functioning order. They have, after all, territories and populations to care for. But providing social functions or taking up responsibilities for unprosperous villages and enterprises can also be part of explicit deals with state authorities. The following quotation echoes a common pattern and perception: "Unprofitable enterprises are compensated by profitable ones. And this is a policy to save the village. Now [a midsize farmer nearby] is buying a village, he has a farm there. They tell him that the farm is unprofitable, why does he need this? He says, 'I'm solving a social problem.' People will leave—the village will die" (Agricultural consultant, Nizhniy Novgorod region, 2021).

In return for solving social problems, enterprises can gain political support or access to state programs, both of which can be of no less vital interest than sustaining relations at a village level. The state owns significant portions of the country's farmland (Uzun 2012), and state authorities play a critical role in approving land and enterprise transactions (Visser, Mamonova, and Spoor 2012). In effect, companies depend heavily on state support if they attempt to expand, but also for their day-to-day operations (Kuns, Visser, and Wästfelt 2016; Wengle 2018). And even if state authorities do not help a business, it will be better if they do not hamper it either.

In Russia, as in most countries, agriculture's profitability hinges on state subsidies. The resulting dependence is increased by the fact that agricultural markets remain relatively unstable and unfavorable for producers. But the distribution of subsidies and other state benefits varies across regions and enterprises. Besides agrarian subsidies and state programs that help them with costly investments in machinery, storage, and processing facilities, or obtaining favorable loans, some enterprises also receive state support for tasks related to "rural development." Relevant programs comprise subsidized wages or homes to attract workers. Not only do enterprises depend on the state to (cross-)subsidize their operations, but the state also depends on enterprises for parts of its rural development agenda. For instance, our potato-millionaire emphasizes how his enterprise mediates state funds: "If the president says, 'We have to develop agriculture,' they very much have to find this object that they might develop" (Businessman, Perm region, 2010). This echoes the historical experience that both Soviet and Russian agrarian and developmental state projects were often grand in their ambitions and scale, but they often were not implemented as designed at a local level (Scott 1998; Smith 2014; Wengle 2022).

Individual entrepreneurs and business leaders can draw various forms of capital from playing such mediatory roles. For businesspeople with political ambitions, getting involved in rural development and agriculture can be a stepping stone to higher political mandates. Both oligarchs in this chapter fall into this category. The owner of the enterprise in Lipenka already held high management posts in the energy sector and was a representative in the regional parliament before expanding into agriculture. Besides energy and agriculture, the web of enterprises under his command comprises food processing, horse breeding and competition, crafts and small industries, hotels, a nature reserve, and further minor businesses across the region. Economic flows in this business web are organized in circuits through which enterprises share and trade their products and resources; these circuits and translations also occur between economic and political operations and forms of capital in the web. As illustrated earlier in this chapter, nonprofitable enterprises are taken over and sustained in exchange for economic and political benefits, and the company boss builds power and authority on his capacity to direct various resources at a regional level—not unlike enterprise directors at village level.

The other industrialist who turned to farming runs a twin rural economic structure that comprises the potato farm and a commercial tour base. He, too, engages in rural development programs. When he was appointed as regional minister of agriculture in 2013, informants with insight into regional policy circles confirmed that he climbed the political ladder not least due to his farm experiment. His potato enterprise has not been a success story, but it had helped him gain political power and status.

Dependencies and resource flows between enterprises and villages, enterprises and the state, and exchanges between economic, social, and political capital are not specific to a particular type of enterprise. However, tapping into many of these flows is easier for larger enterprises and companies. Managers and directors of medium-sized enterprises (controlling less than ten thousand hectares) complain that as agrarian subsidies and rural development programs are increasingly handed over from district to regional and federal bodies, established "good relations" at local and district levels become increasingly irrelevant. Village and district administrations for their part describe how they lose their influence on enterprises that increasingly reach deals with regional rather than local authorities. Hence the upscaling of entanglements aggravates one-sided dependencies on agricultural enterprises. Larger companies also try to capitalize on their real or claimed economic and political strength to legitimize investment projects. They promise to pay wages and taxes, and to revive enterprises and entire villages through their economic and social activity. After similar promises by smaller enterprises and companies may have failed in the past, displaying size and claiming strength is a strategy used to convince local residents and authorities that they are, after all, able to get the job done.

Exploitation

Agriculture has become a historically and structurally disadvantaged sector, and this has implications for agricultural workers, patterns of exploitation, and rural politics. For many workers in Russian agriculture, the situation has improved since the peak of the agrarian crisis. Given the amount and frequency of enterprise bankruptcies over the years, agrarian workers do not tend to criticize agricultural enterprises for exploiting them. The general sense in many rural places is that you are unlikely to make big profits in primary agriculture, and—in contrast to other sectors—if you do, you possibly even deserve it. Rural dwellers engaged in subsidiary household production may very well agree with those managing large farms that the five rubles they get for a kilogram of potatoes won't bring much prosperity to either of them: for producers, it barely covers the production costs, while retailers' markups are around 300 percent. Similarly, rural dwellers described the difference between the 10-ruble selling price for one liter of milk and the 35 rubles they pay in a shop and conclude that agricultural production is hardly profitable.

Class antagonism and complaints about the unequal distribution of profits and benefits are not absent from villages and enterprises, of course. Still, a prevailing basic sense is that primary agriculture disadvantages both workers and enterprises. When wages are low and paid late, workers often understand this as a sign of shared hardship rather than an exploitative strategy. Inequality is seen less as an issue within an enterprise, a village, or agriculture, and more between agriculture and other economic sectors, the rural and the urban, the peripheries and the centers. Some urbanites visiting the countryside show signs of much greater wealth than local agrarian elites. Top managers and directors of big agrarian companies are rather perceived as urban and nonagricultural "outsiders." Rarely are they seen in villages, and if they are, they have often traveled from urban offices in expensive cars or helicopters. Also, rural dwellers know that in many instances companies invest capital that has not originally been made in agriculture.

Which forms of exploitation and politics emerge when enterprises hold powerful local monopolies but are struggling in economic terms? First, such a condition shapes the possibilities and rationalities of employment. Dmitry Ivanovich, whom I portrayed as a *khoziain* in chapter 2, describes the contradiction he faces between employing more villagers or paying them better: "Wages are low and we don't have any [capital] reserves. . . . We could pay [more], for two or three months. Then there would be no diesel, no fertilizer, and eventually economic collapse. I do understand that . . . people do not earn full-value wages, but otherwise, there wouldn't be anything left at all. . . . I have five tractors, and I know I could replace them with one. I can take up credit and buy it and I will have this one tractor. And where will I put these four people? They all work and receive their wages, more or less . . ." (Private farmer, Lipetsk region, 2013).

The quote illustrates a basic rationality that I found many rural dwellers share to some degree: that agricultural enterprises should provide employment as a priority and that decent wage levels are a secondary issue, especially when employment alternatives are scarce. Such rationalities can be used to the disadvantage of workers. Given high levels of informality and low levels of transparency, it is often hard to tell when, exactly, agricultural producers mobilize difficulties in the agrarian sector to veil profits they *do* make or responsibilities they *could* take. But certainly many do, to various degrees.

Another prevalent image frequently used against claims for higher wages and better working conditions is that of rural subsistence. Entanglements between subsidiary household production and large farms can create a squeeze between subsistence and wage labor. In an illustrative instance, I met a farm manager dressed in Armani and driving a Mercedes explaining that villagers were actually alright with minimum wages as they grew most of what they needed in their gardens. In a more general sense, subsistence farming is mobilized as an implicit or explicit legitimation for low wage levels in the countryside. One production manager, who had moved to a village some years before, explains:

> Everybody thinks that people in the village should, for some reason, get less money . . . they think that even specialists, civil servants . . . if you work in a village, you should earn less. I ask them: "And why do you think this should be the case?" . . . and they say: "Well, you all have your subsidiary farming . . .

you live on subsidiary farming." And I tell them: "So, you don't think that people want some better clothes as in the city, eat the way you eat, go to a shop or buy a car? . . . Why do you think that I should earn less than you do?" Go to any shop here and compare the prices to those in the city, the prices here are one and a half times higher. As if [they assumed these goods] arrived here on foot (LFE director, Perm region, 2014).

Rural disadvantage notwithstanding, many enterprises can count on hurdles that keep villagers from leaving the place. A manager explains: "If you live in the village, where else can you go? What choices do you have there? Not a lot. Except from just keep[ing] on working for the company that is there. Unless you would move to the city or would move to Moscow and do something completely different. But many villages, they don't have so much choice" (Production manager, Voronezh, 2014).

While this young expat manager seems to underestimate rural residents' agency, stressing a high level of dependence on local enterprises is appropriate. Rural residents may be attached to place and people, be responsible for elderly family members, or face a lack of opportunities elsewhere. Such attachments can bind them to a particular place, and this dependency can be exploited by enterprises. While daily and weekly commuting and seasonal labor migration are common, especially among men, they often end up in badly paid jobs, and their commuting increases the workload of women who stay in the village with responsibilities for children, elderly family members, or household farms.

The "exchange rates" for transferring rural forms of capital to urban spheres are often unfavorable. The amount you may get for selling a one-hundred-square-meter house in a village will most likely be insufficient to buy a single-room apartment in a town or city. Agricultural qualifications and work experience may be of little value for urban jobs, and those who leave villages may, again, lack access to better-paid alternatives. Private subsidiary agriculture, enterprise support, and land rent will provide a basic livelihood within low-budget village economies, but much less in a city. For instance, one thousand rubles you may receive annually for a land share won't help you much with the two-hundred-thousand-ruble rent for a small flat. Instances of individuals or families choosing to return to their villages after facing difficulties and disappointment in cities are not uncommon. In short, the relative disadvantage bound to agriculture and rural political economies is not something that people can easily escape by leaving. At times, rural dwellers describe themselves as "slaves on our own land,"[5] with nowhere to go.

While agricultural enterprises can exploit rural dwellers' attachment to places that keep them from leaving, they also fear the deterioration of conditions that keep these places livable. Beyond wages, the availability of schools, kindergartens, medical centers and personnel, shops, reasonable streets and transport, electricity, gas, internet, and mobile phone connections all impact whether potential workers will stay in or move to a village. In many places, it seems easier for enterprises to ignore demands for higher wages, or pay wages and taxes months late, than to avoid investing in the village. But this is not enough to keep all rural residents in place and content. The low prestige of agriculture, low wages for hard work, and the perception of instability are frequently named as reasons why younger generations especially leave the country (Kvartiuk et al. 2020).[6] At the same time, the number of persons employed in agriculture, forestry, and fishery in Russia declined by nearly one-third between 2005 and 2014—from over 4 million to below 2.8 million (Rosstat 2015b, 61), and the trend is expected to continue (Wegren 2014, 92–93).[7]

Managers in all enterprises I studied spoke about the risk of running out of crucial workers. They voice the concern that, even if they do not lack workers today, they build on a delicate equilibrium that may very well cause them trouble tomorrow. Younger workers leave villages while those who will not leave are getting older. One Agrokultura production manager reflects that, in some places, "the biggest competition (among agro-companies) is in finding good people. . . . It's not so much about land. . . . On a production level, it's mainly people that they are fighting about" (Production manager, Voronezh, 2012).

Managers and directors I interviewed for this study therefore travel around villages, universities, and training centers to fill vacancies or to hire a specialist on the spot.[8] They invest money and political capital to enable village youths to attend university or to avoid the army if they commit to joining the enterprise later. They organize daily shuttle transport for workers from distant places and build houses for others. And some have considerably increased wages for key personnel such as specialists and tractor drivers. Yet some enterprises already lack workers today, have machinery standing idle because of a lack of personnel, or refrain from expanding production into more labor-intensive sectors for the same reason.[9] As this company director reflects: "We have 120 people working with us. We assume that we will run out of this labor resource. That is, even with the most favorable social situation we can create in the village, there is the objective understanding that the number of workers will decrease every year. We cannot overcome urbanization, that's a global process" (Businessman, Perm region, 2012).

Difficulties to fill certain positions have an impact on enterprise–worker relations. Mangers have to ask recently dismissed workers to return to their former jobs, being unable to find anyone to replace them: "They say that they will dismiss. But how to dismiss? They lack people anyhow" (Private farmer, Rostov region, 2013). Or, from the perspective of an enterprise owner: "[In my] engineering enterprise, [when a worker] comes to work drunk, too late, I will fire him. I have a million-city [a city with more than a million people] behind me. I have constant hiring and dismissal, turnover. Here is a village, here we are stuck. Here we lack people, we don't have the labor resource" (Business-man, Perm region, 2011).

The labor balance varies a lot across places, however. One expat manager compares the employment situation in Russia with agricultural enterprises in Western Europe and complains that, besides core workers, they need to employ "a huge amount of other people that you need, like accountants, security, check men . . . it's just a whole army that you need to keep just the machinery going, which you don't have back home" (Production manager, Voronezh, 2014). An-other manager explained that his farm would be much easier to manage if he reduced the workforce from 125 workers at that time to 30, and at the same time it would allow him to increase salaries for critical workers and specialists. But he fears that the dismissal of a large number of workers may backfire. Guards and watchmen employed on some farms already outnumber tractor drivers several times. A further deterioration of living conditions and spirit could de-stabilize existing local consent and spur appropriation, refusal, and sabotage.

The reserve army in this case is not exactly Marx's ([1867] 2015, 784) re-serve army or surplus population "always ready for exploitation," surrounding an enterprise and keeping rates of exploitation high. Even efficiency-driven managers hesitate to dismiss a "redundant" worker who happens to be a fam-ily member of a "crucial" one, as this may motivate the whole family to leave the village. Also, any further decline of the village population could increase problems in the future. Since administrations' budgets are calculated per reg-istered inhabitant, and schools' budgets per pupil, population decline may re-sult in the further deterioration of social infrastructure, which in turn will in-crease the difficulties to attract or keep critical workers. Unemployment and labor shortages exist alongside each other.

Persistence

Scholars have noted the relative absence of organized movements or resis-tance in the Russian countryside (Mamonova 2016; Mamonova and Visser 2014) compared to other geographic contexts. There have been few publicly

visible protests around agrarian issues over recent decades and hardly any politically organized groups or networks of peasants and agrarian workers within
the country or as part of international networks such as La Via Campesina.
Although agricultural trade unions exist in principle, they play a minor and
rather defensive role and are often accused of being puppet organizations.
While protests are not uncommon in the country in general, they have rarely
included rural areas, and then concerns have tended to be related to environmental issues more than agriculture.[10] One notable exception was a tractor car-
avan, organized by private farmers, heading to Moscow from the Krasnodar
region in the summer of 2016 in protest of raider seizures (hostile land and enterprise takeovers), corruption, and fraud. Protests by farmers are common:
writing letters to authorities; organizing social media campaigns; attempting
to draw media attention through actions such as hunger strikes; or engaging
in more silent and hidden acts of sabotage or appropriation. Most of such acts
that I learned about were quite dispersed, organized individually, and, at times,
opportunistic, aimed at seizing resources for individual enterprises without
further political aims.

Less common, according to my interviews and further sources, are strikes
by workers on large farms. Union organizing and the lawful staging of strikes
are difficult in Russia in general (Matveev 2019a), and the level of political organization among agrarian workers is low (Visser et al. 2015). And yet such
absence of strikes is surprising given the big collectives of workers on large
farms that could form a basis for labor organization, or the fact that a strike by
tractor or combine drivers during harvest periods would allow for substantial
pressure on enterprises as harvest failure would be economically disastrous.
This raises questions about political organization and other factors stimulating or hampering the formation of resistance or organized agrarian politics
more generally and under specific historical-geographic circumstances (Mamonova 2019; Wolford 2010). Rather than attempting to discuss these questions in general, I turn to one specific aspect that corresponds with dispersed
dispossession in particular and will argue for taking struggles for continuation
and persistence seriously as forms of political agency, besides more disruptive
counterparts often framed as resistance in a narrower sense.

Remarkably, the only strike I read or heard about resulted from the firing of
a farm director by the mother company after which the collective of workers
refused to work—until the fired director encouraged them to return to work.
The farm director in question was famous for her support of workers and her
skill in keeping the collective together and operations going. One instance I

witnessed illustrates this vividly. Much had gone wrong on the farm over recent days: a new seeder was standing idle due to a leaking tube, and so was one
urgently needed tractor with a bug in the navigation system. The company engineers had not been able to organize spare parts yet. Two drivers refused to
work because the newly installed computers on their tractors miscalculated
the hectare coverage and fuel consumption in a way that would have earned
them negative wages.[11] Accusations of theft had been passed on to the main office by an expat manager although they later turned out to be wrong.

The farm director invited one of the mother company's production managers to her office where she had gathered a dozen key farm personnel. Not hiding
her anger—not about technical difficulties, which occur in large-scale farming,
but more about management's mistakes in coping with the situation—she began to enact her role as a *khoziaika*[12], master and caretaker, and recover her
authority and the workers' dignity. Employing some brilliant rhetorical strategies, she redirected the accusations from the collective toward management
failures at higher levels: a second glance or an inquiry with a farm specialist
would have resolved the allegation of theft on the spot and without causing
a scandal. Solutions proposed by company management to get staff and machines back to work ignored the situation of workers afraid of losing wages and
reluctant to be employed on other machinery. Fiercely demanding respect for
the workers, she came forward with a solution that all parties could (or had to)
agree on. In a well-staged, on-the-spot phone call, she even managed to order
the urgently needed spare part that the company could not get hold of, claiming back some of the competence over machinery that had been transferred to
the head office. She instantly filled the gaps she had just brought to light and
reclaimed authority, showed herself to be a skillful mediator, and constructed
a close bond between herself and the collective.

I suggest that the political moment here—and by extension the reaction
to the director's dismissal—has parallels to the defense of kolkhoz relations
discussed in chapter 2. In both instances, concerns and action were directed
toward the maintenance of arrangements and agreements that villagers and
workers relied on for employment options, working conditions, and some social security. The shareholder collective in Setovka mobilized to keep a local enterprise and the associated support structure intact, and a workers' collective under Agrokultura mobilized against the dismissal of a farm director
standing up for workers. These can be understood as "weapons of the weak"
(Scott 1985) insofar as in both cases the collectives would have been in a weak
position to engage in open, organized forms of resistance. Rather than inter-
rupting or sabotaging operations and structures, however, actors here aimed

at stabilizing certain existing arrangements. Pressure to collaborate with established enterprises and companies follows from the view that things would be worse without them.

Such stabilizing tactics should not be confused with passivity or the absence of political agency. In Saba Mahmood's terms, "What may appear to be a case of deplorable passivity and docility . . . may very well be a form of agency. . . . Agentival capacity is entailed not only in those acts that result in [progressive] change but also those that aim toward continuity, stasis, and stability" (Mahmood 2001, 212). Writing about rural Latvia, and thus closer to this study's context, Dace Dzenovska (2018, 21) describes how rural residents act to postpone what they call "slow extinction" in an attempt to maintain "life in a harsh present with hope, but not certainty, that life would go on." Similarly, for this study, I would stress the importance of acknowledging the practices described here as agency.

Dispersed dispossession provides a background against which tactics that aim toward continuity and stability appear plausible and become graspable as adaptive and creative forms of *agency* that respond to disruptive changes and high levels of uncertainty. I don't suggest that such tactics were, per se, politically effective or emancipatory. But they make sense under given circumstances. As Maria Todorova writes about post-Soviet coping strategies, "The longing for security and stability often leads people toward stupidity, but it is not a stupid longing" (Todorova 2010a, 7). Dispersed dispossession forms the horizons of imagination, expectations, and plausibility. As a matter of workers' experience, a nonworking enterprise often causes much more trouble than a working one. Farm operations stagnate and collapse regularly, for various reasons, but rarely for the benefit of workers. A politics of persistence aims at keeping changes predictable, authorities accountable, and decision-making inclusive. It may be modest in its concrete aims but it is, at the same time, quite fundamental in that it targets relations that form the *basis* for security and predictability, as well as agency. This is not to say that dispersed dispossession rendered more coordinated, proactive, or radical forms of political mobilization impossible or would fully explain the relative absence of organized movements in rural Russia. Coordinated resistance needs to be organized, and whether or not it will occur in the face of dispersed dispossession depends, as in other instances, on factors such as leadership, institutional hosts able to mediate and organize mobilization, experience, and other resources for collective action to draw on (R. Hall et al. 2015; Motta and Nilsen 2011).

How rural residents usually criticize what they experience, and what they have experienced in the past, further helps to make sense of the politics or persistence under these specific circumstances. Some of the fiercest and most straightforward criticism of enterprises and investors I encountered was directed against those who not merely shut down a local enterprise but also plundered and sold off productive infrastructure, thus depriving local populations of a basis and means of production and value creation (chapter 3). Harsh criticism is also directed against enterprises and companies that draw substantial benefits from state programs and subsidies but do not use them to the benefit of workers and villages. Instances include such companies that bought up farms with government support without developing them. Sometimes they are accused of using such deals merely to "grab" state resources: "Like a dog on a heap of hay, it does not eat but does not give anything to anyone else either" (LFE director, Lipetsk region, 2012). Such criticism resonates with studies that emphasize the role of "insider rent" (Dzarasov 2014) in Russian capitalism: the degree to which elites are able to tap into state-controlled resources to privatize benefits from them.

Rural actors measure the "behavior" of such enterprises and companies against investment promises. Many would emphasize that the term "investor," loaded with positive connotations, should not apply to those who do not live up to promises to revive production, to provide employment and broader social supports, and hence contribute to local development—promises that have often been made to legitimize investment projects in the first place. Company owners and top managers visiting a village on a helicopter once a year, avoiding meeting villagers, exemplify management acting beyond rural populations' reach, and decoupling of business and population interests. Such projects are criticized for profiting from state subsidies and the availability and cheapness of resources such as farmland and farms, but not to the benefit of local communities. Rural dwellers in these situations articulate anger and frustration since they find themselves disregarded and betrayed in various roles at the same time: as owners (with property that makes no difference), as workers (left without jobs), and as citizens (with little benefit from agricultural subsidies and rural development agendas, and without political influence). They lament the loss of a place and role they think they should have within a political economy, and they criticize how companies exploit and perpetuate patterns of dispersed dispossession that for many began with the disintegration of the Soviet agrarian system and for some even before that.

Chapter 6

Reconnection

The Idea of dispersed dispossession is significant beyond the context of this study. While the histories of colonialism and totalitarianism continue to matter and to cause harm (Kuzio 2023; Stoler 2016), the concept resonates with a wide range of circumstances. Further, in an era in which the economic order is increasingly described as post-neoliberal (Berndt and Boeckler 2023; Bishop and Payne 2021), authoritarian and totalitarian regimes are on the rise (Koch 2022), austerity and systemic crises threaten the fabric of social life (Berlant 2022; Ryabchuk 2023), and environmental crises directly affect ever more people (Dankelman and Naidu 2020; Tsing et al. 2017; Wang et al. 2023), rethinking concepts of rural dispossession, and dispossession more generally, is timely and necessary. The idea of dispersed dispossession should help illuminate mechanisms and dimensions of dispossession that elude other concepts and framings. This study emphasizes five such dimensions. First, the concept captures the deterioration of state- or community-mediated collective goods, support systems, material infrastructures, social contracts, and the separation of further webs of relations constitutive for well-being and agency. Second, it captures drawn-out processes of dispossession in which preexisting harms and injustices accumulated over historical periods and political-economic systems are perpetuated and exploited. Third, rather than by direct seizure, dispersed dispossession works through the fundamentally unequal capacities to navigate disintegration and to repurpose, revalue, and appropriate devalued and degraded goods. Fourth, it shapes the horizon of conceivable alternatives and plausible promises. Finally, it comes with profound implications for the conditions and conceptualization of resistance and agency. I conclude by revisiting these points.

Relational Goods

As we have seen, dispersed dispossession is less about the separation of rural dwellers from land alone, or the violation of property rights, but rather about changing political-economic, social, and physical landscapes and actors' capacities to navigate them. One can choose different historical starting points for telling this story—a choice with a profound impact on the narrative. This section emphasizes the post-Soviet reforms while the following sections address how further pasts and futures are folded into the present. Even decades after their onset, post-Soviet land and agricultural reforms remain significant for current rural relations. Rural actors themselves still frequently refer to them to make sense of the circumstances they encounter in the present, with many interpreting them as a starting point of a series of changes and developments that led to lasting uncertainty and instability and that deprived them of something other than individual property. The post-Soviet disintegration is part of the genealogy of rural conditions in the 2010s.

The reforms' results should not be confused with reformers' declared objectives. Both in letter and in effect, however, these reforms aimed far beyond redistributing land access; they aimed at rearranging the system of agrarian production and rural life and redesigning the countryside. The logic of decollectivization was to undo the historic evils and mistakes of collectivization, replacing central planning with economic freedom, markets, and entrepreneurial initiative, and Soviet-style large farm enterprises with private farms (Allina-Pisano 2008; Hann 2003; Wegren 2009). Both the implications *and* partial failure of this agenda shaped the meaning and mechanisms of rural dispossession in Russia in the 2010s. As land entitlements failed to play the role of a silver bullet to reorganize the agricultural system, land relations became complicated (Lerman and Shagaida 2007; Shagaida 2010). As we have seen, many rural dwellers were unable to become the kind of economic subject envisioned by market reformers—private farmers cultivating their own land. Accordingly, they identify the roots of their deprivation not so much in losing access to land but rather in their limited capacities to secure decent livelihoods under circumstances they would describe as unjust for agricultural producers in general and smallholders in particular. Land entitlements, in many cases, did not serve their interests very well because they could not use or keep them. They could not use them if benefiting from land rights would have required access to other resources—such as infrastructure, machinery, subsidies, insurance, markets, agronomic, managerial, or legal expertise—that they were lacking or that they lost at the same time they obtained property titles.

This occurred most profoundly in places and regions less favorable for agriculture. In more favorable agricultural regions, rural dwellers often could not keep land entitlements. Here, agriculture drew earlier and stronger business interest (Ioffe, Nefedova, and Zaslavsky 2006; Visser, Kurakin, and Nikulin 2019; Wegren, Nikulin, and Trotsuk 2023), and rural residents were more directly dispossessed of land by agricultural companies that exploited diffused and vague property relations and corruption in the legal and political system (Visser, Mamonova, and Spoor 2012).

The story of dispersed dispossession is hence also one about the limits and failures of land reform and the limits to individual property in land more broadly. Rather than security, rural residents had gained "dispersed ownership" (Kurakin 2015, 153). If we were to tell the story of rural dispossession in post-Soviet Russia with a narrow focus on landed property, as a story of rural residents "only" losing their land, this would in some sense extend the market reform's *failed* basic promise—that property titles would provide a sufficient basis for a private small-scale farming sector to develop and that farming households would be provided with a stable income and a place in a restructured national agrarian system.[1] Some rural dwellers indeed speak of land titles as symbols of reform failure and hence as part and parcel of the process that deprived them. Contrary to initial reform promises, property titles did not create independent peasants but instead revealed their dependence on sustaining relationships mediated by the state, agricultural enterprises, or local communities. Much of the reform was perceived as a crisis, and crises can reveal people's dependence on various enabling and sustaining relationships that are denied in great parts of modern, and especially liberal, world views (Hoppe 2024). Property-based reform promises failed not least due to their implicit reductionism, presupposing and envisioning counterfactual self-sufficiency if property rights were granted.[2]

The concentration of agricultural assets that began by the turn of the century and intensified in subsequent years does not usually displace subsistence farming or pose immediate threats to individual land rights, as the land that companies acquire has largely been worked by large enterprises since Soviet times. Dispossession here usually does not constitute an event or boil down to a separation from farmland as a primary theft. Rather, it works through the separation of complex webs of relations. What makes the issue of land access rather secondary for many rural dwellers in Russia is the breakdown and lack of a broader array of supports that would enable them to benefit from it in the first place. These are not merely supplementary means to the realization of farmland potential but resources in their own right.

We have seen that the goods at stake in dispersed dispossession can resemble state-mediated public goods or community-mediated commons. Often, they don't fit these categories, a point to which we'll return below. In broad terms, the objects of dispersed dispossession can be defined as relational goods (Donati 2019). Rural residents may demand them from the state, co-create them collectively, or lament their absence. We have seen, for instance, how communities fight for the preservation or restoration of ways of governing an enterprise as a *khoziaistvo* rather than a business, aiming toward need fulfillment more than production. Such relations can be paternalistic (Rogers 2006), but we have also witnessed how rural dwellers take an active role in restoring and reinventing collective arrangements, and claim their role in and benefits from a *khoziaistvo*. From this perspective, rural residents cling to large enterprises not due to an abstract or nostalgic preference for large-scale farming, but because the latter function as mediators of enterprise-controlled and state-provided resources vital for rural populations and institutions such as village administrations. In this regard, the goods mediated through a *khoziaistvo* can be understood as relational goods that both consist of and emerge from social relations (Donati 2019), and which collectives can demand but also co-create.

An increased sensitivity for relational goods can benefit rural and agrarian studies more broadly, not least to broaden and deepen concepts of rural dispossession that often focus on land (Edelman and Wolford 2017). Landed dispossession is the most prominent and most broadly theorized form of rural dispossession.[3] Many studies find, or assume, that rural dispossession follows, temporally and causally, from the appropriation of farmland by powerful states or private investors. This is often presented as straightforward and obvious. Michael Levien (2013b, 379) offers a compellingly clear and conceptually elaborate summary of some often implicit assumptions when he describes land as "essentially a zero-sum asset" of finite supply and under high current demand that "can either stay with a farmer or be given to a capitalist." He assumes that the dispossession of land "constitutes a total and one-time threat to people's means of production and subsistence . . . a sudden, exogenous and irreversible threat to people's livelihoods, homes, and ways of life" (Levien 2013b, 363). He concludes that the dispossession of land comes with "inescapable transparency" and "cannot be obscured" since "any farmer can see perfectly clearly the threat this poses to his or her existence" (Levien 2013b, 362).[4]

I do not wish to challenge the accuracy of such findings for their specific contexts, and I acknowledge that agrarian and rural studies do consider goods and resources beyond land. It still seems worth emphasizing that the distinct

and context-specific significance and role of land relations need to be studied in a way that does not collapse the assumption and diagnosis into one.
If land becomes the unquestioned object and common denominator of rural dispossession, it may sometimes turn into an empty signifier and foreclose
rather than stimulate explicit investigation.[5] The problem then is not only with
empirical inaccuracy but also with the very scope and solidity of such critique. When ideas of rural dispossession are narrowed down to land grabs, this
brings the risk of bracketing other forms of dispossession and assuming that as
long as there is no land grab, there is no problem (Vorbrugg 2019). The peasant or local landholder then figures as the only kind of potentially dispossessed
subject—and not the wage laborer or the unemployed, the self-employed depending on state support, or the worker leaving behind land and family and
migrating to a city, often in possession of land titles and still without sufficient
income. It is characters of the latter kind, however, who figure predominantly
in our study.

In Russia, farmland takeovers are often not coincident with the loss of
means of production or subsistence; they are not transparent, such that people do not know for sure what or who deprives them, or how; and they are
commonly not understood as a zero-sum game in which investors grab what
should belong to the peasants. It is a matter of historical experience for many
rural residents that individual land rights or access did not substitute for agricultural subsidies and rural development programs, or for local arrangements,
including kolkhoz relations, that would provide security and support. This
does not mean that land relations were irrelevant. Personal subsidiary farming (food production on private plots) remains important for many households. Besides agriculture, land is used for various purposes, including fish-
ing, mushroom and berry picking, beekeeping, and rural tourism. Residents
are also attached to rural places and land for social, cultural, and environmental reasons. Many say they enjoy the relative calm and freedom in the countryside, including the distance from state authorities. Land relations do matter in rural Russia. However, I am cautious about framing them as a nucleus
that would define livelihoods, or around which rural livelihoods would "naturally" evolve.

Dispossession after State Socialism

The idea of dispersed dispossession emerged from a study in the Russian countryside. While it is not unique to the Russian or "postsocialist" context, and
not the only form of dispossession one would find there, it is contingent on

historical context, including the implications of state socialism and its demise. The question of dispossession after the demise of state socialism has been academically addressed early, recurrently, and prominently (Allina-Pisano 2007, 2008; Humphrey 1996; Kalb 2009; Kalugina 2007; Nazpary 2002; Verdery 2003).[6] Notions of "cultural" (Creed 2011) and "moral" (Hann 2011) dispossession emerged from these debates. While these studies offer both important empirical insights and original conceptual contributions, interestingly they have remained relatively disconnected from most of the broader debates on dispossession in the social sciences.[7] Most studies of postsocialism have engaged rather superficially with dispossession as a concept and the theoretical traditions underlying it, while postsocialist contexts are largely ignored within more general debates. As a result, there remains a gap between empirical studies of dispossession in the region—which tend to use the term in a descriptive manner and as if it was self-evident—and broader debates on dispossession that largely bracket (post)socialist contexts and thereby wrongly imply that they had little or no theoretical significance.[8] This gap is more than a coincidental omission. It rather reflects some distinct challenges in bridging these debates.

In academic debates within Russia, the question of rural dispossession in the post-Soviet period has not been addressed systematically and has remained surprisingly absent (Kalugina 2015, 231). Context-specific theoretical and methodological preferences only partially explain this. Russian scholars' hesitance to draw on critical theoretical traditions, labeled as Marxist, is sometimes taken to explain prominent gaps between "Eastern" and "Western" post-Soviet academic discourses (Ėtkind 2011; Tlostanova 2012). In Russian rural studies, however, a significant left-leaning tradition exists and prevails.[9] These scholars, as well as their colleagues in the liberal camp, do not principally shy away from criticizing failed policies, unscrupulous businesses, and other drivers of rural deprivation. But they rarely apply a language of dispossession, arguably because it can appear ambivalent. The post-Soviet reforms granted agricultural workers property rights rather than depriving them of ownership, which complicates the application of property-based understandings of dispossession. This has led some to argue that dispossession in postsocialist settings can be hidden rather than obvious. Katherine Verdery (2003, 76) found that underlying "the rise of responsible owners and entrepreneurs . . . lurked forces that dispossess" in Romania—a finding that holds true for Russia, too. I would emphasize, however, that dispossession seems elusive here due to the limits of conceptual language rather than the invisibility of its effects.

Interestingly, while dispossession in a liberal and legal sense translates clumsily into Russian, one of the several terms for deprivation captures part of the idea of dispersed dispossession quite well. *Obezdolivanie*, literally and in its older meaning, means being bereft of a *share* in something rather than individual ownership.[10] This book has aimed to address the need and under-explored potential for theorizing dispossession along the lines of losing one's share in collective goods and place in social arrangements.

For the absence of post-Soviet realities from broader critical debates on dispossession, it is important that while concepts of dispossession may appear as universal, they are rather bound to distinct historic-geographic contexts. Robert Nichols (2020, 51) identifies "two contexts and two conceptual lineages behind the language of dispossession: one European and one Anglo-colonial," where the first refers to the historical transition from feudalism to capitalism, and the latter to the appropriation of Indigenous territory through property-based "legalized theft." These conceptual lineages do not fit Russia and other former socialist contexts very well. Historically, Russia did not transition from feudalism to capitalism, but to state socialism. Until recently, Russian colonial history has rarely been acknowledged. It has been discussed and theorized mainly in countries with historical experience of it, but these debates have not traveled well beyond these contexts and have hardly impacted conceptualizations of dispossession. The absence of insights from the region in debates on dispossession reflects the more general marginalization of the "Global East" (M. Müller 2020) as a space from which significant questions or original concepts and theories may emerge.[11]

Studies of agrarian change in Russia based on extensive fieldwork have become rare since the beginning of the 2010s.[12] Conceptual contributions have not been a main priority of most recent studies of rural change in Russia or have received only limited attention in international, mainly anglophone, debates. Such hurdles notwithstanding, some themes in the literature on post-Soviet dispossession seem well suited to connect to more general debates. Earlier scholars have revisited and extended concepts such as that of property (Hann 2005; Verdery and Humphrey 2004; Verdery 1999) or neoliberalism (Collier 2011; Hirt, Sellar, and Young 2013) through the lens of postsocialist privatization. I want to suggest that, similarly, we can revisit and extend concepts of dispossession. The dispossession of *collective* goods, meaning, options, and agency has been a recurrent theme in studies of postsocialist privatization. Jessica Pisano, for instance, found that during privatization, agrarian "worker-shareholders were dispossessed of the land and farms they had collectively regarded as their own" (Allina-Pisano 2008, 185). Caroline Humphrey (1996, 72) suggested that the "dispossessed" in Russia "are created by the specifically post-Soviet political domains of which they are no longer a part."

Such dispossession has often been treated as a historical and regional specificity, but its significance extends beyond regional framings. Understood as "part of a historically specific transition from one form of social organization to another" (Nichols 2020, 77), immanent in "microlevel practices that worked to dismantle one infrastructure of life and replace it with another" (Nichols 2020, 45), postsocialist dispossession corresponds very well with historical instances of settler colonialism or the great enclosure, or systemic ruptures and crises: it relates to changes at a societal level and to the infrastructure of life. This resonates with findings that contemporary dispossession elsewhere also works through "social relations already configured and disposed by imperial conquest and racial capitalism" (Byrd et al. 2018, 1) or can occur as an unexpected and unplanned piecemeal erosion of social relations (Li 2014a; Povinelli 2011). It also resonates with reflection on life and deprivation on a "damaged planet" (Tsing et al. 2017), environmental damage that has been caused by both capitalist and state socialist systems (Gille 2022; P. R. Josephson et al. 2013).

In this respect, this study speaks to a growing literature that emphasizes conditions of prolonged crisis, deteriorated livelihood bases, and systemic disadvantage over eventful dispossession. Concepts that have been coined and used to address such conditions include abandonment (Biehl 2013b; Povinelli 2011), duress (Stoler 2016), and structural, slow, silent, and ordinary violence (Das 2007; Galtung 1969; Nixon 2011; Watts [1983] 2013). They have been related to deprivation rooted in colonialism, imperialism, racism, capitalist exploitation, multiple crises, structural adjustment, pollution and ecological deterioration, and austerity in the Global North, South, and East. I laid out my reasons for sticking to the concept of dispossession in the introduction.

Appropriation

Dispersed dispossession creates specific conditions for appropriation and concentration, devaluing and freeing assets that then become easy to seize. In post-Soviet Russia, privatization *alongside* the disintegration of the agrarian system, the mass bankruptcy of enterprises, and the devaluation of labor and further agricultural assets set the conditions for the growth of huge agricultural companies—the infamous "agroholdings" (Rylko and Jolly 2005; Shagaida 2012), also mocked as "oligarkhozes" (Nikulin 2011). They exemplify a massive concentration of land control, market shares, state subsidies, and political influence for powerful companies. Seen from this perspective, the story of dispossession can be told as one of accumulation: the powerful and privileged gained opportunities for appropriating available and undervalued assets. Rural residents formally gained property titles, which, however, turned out to be relatively useless or insecure. Concurrently, they lost social security and guarantees, and their place as members of enterprises, villages, and the national economy. This echoes a more general historical pattern in which the creation of property relations and dispossession are part of the very same process in which the transfer of property and the transformation into property go hand in hand (Nichols 2020, 31).

Yet the genealogy of "concentration" (Clapp 2023) of assets, control, and power in the Russian agricultural system begins before privatization. The "collectivization" under Stalin (the creation of large farms and industrialized agriculture through the dispossession of peasants) and "decollectivization" during market reforms (the freeing of agricultural assets through the distribution of property titles, for instance) were opposed historical forces that, nevertheless and ironically, both played a constitutive role in the concentration of agricultural assets and power that we find today. As we have seen, agribusinesses and investors draw advantage and opportunities from villages, enterprises, and fields formed for and through large-scale industrial farming over decades. The dispersion of state and collective farms—one declared goal of post-Soviet reforms—eventually reverted to even greater concentration as far as large producers are concerned. A homogenization of production occurred in parallel. While large Soviet enterprises produced a range of products, also to cater to local needs, their successor enterprises often gradually cut back to focus on the most lucrative ones, and larger companies restructured farms they bought to produce a single or just a few products.

They also benefit from a relative abundance of farmland created by successive Soviet governments pumping trillions of gas- and petro-rubles into the expansion of the cultivated areas (P. R. Josephson et al. 2013; Nefedova 2014). This abundance, together with the massive devaluation in the post-Soviet agricultural crisis, turned agricultural land into a category of "Cheap Nature" (Moore 2015)—a resource, created outside of capitalist relations, hugely undervalued and easy to appropriate and exploit. The dispersion of land and enterprise ownership in the post-Soviet period, the distribution of land entitlements to individual owners, many of whom could not really use them individually, created opportunities to appropriate devalued agricultural assets. Domestic elites were the main beneficiaries. Their group composition changed much less than the political-economic systems from which they derived their privilege (Barnes 2006; Dzarasov 2014), which is another continuity in concentration trajectories across political systems and ruptures.

While this is an example of assets that have been produced outside of capitalism being absorbed into capitalist relations, I would argue that their freeing through crisis and devaluation itself can be understood more accurately as historically contingent rather than a function of capitalist accumulation. The appropriation of devalued resources was not always straightforward either. Over the chapters, we have seen projects to control and channel resources "without immediately capitalizing" them (Moore 2015, 95). Companies' motivations to appropriate farms and land were diverse, and economic and political benefits were not always immediate. If disintegration and devaluation are drawn-out processes, the same is true for appropriation through reintegration, recombination, and revaluation. Dispersed dispossession is thus characterized by repetitive rounds of promise, failure, abandonment, integration, and appropriation. Different types of dispossession can occur in parallel in the same political-economic context, however, and instances of direct land theft are also reported in rural Russia. In those instances, state–business entanglements provide impunity for companies that dispossess rural dwellers by force.[13] Such incidents have been reported to be most common in southwestern parts of Russia and around Moscow (Nikulin 2012; Visser, Mamonova, and Spoor 2012; Visser and Spoor 2011).

Dispersed dispossession also resulted in partial codependence between rural residents and enterprises. Agriculture is a risky and not always profitable business in Russia, and "official" agricultural subsidies are low in international comparison. However, many of the more successful companies tap into other resources, use various diversification and hedging strategies, or are part of varied business conglomerates. Those characterized by deep regional embeddedness, multisector configuration, and entanglement with politics and developmental agendas echo the Soviet model of territorial-production complexes (Rutt 1986) and are better understood as complex hybrids than pure capitalist companies or agrarian producers (chapter 5). Enterprises strongly entangled with rural development policies are rewarded for taking on social functions. When they mediate state subsidies and rural development programs, or take over social responsibilities and services, they respond both to the need to maintain a degree of livability in villages for the workers on whom they depend and to demands from those parts of the state apparatus that promote developmentalist promises (Matveev and Zhuravlev 2023; Wengle 2015). State actors, in turn, rely on them to implement development agendas and keep political ties on the ground.

The form and extent of social provision by agricultural enterprises change over time and vary across regions (Nefedova 2014; Ryzhova 2022; Visser, Kurakin, and Nikulin 2019). Strong agribusinesses in favorable agricultural regions tend to cut back and formalize kolkhoz-type services as they can pay higher wages, invest in machinery that reduces their dependency on workers, and operate in an environment in which the survival of a village does not fully depend on their support and guarantees. Local needs are changing, too. Where local administrations can get funds for renovating a school from state programs, there is no need for an enterprise to take up that task. Where rural residents give up subsidiary farming, they do not need companies to work their fields or provide fodder for their animals. They may be interested in better roads or mobile data connection, however. Infrastructural development of this kind goes beyond what local enterprises can provide. In contrast, large companies or powerful businesspeople closely entangled with state authorities can facilitate larger development projects, as we have seen. In short, state–business symbioses change and may be upscaled, but they persist.

This echoes studies that find that the current economic policy regime in Russia "represents a mix of different paradigms" (Matveev 2019b, 29), including the concurrence of state developmentalism and "withdrawal from previous social obligations" (Kulmala et al. 2014, 540). It helps to situate Russian agribusinesses within the broader variations of capitalism and to differentiate the story of concentration and dispossession in Russia from finance-driven or neoliberal pathways elsewhere.[14]

Horizons

Dispersed dispossession unfolds in drawn-out temporalities rather than clear-cut events. We have seen how arrangements that have stopped working for the present also lost their capacity to carry a promise for the future. With Akhil Gupta (2018, 69), we can argue that the "temporal structure" of such situations is specific. He uses the notion of "suspension" to describe an indeterminate state that is not merely a transformational moment between a beginning and end point, but one that "needs to be theorized as its own condition of being" (Gupta 2015) to better understand how an indeterminate present corresponds with an open or uncertain future. Related observations have been made and theorized for former socialist settings. Dace Dzenovska (2020, 23) conceptualizes the "interstices of the old world and the new" as emptiness, or an interregnum. As the old is withering away and the new cannot emerge, the present itself becomes relatively unstable and open, inscribed with loss and possibility (Dzenovska, Artiukh, and Martin 2023).[15] This study's contribution to a better understanding of situations characterized by such suspension is twofold: it reflects on their impact on rural imaginaries and agency, and it demonstrates how businesspeople and politicians frame such situations, including the history of failed improvement promises, to justify projects that promise to fix them in the future (Barry and Gambino 2024).

We have seen how the suspension of credible political promises is part of what shapes both material conditions and social imaginaries. It has to do with the succession of powerfully imposed but often spectacularly failing schemes (Scott 1998; Smirnova 2019). The Soviet system obviously failed to meet its high-modernist development targets and ideological promises (Buck-Morss 2000; Scott 1998; Yurchak 2006). Market reforms resulted in sharper inequalities and failed to bring about the promised kinds of agricultural modes of production and subjects. Agribusinesses often failed to meet promises to both shareholders and local stakeholders, and even to achieve profitability. Dispossession was partly implied in these projects, an effect of their failure, or both. The situation is historically complex, and Russian public discourses addressing it are not coherent.[16] For many rural residents, it seems difficult to make sense of this situation, but many ascribe their deprivation, or the state of suspension they find themselves in, to schemes and promises that *didn't* work.

This perception shapes the horizon of possible and desirable alternatives. Even those who continue to emphasize certain benefits of the Soviet system show awareness of its downsides and the fact that there is no way back to it. But promises related to the market and land reforms did not materialize either, and many rural dwellers lost faith in the option of smallholder farming long before they lost land titles to agricultural companies. Similarly, the promise that a restructured post-Soviet economy would provide pathways from villages to cities, and from agriculture to other economic sectors, materialized for some but was impossible or unfavorable for others. With subsistence agriculture providing a poor alternative, and peasant farming a difficult or unrealistic one, rural residents did not become the kind of peasant farmers envisioned in market reforms.

The sense of inhabiting a situation shaped by repetitions of failing improvement promises may lead to disillusionment or cynicism. Yet situations of suspension are not situations of stagnation, as they open specific possibilities for specific actors. For instance, even though contemporary agricultural companies' business models are different from historic kolkhozes, they can still build on the unpopularity of market reforms among rural populations. Carrying on with large-scale agriculture, they promise that this will preserve local farms, provide jobs, and prevent further deterioration. The relative common sense of being caught in a present ripe with precarity and crises of everyday reproduction (Nikulin and Trotsuk 2016) can be turned productive for some. It is mobilized and exploited by politicians out for votes and companies out for land and cheap labor, with both promising development, improvement, and employment to those who become part of their respective projects. As the threat of further deterioration lingers, promises to fix the situation and revive large farms, local agriculture, and villages have become common. Such promises can relate to a longing to reverse disintegration, reinstall infrastructures, agency, even a lost sense of temporality, bringing back prospects for a future that seemed lost or at least uncertain.[17] Material infrastructures often appear as "the most concrete things that could establish a link between the past, the present, and the future" (Dzenovska 2018, 22), and the promise to revive deteriorated infrastructures can be mobilized to legitimate all kinds of projects, including exploitative and extractive ones.[18]

Remembering past empty, nonperformative, or failed promises, many rural dwellers show healthy mistrust and skepticism toward such promises made by authorities or companies. They address the repetition of a long list of unfulfilled promises, failed schemes, and crises. And yet, many see themselves depending on the state or companies (or hybrids of both) perceived as powerful enough to fix persisting and deeply ingrained problems. On an ideological level, therefore, it can be said that dispersed dispossession works "through multidirectional temporalities of threat and promise" (Ahmann 2022, 301). One of the often implicit and sometimes explicit threats brought forward by state authorities and company representatives is to not intervene, to leave things as they are, or allow further deterioration. Keeping enterprises and villages going is an effort that must be made by someone willing and able to do so. When forms of local self-governance and economic subsistence have deteriorated and been replaced by centralized hierarchies and economic or political dependency, any local agency to revive a place can seem highly constrained (Farmer 2004; Kovács 2016; Li 2014a; Watts [1983] 2013). Rural residents do criticize companies and politicians for perpetuating existing deprivations and not living up to those improvement promises that played an important role in legitimizing investment projects in the first place. And yet a perceived lack of alternatives keeps them dependent on such actors. Joan Robinson (1962, 45) provocatively stated that the "misery of being exploited by capitalists is nothing compared to the misery of not being exploited at all." I heard similar assessments, put forward in more blunt and bitter forms, in many places across rural Russia.

This book demonstrates how the continuous failure of promises, expectations, and hopes does not necessarily or immediately destabilize the workings of companies, or larger economic and political projects and systems. This is not unique to rural Russia. Lauren Berlant (2011) has shown how "cruel optimism," the attachment to unachievable promises and fantasies, is immanent to the workings of late liberal capitalism. The conditions, promises, and longings that we have dealt with in this study are different. I found little hope for models of capitalist/democratic development of the Western type, also compared to studies of rural change in other former state-socialist countries (Dzenovska 2022). The kind of "cruel optimism" we saw in this study is less teleological and future-bound. Rather, it mirrors the circular and recursive temporal patterns of dispersed dispossession itself. Promises of a better future take a detour to the past as they pledge to fix past deterioration and restore what many deem was lost: security, predictability, collectivity, and the basis for hope.[19] Promises of this kind are made to seem plausible against the backdrop of disintegration, and they create and reiterate imaginative horizons of a better future in which some of the lost accomplishments of the past have been restored. But promise-making also comes with its own history. The disappointment of earlier promises generates a longing for new ones and at the same time undermines their credibility. Situations of this kind are full of internal contradictions.

Promises to fix problems in the present by "returning" to a better past are always dubious. But in our case, any promise to restore a situation "before dispossession" is particularly implausible because, as I have argued, dispersed dispossession is best understood as perpetuating and exploiting historical injustice, degradation, and failures, the underlying causes of which span different political-economic phases. In this understanding, there never was an intact situation before dispossession "to return to." Also, the recursive quality of dispersed dispossession is related to the recursive workings of reform, developmental or investment projects that create new realities that cannot be reversed. Answers to dispersed dispossession therefore cannot lie in the past. The traditionalist and revisionist political ideologies and projects[20] denying this are dangerous but common in (rural) Russia and the broader "region" (Bluhm and Varga 2020; Mamonova 2019). They are an obvious part of current Russian state propaganda and ideology and may explain some of the compliance with a regime become fully totalitarian. It would be inadequate, however, to explain such elements away through post-Soviet "nostalgia" or related diagnoses of Russian or "Eastern" attachment to the past. This study demonstrates how many rural residents—guilty of nostalgia, passivity, and compliance according to many popular accounts—critically reflect on the past or at least on aspects that are or were close to their experience or occurred in places where they live. It is important not to project inconvenient ideologies on convenient suspects. Some Western popular discourses tend to project a distorted relationship with the past onto Eastern Europeans, and some Russian urban discourses apply a similar pattern to Russian villagers. This study shows that the picture is more complicated. We may be well advised to approach the misuses of misrepresented history as part of a larger ideological project rather than the disposition of a certain population.

Dispersed Agency

What I have described as persistence in the previous chapter does not turn villages into places of stagnation. For most actors, passivity and stagnation would be bad options. Russian villages can be understood as sites of permanent reinvention. Oligarchs reinvent themselves as sovereigns of a village. Agricultural producers try to reinvent agriculture with new technologies, products, and ways of producing. Some villages are being reinvented as places of leisure rather than agriculture. And rural dwellers, too, reinvent themselves all the time: from workers in the regulated kolkhoz system to self-employed service providers or small entrepreneurs, commuters or new urbanites. Here, we see concurrences of continuity and change rather than a conflict between them. Conflicts evolve around how to organize changes, who benefits from them, and what will support rural dwellers to find their way through them. These practices and negotiations have often been characterized as mundane, "quiet," or "silent" (Mamonova 2019; Visser et al. 2015; Visser et al. 2019) to differentiate them from open forms of resistance. It could be added that they often remain silent about future promises and big visions, and that discourses formulating visions for rural development in Russia have rather been driven by experts (Nikulin and Trotsuk 2016; Vorbrugg, Fatulaeva, and Dobrynin 2014).

We have discussed various tactics by which rural residents react to dispersed dispossession. Villagers often attempt to maintain, restore, or reinvent social contracts, material infrastructures, and institutions that would provide some security and predictability and a basis for individual and collective agency. If dispersed dispossession works through feedback loops, constraining agency, and creating vulnerabilities and dependencies that reinforce further dispossession, these tactics aim to break this cycle. Renovating a cultural center or a school helps to revive a place, and consolidating social contracts and relations of trust and responsibility enhances capacities for collective action. Relating, realigning, repairing, and regenerating are ways of acting that lay the ground for actions to take and things to emerge in the future, forms of agency that act back on their own conditions. If successful, they strengthen the capacity for collective agency. They can provide a basis to organize against intentional theft, but also against those forms of deprivation more characteristic of dispersed dispossession, such as authorities' and apparatuses' "indifference to arbitrary outcomes" (Gupta 2012, 6). They are, in terms of a theory of access discussed earlier, concerned with the social and material *conditions* that underly "the *ability* to derive benefit from things" (Ribot and Peluso 2003, 153).

In the introduction, I framed such ways of acting as (re)assembling. We now see how this framing resonates with conceptualizations of agency in former socialist contexts described as maintenance, endurance, repair, recombination, and small but significant deeds (Dzenovska 2018; Nikulin and Trotsuk 2022; Ringel 2018; Stark 1996). It further resonates with notions of endurance, but also the limits to and exhaustion of agency under conditions of abandonment and crises of everyday reproduction (Biehl 2013b; Das 2007; Povinelli 2011; Stoler 2016). In some ways, it also resembles practices of commoning. However, while such practices are relatively common in various former socialist countries, people and movements rarely use the label "commons," in part, arguably, because of the uneasy association with state socialist collectivization (Toto et al. 2023). Also, although strong traditions of rural commons existed in pre-Soviet Russia (Lindner 2008; Smirnova 2019), there is no living memory of this time, and the occasional references to these historical commons, the *obshchina*, remained rather vague and partly disputed in my conversations with rural residents. More frequent than references to "the commons," *obshchina*, are references to "the communal," *kommunal'noe* or *obshchestvennoe*. These notions were in heavy use in the Soviet period. As we have seen, however, current uses adapt them to current conditions and reinvent them. They may be better understood as relational goods: this turns their relationship to specific historical forms into an empirical question rather than an implication of the concept. As they refer to forms of provision and support that can be demanded from the state or an enterprise or organized by community collectives, they blur, on a practical level, the boundary between the commons often associated with micro-politics, and public goods associated with state-provided social welfare. It is the first of these options, demanding support from authorities, that tends to be emphasized by those who characterize rural populations as dependent, compliant, or passive. A focus on reassembling sheds light on the more proactive forms of agency that exist, even though they may be relatively quiet or hidden (Jehlička et al. 2020; Jehlička 2021).

This is not to romanticize such forms of agency or suggest that they were prevalent in the Russian countryside. Indeed a lack of collaboration has been identified as among the reasons why local political or social initiatives have failed or why rural residents have failed to resist resource takeovers (Mamonova and Visser 2014; Ryzhova 2022). Studies that illuminate tendencies of political passivity and compliance that underly the relative absence of rural social movements or open forms of resistance remain important, not least because they help us better understand the popular support for authoritarian and populist regimes and politicians (Kovács 2022; Mamonova 2019). However, we should avoid reproducing clichés of apathetic villagers and collective paralysis because they are inaccurate, unfair, and do not provide good explanations (chapter 2). We should aim, rather, to better understand the forms of agency that *do* exist, beyond narrow understandings of open resistance. We have seen, for instance, that the quasi-absence of land rights movements is understandable given the limited use and worth that most rural dwellers in Russia derive from land rights. Why should they struggle for something most strongly associated with a range of broken promises and unfulfilled expectations? As an alternative to noting the absence of certain forms of political agency, we may focus on existing forms and conceptualizing tactics of reassembling that respond to dispersed dispossession *as agency*.

This is significant for studies of rural Russia, broader rural and agrarian studies, and crisis-ridden contexts in general. Lauren Berlant (2022, 25) argues that the "question of politics becomes identical with the reinvention of infrastructures" under conditions of prolonged crisis and institutional failure that lead to "infrastructural collapse" (Berlant 2022, 96) of things like roads, economies, health systems, social relations, moral economies or options, and imagination for political agency and claim-making. In such moments of crisis, in her words, "politics is defined by a collectively held sense that a glitch has appeared in the reproduction of life. A glitch is an interruption within a transition, a troubled transmission" (Berlant 2022, 24). Infrastructure is important to manage the contingency and violence immanent in such conditions. In this perspective, infrastructure and its relation to a changing world are processual: infrastructure is what "binds us to the world in movement" (Berlant 2016, 394),[21] a form of mediation, or "a technology of engagement" (Berlant 2022, 105). This resonates with rural residents' attempts, described in this book, to repair, restore, and reinvent various infrastructures to navigate situations complicated by ruptures, contingency, and the disintegration of sustaining relations. Such a broad understanding of infrastructure is helpful to emphasize the importance of systems of reproduction in crisis, and of concrete relations and resources that sustain lives and agency under such conditions. It helps to understand how infrastructures are at the heart of struggles around dispersed dispossession.[22]

This reflects subjects' dependence on powers beyond themselves and its implications for conceptualizing dispossession. If we understand social beings as always in relation to and depending on others—humans, things, supporting environments and structures—they are never self-sufficient or in full possession of themselves. As Butler and Athanasiou (2013, 4, my emphasis) put it, "If we are beings who can be deprived of place, livelihood, shelter, food, and protection, if we can lose our citizenship, our homes, and our rights, then we are fundamentally dependent *on those powers that alternately sustain or deprive us*, and that holds a certain power over our very survival." Or, as Berlant (2022, 3) puts it, "no one was ever sovereign, just mostly operating according to some imaginable, often distorted image of their power over things, actions, people, and causality." Understanding dependence as a part of the human condition while acknowledging the very unequal distribution of its concrete forms helps us better understand the situation that actors in this study find themselves in. Their dependence on institutions, material infrastructures, social contracts, and various supports is context-specific but not exceptional. This is why various forms of practical, technical, medical, educational, and economic support, and the infrastructures, institutions, and agreements on which they depend, should count as objects of dispossession. One benefit is the opening for understandings of political agency that do not presuppose contrafactual individual self-sufficiency and independence. Arturo Escobar and others have shown how acknowledging and fostering "interexistence and interbeing" (Escobar 2018, 175) can become the basis for a politics of the relational and societal transitions. In this study, rural residents' efforts to sustain or restore various infrastructure and supportive relationships shed light on them as both stakes in dispossession and conditions of political agency. It is thus that they may also provide a basis for hope, recovery, and a progressive politics of healing and justice.

NOTES

INTRODUCTION

1. The Moscow School of Social and Economic Sciences (MSSES), founded by the great scholar of Russian peasantry Teodor Shanin.

2. Stefan Dorondel (2016) has coined the notion of disrupted landscapes.

3. See Nastassia Astrasheuskaya, "Russia Starts to Sow Seeds of 'Wheat Diplomacy,'" *Financial Times*, September 2, 2021, www.ft.com/content/4d925bae-fa89-4e64-9063 -0c01e3b5690c.

4. Ukaz Prezidenta RF ot 30.1.2010 N120. Ob utverzhdenii doktriny prodovol'stvennoi bezopasnosti Rossiiskoi Federatsii.

5. Putin's rhetoric on the issue, too, has changed greatly since 2003, when he infamously stated that a northern country like Russia could benefit from a warming climate, "spend less on fur coats, and the grain harvest would go up" (Pearce 2003).

6. The agrarian change literature scrutinizes such processes and has described them as land grabs (Borras et al. 2011), exclusion (D. Hall, Hirsch, and Li 2011), and dispossession of land (Levien 2018) or expulsion (Sassen 2014). While engaging with these debates, this study is cautious of the limits in applying them to the Russian case and puts forward the argument that rural dispossession in Russia requires contextualization.

7. See the interventions by Edelman, Oya, and Borras 2013; Oya 2013; Scoones et al. 2013; Vorbrugg 2019.

8. Notable monographs include those by Tania Li (2014a), Alice Beban (2021), Michael Dwyer (2022), Jo Guldi (2022), and Andrés León (2023).

9. For critiques, see Allina-Pisano 2008, Spoor 2012, and Varga 2023.

10. Arguably the last large-scale "land grab," understood as a forced separation of rural populations from farmland they had previously controlled more directly, was the Stalinist collectivization in the 1930s (chapter 2).

11. Dispersion and accumulation are antonyms that, at a metaphorical level, point to the relationship between dispersed dispossession and capitalist accumulation. I think of such metaphorical connections as potentially generative of interesting questions to spur empirical investigation and conceptual reflection. They do not provide any useful insights before such inquiry is done.

12. For instance, Elizabeth Povinelli (2011, 4) speaks of uneventful "dispersed

suffering"; Ann Stoler (2013, 12) of the "dispersed effects" of colonial histories; and Robert Nixon (2011, 2) characterizes "slow violence" as "dispersed across time and space." Hannah Appel (2019, 5), drawing on Povinelli, conceptualizes liberal capitalism as a project that articulates in "dispersed and competing" experiments. Such uses are informed by traditions of thought that emphasize discontinuity and rupture the "microphysics of power" (Foucault [1976] 1986) and multiplicities (Deleuze and Parnet 1987).

13. I thank Dace Dzenovska for her advice to think more systematically about this cluster of terms.

14. *Razvalili* (broke up) and *razobrali* (took apart) were the most common such terms I encountered in my fieldwork (see chapter 3). The common use of such terms has been observed and interpreted before (see, e.g., Paxson 2005; Rogers 2006).

15. This means that crisis dynamics here cannot be pinned down to a crisis of neoliberal accumulation (Harvey 2003), or the multiple crises of food prices, energy supply, ecology, finance, and investment, which have driven the global "land rush" (McMichael 2014). It is distinct from other crisis constellations often cited to explain rural dispossession. For different analyses of how intertwined crises of the Soviet and post-Soviet periods shaped the current Russian political economy more broadly, see the work of Andrew Barnes (2006), Ruslan Dzarasov (2014), Boris Kagarlicky (1992), and Alexei Yurchak (2006), among others.

16. Privatization in Russia has been described as a major case of shock therapy. While some authors with a global perspective emphasize the opportunities thereby created for Western businesses (Klein 2007; Harvey 2003), many with a country-specific focus also stress the role of and benefits for Russian elites (Dzarasov 2014; Matveev 2019b; McFaul 1995).

17. One finds variations of this theme in the literature on postsocialism (see, e.g., Ashwin 1995; Dzenovska 2020; Humphrey 2002).

18. While I do not use the notion of "the dispossessed," I follow Humphrey's (1996, 75) conceptualization of post-Soviet dispossession as far as I also emphasize the separation from basic societal functions and units.

19. In this respect, dispersed dispossession is inspired by notions of violence "built into structure" (Galtung 1969, 171) rather than manifesting through immediate action. This does not suspend questions of responsibility but rather extends their scope beyond a narrowly defined direct and intentional dispossessive action.

20. Felix Ringel (2018), borrowing from Jane Guyer, discusses a related phenomenon as enforced presentism.

21. Dzarasov (2014), among others, has argued this in detail. Recent examples include how swiftly "businesspeople" in Russia managed to acquire and capitalize on the highly undervalued assets left behind by Western companies that quit the Russian market because of Russia's war on Ukraine and the international sanctions that followed. Ironically, of course, it had been the opportunity to acquire highly undervalued assets and exploit a political-economic crisis that drew many of these Western companies to invest in Russia in the late 1980s and 1990s.

22. Examples include reflections on "renewal" (Gunko et al. 2021) and "recombination" (Stark 1996). Similar ideas are expressed in concepts without the prefix re-, such as maintenance and endurance (Dzenovska 2018; Ringel 2018), quiet food sovereignty

(Visser et al. 2015), and small deeds (Nikulin and Trotsuk 2022). I am grateful to Dace Dzenovska for pointing some of this out for me.

23. Examples from different theoretical traditions include Giddens's (1984) duality of structure, actor-network theory (Latour 2005), or conceptualizations of infrastructure (Anand, Gupta, and Appel 2018; Berlant 2022). While differing greatly in terms of their theoretical basis and analytical aims, these approaches not only offer various ways of bridging the conceptual binary between structure and agency, they also offer important arguments for how agency matters for structures and how structures matter for agency.

CHAPTER 1. TRACES

1. Approaches of this kind are popular in anthropology, but also in human geography (see, e.g., Ouma 2015 and Verne 2012, among many others).

2. Ioffe, Nefedova, and Zavlavsky (2006) provide an encompassing overview of regional differences. For an overview of differing economic agricultural indicators, see Wegren, Nikulin and Trotsuk (2023).

3. I rarely refer to the characters in this study by their names and mostly refer to their roles instead. This is because of the large number of characters and the fact that some appear in different chapters. When I use names, they are anonymized, using the form in which I would have addressed people in reality: in Russian, you would address someone with first name and patronymic if you do not know them well, they are older than you, or have authority over you. You address peers with their first name, and friends and family often with nicknames.

4. Todorova uses this German term in the original, which signifies ways of coping and dealing with the past, including redress or retribution.

CHAPTER 2. KOLKHOZ

1. Economic relations between state and enterprise were more immediate in state-owned farms, where wages were more strictly standardized and there was a "direct exchange" between state and farms in which the former provided inputs (such as fuel, fertilizer, infrastructures, money) and wages, and received the farm's produce. Collective farms were bound to state-issued production plans, but they were part of more complex and hybrid webs of economic exchange.

2. Laying out the tasks of collective farms, the entry in the *Great Soviet Encyclopedia* gives roughly equal weight to agricultural production; tasks including the increase of production through mechanization and electrification; and social tasks. It states that collective farms, "under the leadership of the party organization, [are required] to work on the communist education of collective farmers, their involvement in public life, and the development of socialist competition; to more fully satisfy the growing material and cultural needs of the collective farmers, to improve the living conditions of their lives, and to gradually transform hamlets and villages into well-maintained settlements" (own translation, original available online at http://bse.sci-lib.com/article063068.html).

3. Stephen Collier (2011, 81) offers an insightful reflection on the parallels between the words *khoziaistvo* and economy: "The Russian word *khoziaistvo*—an essential term

in many contexts—shares some of the semantic constellation of the English word 'economy' in its original usage. Comparison of the two terms is illuminating. 'Economy,' as is well known to economic anthropologists, for whom these distinctions were once crucial, originally referred to the *nemein*, or management, of the *oikos*—the household. But it could be used in other domains as well. As the *Oxford English Dictionary* defines this now basically obsolete range of uses, economy concerns '[t]he management or administration of the material resources of a community . . . or other organized body; the art or science of managing such resources.' In Polanyi's sense, these prior usages referred to forms of *substantive* economy—instituted mechanisms of need fulfillment—not to the *formal* understanding of economics that emerged with the rise of liberal political economy. Similarly, the Russian root *khoz* originally referred to the household, and is closely linked to problems of management: a *khoziain* is the head of a household or of some other substantive economy; the verb *khoziaistvovat* is the activity of managing and transforming a *khoziaistvo*. *Khoziaistvo*, as a noun, can refer to a farm, a household, or virtually any nexus of production and need fulfillment—that is, to almost any unit of substantive economy. But *khoziaistvo* can*not* imply the formal meaning of 'economic.' Thus, while there was a '*narodnoe khoziaistvo SSSR*'—in the standard translation, a national economy of the Soviet Union—it is somewhat discordant to call post-Soviet Russia's market economy a '*khoziaistvo*.'"

4. Political relations between Bolsheviks and peasants at that time were tense. The former assumed that they had to fundamentally transform the agrarian economy—in the mainly agrarian society that the USSR at that time still was. In the medium term, the plans to instrumentalize peasants for industrialization and state-socialist development backfired politically and economically. Peasants slaughtered tens of millions of farm animals to avoid surrendering them to collective farms, and yields of most crops fell substantially. It is also reported that although power used in agriculture increased fourfold between 1913 and the late 1950s due to the employment of large machinery, agricultural productivity rose above prerevolutionary levels only in the 1960s (Ioffe, Nefedova, and Zaslavsky 2006, 23–24).

5. Scientific figures range from about 2.2 million to 5 million victims in Ukraine, which at that time had a population of 29 million. These numbers are lower than those that have been claimed by some politicians. The remaining variation is due to both questions of categorization (if they count deaths by starvation or more complex numbers of excess deaths) and the availability of historical evidence. Some central questions around the historical responsibility remain contested not only between strongly differing Ukrainian and Russian official accounts, but also among historians and commentators. The interpretation of the great famine as genocide long counted as contested (Lewin 1975). However, that a plausible case of genocide can be made already speaks of the gravity of the consequences and political allegations and an increasing number of nations and researchers acknowledge this classification (for one useful overview, see "Holodomor," University of Minnesota, Holocaust and Genocide Studies, https://cla .umn.edu/chgs/holocaust-genocide-education/resource-guides/holodomor).

6. From the late 1980s, the Gorbachev government passed pieces of legislation intended to stimulate the enhancement of economic freedoms and transfer of responsibilities to local actors: local administrations gained responsibilities; collective enterprises gained freedoms such as selling part of their produce independently; and rural dwellers

were provided possibilities to organize production beyond the state and collective enterprises (Lindner 2008, 150–53).

7. Rural dwellers frequently describe how local and regional markets were easier to access and more lucrative for them in late Soviet times than in the third decade after market reforms began. The vanishing of local marketplaces, increased presence of supermarket chains, and stricter regulations and quality checks on produce sold to processing enterprises foreclosed options of direct sales and increased the dependence on middlemen.

8. Russia has witnessed four major land reforms over the twentieth century: the Stolypin reforms, which began in 1906 and allowed peasants to convert communal land into private property; the Bolshevik reforms in the 1920s, which expropriated landlords, the tsarist state, and the church; and Stalinist collectivization in the 1930s. The latter transferred land control from villages and small farms to state-controlled large farming enterprises. Hence the last of the great land reforms, which started during perestroika and was in process into the 2000s, can be understood as a means of decollectivization and abolishment of the (post-)Stalinist model of organizing agriculture (Wegren 2009, 12–13).

9. For details, see Allina-Pisano 2008, Lerman and Shagaida 2007, Shagaida 2010, and Wegren 2009.

10. Personal subsidiary farming was also part of the Soviet agro-industrial complex, not only a compromise with the peasantry's demands for private production (Pallot and Nefedova 2007, 23), but also a necessity to compensate for industrialized agriculture's failure to meet production targets (Lindner 2008, 87–93). It is estimated that in the mid-1960s, more than 60 percent of the total potato and egg production, and around 40 percent of vegetables, meat, and milk, were covered by private households—kolkhoz and sovkhoz workers and, to a lesser degree, urbanites—and not state farms (Lindner 2008, 90–93; Wädekin 1973).

11. Federal'nyj zakon No. 101. Ob oborote zemel' sel'skokhoziaistvennogo naznachenia [Federal Law No. 101., On the turnover of agricultural land]. http://gov.cap.ru/SiteMap.aspx?gov_id=532&id=1312983.

12. This does not necessarily imply any hostility toward external investment per se. For instance, the mayor who played a central role in problematizing and politicizing the attempted takeover of farmland in Setovka arrives at an almost opposite conclusion when speaking about the effects of the same investment projects for the neighboring village: "At least some enterprise, that is, some kind of future for the village. If there is a producing enterprise, this means a future for the village. . . . This is an unmatched benefit for the village" (Village mayor, Perm region, 2010). She even praises the investor for the benefits he had brought to Setovka, the very village that saw itself put under threat by his expansionist aspirations. She describes how she expresses her gratitude to the investor "at all meetings and all levels" for bringing funds for a new road and gasification, which also benefited Setovka (Village mayor, Perm region 2010). The main actor in Setovka's public mobilization did not oppose investment activity as a matter of principle. Where there is no running enterprise left, and if they do not endanger running structures, she appreciates such projects.

13. Assembly protocol 2007, lease contract 2001.

14. For urban contexts, see Gunko et al. 2021; Collier 2011; Crowley 2016.

15. Pallot and Nefedova (2007, 113), too, speak of mutual obligations and support between large farms and rural populations as a "social contract."

16. A *khoziain* is a master, owner, or landlord, but also a head of a family or household. Directors upholding kolkhoz functions and taking an active part in them are often referred to by this term.

17. *Khoziains* of large farm enterprises have been portrayed similarly in other studies (see, e.g., Rogers 2006; Paxson 2005).

18. *Assotsiatsia krest'ianskikh khoziaistv* 1992–98, *Tovaritshestvo na vere* 1998–2008.

19. The farm director, for his part, explains that former co-owners left, one by one, during times of economic hardship and risk. He also depicts this sort of enterprise privatization as process driven and shaped by state policies. For instance, the way in which Russia's WTO accession in 2012 was translated into state agricultural policies resulted not only in the overall cut in agricultural subsidies but introduced a new subsidy calculation scheme based on the area of formally owned farmland, which increased the pressure on enterprises to formalize land. Fully privatized enterprises also often find it easier to obtain bank credit than others such as cooperatives.

20. The assembly defined the physical location of land titles under formal enterprise control, which was fertile land in favorable sites. Other parts of the land bank in unfavorable locations were defined as ready for formalization by any other actors, private shareholders, or external enterprises—which is a common way for solving such issues (Allina-Pisano 2008; Lindner 2008;). A sequence from the protocol of an assembly in 2011 demonstrates that the strategy had the intended effect: "[Company lawyer]: I speak in the name of [the investing company in the neighboring village]. We made ourselves familiar with the land defined for immediate allotment. Our enterprise is not satisfied with these land plots, as they are the least fertile, most distanced. We would like to reconsider the [2007 assembly's] decision. [Assembly chairperson]: The decision has not been disputed by anyone, the period [for doing so] has passed, and the fact that [your company] is not satisfied with the allotted land plots is no reason for a reconsideration of the former decision. ['Kolkhoz' director]: I suggest taking the proposed new vote on land allotment off the agenda." The only vote against the director's proposal came from the investing company.

21. Assembly protocol 2007, from village administration archive.

22. The monetization in Setovka partly followed patterns that also could be observed in other places. Enterprises' technical services and natural products may no longer match rural dwellers' needs, for instance, when they give up household subsidiary production. When enterprises shift to producing mainly a single crop, they have less to offer for local use. When they employ ever larger machinery, it can become useless on tiny household plots, and monetary rents become much more practical. Many farm managers are ambivalent about the provision of services, even if they can be inexpensive for them and important for villages. But they also go along with additional organizational efforts. The demand for work- and skill-intensive services can increase with the modernization of village and household infrastructures, and enterprises have little spare capacity during periods of intensive work on the fields. Setovka's enterprise director planned to get rid of service provision by outsourcing it to an individual entrepreneur or private enterprise (LFE director, Perm region, 2014).

CHAPTER 3. RUINS

1. Overgrown fields also became an unresolved problem with various material consequences for landowners, who can be fined for the degradation of farmland and choose to burn succession vegetation to avoid fines. They thereby have unintentionally caused many of Russia's large forest fires over recent years (Glushkov et al. 2021).

2. Many agrarian economists, environmental historians, and others agree today that cultivating much of the now abandoned farmland was a rather bad idea from the start. The Soviet agrarian system was extremely expansive, and, not unlike prerevolutionary Russian agriculture, there was a preference for incorporating new lands over improving production on already cultivated land (P. R. Josephson et al. 2013). In effect, much of the land farmed in Soviet times was located in regions that are too cold or too dry to provide favorable conditions for agriculture, which is one of the reasons why taking such land back under cultivation would make little sense from an economic viewpoint (Shagaida et al. 2018; Uzun, Shagaida, and Lerman 2019). Recently, there have been attempts to reframe abandoned farmland as something much more positive, namely, potential forests with social, ecological, and economic benefits (Vorbrugg, Fatulaeva, and Dobrynin 2024).

3. Gerry, Nivorozhkin, and Rigg (2008) diagnose the "ruralization of poverty" in Russia on the basis of data that includes monetary wages but also noncash payments, consumed or sold home production, government or charitable benefits, and informal gifts.

4. Russian state statistics have been criticized as relatively unreliable for various reasons (Ioffe 2005; Ioffe, Nefedova, and Zaslavsky 2006). The numbers presented here hence may suggest an unrealistic level of accuracy. The broader tendencies have been confirmed by studies that draw on various sources and methods, however.

5. The fall among the urban population was comparable, while average rural life expectancy has been constantly one to two years below urban levels over the last three decades (Rosstat 2010, 101).

6. These trends coincide with Russia's embargo on agricultural products from the United States, Canada, the Europena Union, Norway, and Australia, announced in summer 2014 in reaction to Western sanctions against Russia after the annexation of Crimea earlier that year. The embargo did have a stimulating effect on Russian agricultural production, most of all for pork and poultry producers (Wengle 2016). The production increases in field crops emphasized here are more strongly related to longer term developments in production, global demand, and prices.

7. Several monographs discuss economic and social aspects of the Soviet food system in detail (Humphrey 1999; Smith 2014; Wädekin 1973). Studies in agrarian and environmental history, land system sciences, and other fields cover environmental aspects (P. R. Josephson et al. 2013; Wengle 2022; Matasov et al. 2019).

8. Generalized claims about a depopulating countryside are not in line with state statistics on the issue, according to which the share of the rural population has been relatively constant over recent decades and only dropped from 38.9 million in 1990 to 37.6 million in 2018 (Uzun, Shagaida, and Lerman 2019, 478).

9. The historic roots and prevalence of such representations have been well documented (see, e.g., Ciută and Klinke 2010; Neumann 1999).

10. Such power-laden "regimes of truth" (Foucault 1977) constitute distinctions between true and false, which also means that there is no simple and straightforward way to answer the question about a stereotype's "correctness."

11. In the nineteenth century, the Slavophile and Narodniki movements, famous thinkers and writers such as Alexander Herzen and Leo Tolstoy, and a broad range of poets and painters cherished and arguably idealized village life. Part of this was the romanticization of the countryside as a place of tradition, nature, relative autarky, and collectivism—in contrast to crowded, more regulated, and dependent urban life. But the association was not strictly or exclusively traditionalistic or conservative; the village was also being imagined as a place of possibility that allowed for the realization of visions of a better and more ethical life. This spurred a variety of movements to the countryside and rural commune movements across different time periods.

12. Peasant village communities in Imperial Russia (see Bartlett 1990; Pallot 1999; Smirnova 2019).

13. I was probably the first representative of a German institution setting foot in some of these villages' ground since the Wehrmacht had left the place or the nearby front line. This was how, in some instances, elderly people commented on my presence, which apparently triggered their memories of the war, which, in some of these places, killed people in almost each family and sometimes a quarter of the entire village population.

14. Relatedly, in the literature on post-Soviet restructuring, one finds numerous descriptions of how change becomes disorganized and caught up in repetition or regression, a future at times turning "backwards," and a fracturing of the ground on which anticipation and expectation could be built (Ashwin 1995; Humphrey 1999; Petrovic 2010; Pine 2007; Verdery 1996).

15. In his "Birth of Biopolitics" lectures, Foucault suggests that Marx, in his conceptualization of labor as commodified, abstract, and alienated, to a certain degree perpetuated a theoretical flaw of classical (liberal) political economic theory, which tends to ignore the relevance of labor by reducing it to abstract categories. From the workers' viewpoint, Foucault argues, labor will not appear as an abstract and alienated commodity, but rather as a form of capital providing the capacity to generate steady income (Foucault 2008, 224–26).

16. Recombination is understood as a productive strategy of actors maneuvering situations of uncertainty, characteristic for periods of systemic change. Strategically exploiting ambiguities in overlapping legitimating principles and orders of worth, they acquire agency and at the same time contribute to the emergence of new organizations and institutions (Stark 1996).

17. Correctives to such bias have been proposed under different labels, such as the notions of expulsion (Sassen 2014), displacement (Werner 2015), or disarticulation (Bair and Werner 2011).

CHAPTER 4. POTENTIAL

1. It is thus that this concentration of agricultural assets and massive growth of large agricultural companies has been related to the global land-grab debate as one important case (Edelman, Oya, and Borras 2013; D. Hall 2013) or even a prototypical example of the large scale of land grabs more generally (Grain 2008; Sassen 2010). Studies with a more regional focus on Russia also framed such accumulation as "land grabbing" or a "land rush" (Atkin 2009; Visser and Spoor 2011; Visser, Mamonova, and Spoor 2012; Wengle 2018).

2. Companies such as BEF built their land control on legal constructs involving (sometimes great numbers of) daughter companies since foreign companies are not allowed to own land in the Russian Federation (Shagaida 2010). From a legal angle, their massive land banks always stood on somewhat shaky ground, firm under current regulations but prone to change.

3. Luyt and colleagues (2013, 22) summarize: "Initial assumptions of attractive operating returns were based partly on the notion that agriculture in most of the region was outdated and undercapitalized and that investment in modern management and equipment would result in a relatively rapid turnaround in productivity and profitability. This was further supported by the assumption of sustained higher agricultural commodity prices."

4. Big promises, high expectations, and the image of pioneering but solid investment are not unique to Russian agriculture but characteristic for the new interest in the sector over recent years more generally. They combine scenarios of a growing demand for food, fodder, and agri-fuels (spurred by peak oil), and the limits to the availability of agricultural land (peak soil) and productivity increase, and turn this into claims of "naturally" profitable and secure investments (Fairbairn 2020; Ouma 2020).

5. The interview was conducted in 2011 and refers to a project based in Perm region, which is not among the country's more favorable ones, and business interest in agriculture and farmland emerged late in comparison with some other regions.

6. Trigon Agri –50 percent, Alpcot Agro –63 percent, Blackearth Farming –76 percent (Luyt, Santos, and Carita 2013, xxvi).

7. By that time, to become bigger was no longer "an objective in itself" (Production manager Voronezh, 2012) for Western investment companies, and selling assets to pay off debts, selling nonprofitable or unstable farms became more frequent. Many companies did not work their entire land banks anyhow and thus could intensify production within existing boundaries; some would reshuffle, consolidate, and concentrate land banks, or even cut back the area of cultivated land to reduce expenditures, both by selling off land in less favorable (distant, less fertile, climatically risky) locations and by letting fields lie fallow.

8. Many of the largest agricultural producers today are Russian holding structures that started as food-processing or commodity-trading companies, deepened their vertical integration, and successively bought up their supply base, some of them before the turn of the century (Barnes 2006, 155–63). Other—often newer—players are vertically integrated holding companies that were designed to include a broad range of the production chain. Most companies controlling large land banks by the late 2010s had a

strong base in processing (mostly sugar, dairy, meat, or vegetable oils), trade, and agricultural machinery (BEFL 2019). Few of these companies had significant shares of foreign investment capital (BEFL 2013, 2015b; Novirost 2013).

9. The ruble was devalued by the government and lost two-thirds of its value within less than a month.

10. Agricultural enterprises are relieved from paying taxes on profits, and thus formally shifting profits to the production side within one vertically integrated holding company by increasing sale prices would allow these holdings to save on taxes (Nefedova 2014, 95).

11. *O finantsovom ozdorovlenii sel'skokhoziaistvennykh tovaroproizvoditelei*; Federal Law N 83-F 3; July 9, 2002.

12. Significant portions of agricultural subsidies go into agricultural loans and rural infrastructural investment (in a state agricultural program from 2007 to 2012, half of the budget was for supporting loans). The portion of loans going into modernizing production infrastructure is substantial but held to be too low to cover structural deficits (Nefedova 2014, 332).

13. The proverb goes back to a famous sixteenth century drawing by Pieter van der Heyden. I am grateful to Alexander Nikulin for suggesting this metaphor.

14. Companies' financial reports publish the income of board members but do not differentiate between wage categories in the operational business. Hence estimates on these are based on fieldwork insights rather than statistics.

15. For related arguments in other contexts, see Barry 2013 and Appel 2019.

CHAPTER 5. TACTICS

1. This is famously expressed in Marx's bee-architect allegory. He writes: "What distinguishes the worst architect from the best of bees is this, that the architect raises his structure in imagination before he erects it in reality. At the end of every labour-process, we get a result that already existed in the imagination of the labourer at its commencement" (Marx [1867] 2015, 12).

2. Arendt writes: "Thinking and working are two different activities which never quite coincide; the thinker who wants the world to know the 'content' of his thoughts must first of all stop thinking and remember his thoughts. Remembrance in this, as in all other cases, prepares the intangible and the futile for their eventual materialization; it is the beginning of the work process, and like the craftsman's consideration of the model which will guide his work, its most immaterial stage" (Arendt [1958] 1998, 90–91).

3. A speech act that brings into being what it declares is an illocution.

4. Enterprises' social contributions have become harder to quantify in the post-Soviet period. They appear in statistics when enterprises receive formal payment for and keep an official account of services to village administrations and households, but not if they provide them as an informal substitute for outstanding wages, taxes, or land rent. More recently, however, there has been a tendency to formalize such services (Lindner and Vorbrugg 2012; Moser 2016; Visser, Kurakin, and Nikulin 2019).

5. "Slaves on our own land" is a formulation commonly but not consistently used in rural Russia (see Allina-Pisano 2008, 3; Humphrey 2007; Lindner 2007). In the given context, it was used to point to the paradox that landownership may not bring you

much freedom if you cannot make a living from it, and options to move elsewhere are limited.

6. One should add that the Russian countryside has seen a trend of steady out-migration since early Soviet times, and that there is no statistical data on the number of persons leaving rural areas and moving to cities permanently nowadays (Nefedova 2014, 28).

7. Rural unemployment rates are not well covered in the official statistics, and they are partly contradicted in the literature: Wegren finds that more than one-third of rural dwellers were unemployed in 2010 (Wegren 2014, 92–93), while Nefedova speaks of 9 percent rural unemployment in 2011 and contrasts it with 5.3 percent in cities (Nefedova 2014, 71). Kalugina and Fadeeva (2009) estimate rural unemployment at 55 percent.

8. Labor shortages occur among those with various qualifications. Still, many analysts (Kalugina 2012; Kvartiuk et al. 2020) and enterprise representatives emphasize the deterioration of agricultural educational institutions and standards following the collapse of the Soviet system and the outmigration of the "most capable" members of the rural population and college graduates. According to different statistics, only one-third of the students graduating from agricultural subjects at state colleges and universities started work in agricultural occupations, and only one-fifth returned to villages in 2006 to 2007 (Skul'skaia and Shirokova 2009, 97).

9. Much agricultural labor is seasonal, and a deficit in the agricultural workforce during harvest times was evident already in the 1980s, when Soviet soldiers and students had to help out in field operations (Nefedova 2014, 69).

10. Some of the biggest and most sustained protests over recent years were organized around issues of elections, corruption, and planned reforms such as the national pension reform. Protests in rural areas included those against planned waste incinerating plants and landfills or issues of water pollution, often organized by networks that included both rural and urban actors.

11. Part of the surveillance of operations and workers is based on smart applications of machinery. In this instance, the application would calculate if fuel consumption corresponds to the covered acreage, and a mismatch would be taken as an indicator of fuel theft.

12. *Khoziaika* is the female form of *khoziain.*

CHAPTER 6. RECONNECTION

1. See *Poverty as Subsistence* by Mihai Varga (2023) for a related argument on Romania and Ukraine.

2. This resonates with broader and often more normative calls to conceptually decouple dispossession from property so that the critique of dispossession does not reify individualistic, liberal, or legalist property relations (Balibar 2014; Butler and Athanasiou 2013).

3. Much of this theorization draws on long-established intellectual traditions that emphasize land's particular status and central role in relation to both human existence and capitalist relations. The two classical references here are Marx's ([1867] 2015) "so-called primitive accumulation" in the first volume of *Capital,* and Polanyi's ([1945] 2001)

conceptualization, in the *Great Transformation,* of land as a fictitious commodity, in tension with marketization and capitalist appropriation. For both Marx and Polanyi, changing land relations form part of broader arguments about historical shifts toward market capitalism.

4. Levien's conclusion rests on a deliberately narrow definition of dispossession by "extra-economic" forces. For broader understandings of dispossession, an extensive literature shows how the dispossession of land does not always take such open forms (D. Hall, Hirsch, and Li 2011), but it may be immanent in emergent market and property relations (Li 2014a; Verdery 2003); enforced through state regulation and law (Whitehead, R. Jones, and M. Jones 2007) or material infrastructures (Blomley 2003, 2007); and legitimized through modernization, development, or improvement narratives (Gidwani 2008; Hart 2002; Li 2007; Nichols 2018).

5. The point goes beyond the question of landed property. Most critiques of landed dispossession in critical agrarian studies do not presuppose private property, but they may consider the establishment and enforcement of property rights (Blomley 2003) as among the processes that cause dispossession regardless of whether or not formal property titles existed before (D. Hall, Hirsch, and Li 2011; Peluso 1992), or address the denial of land rights rather than land seizure (Adnan 2013). This echoes a twist in Marxian thinking that allowed the perspective on the relationship between property and dispossession to be reversed and the separation between producers and means of production to be viewed as what establishes private property and capitalist relations in the first place (Nichols 2018). It also echoes Polanyi's ([1945] 2001) contribution of showing the limits to attempts at commodifying land, which remains a fictitious and unruly commodity rather than a good that could be appropriated smoothly (Wolford 2007). And yet, even if we exchange landed property for land access, a narrow focus on land relations risks presupposing wrongly that subjects or communities could thrive from land access alone.

6. With increased general attention to dispossession in the social sciences, more studies followed recently (Khalvashi 2018; Kušić 2024; Triantis 2018).

7. Exceptions include Chari's and Verdery's (2009) work in which they discuss Harvey's notion of ABD in relation to state socialism and its collapse. Even here, however, we see an existing notion of dispossession being applied to the context of (vanished) Second World rather than developed from within it.

8. Studies of post-Soviet rural poverty and inequality have been more common (Gerry, Nivorozhkin, and Rigg 2008; Spoor 2008; Wegren 2014), but arguably these phenomena, too, remain not well understood (Wengle 2022, 32).

9. It is often associated with Teodor Shanin who, besides (co-)founding the *Journal of Peasant Studies* and the Moscow School of Economics and Social Sciences, also shaped the field of Russian rural studies.

10. I am grateful to Alexander Nikulin for pointing this out to me.

11. Similar points have been made by numerous authors recently (Cima and Sovová 2022; Jehlička 2021; Kangas and Salmenniemi 2016; Karkov and Valiavicharska 2018; Müller 2020; Tlostanova 2015, 2019). One part of the diagnosis is that international, often anglophone, audiences were not very perceptive of conceptual and further broader insights from the broader region of former state-socialist (South) East European and Central Asian states. Another is that scholars in Eastern Europe and the broader

"region" work under relatively unfavorable practical and material circumstances and are trained in academic traditions that often may not be compatible with the current trends and demands of anglophone academic debates (Trubina et al. 2020). Seeing such constraints more clearly is intended to bring more attention to the substantial conceptual and theoretical work from and on "the region." Vivid examples include work that emerges at the intersection of postcolonial and postsocialist theorizing (Chari and Verdery 2009; Kangas and Salmenniemi 2016; Karkov and Valiavicharska 2018; Mignolo and Tlostanova 2006). Recently, Russia's 2022 invasion of Ukraine has spurred and mainstreamed debates on decolonizing knowledge production in Ukraine (Oksamytna 2023), as well as in Baltic, Central Asian, and other countries.

12. While there are a number of studies that build on extensive fieldwork in the Russian countryside conducted in the 1990s and early 2000s (Allina-Pisano 2008; Lindner 2008; Nefedova and Pallot 2006; Pallot and Nefedova 2007; Shanin, Nikulin, and Danilov 2002; Visser 2008; Wegren 2005), much of the more recent work by both Russian and international colleagues is based on quantitative methods, surveys and statistics, web research, expert interviews, and short field visits, and/or provides general overviews or comparison between regions. Others analyze and evaluate ongoing juridical reforms and institutional change (Leonard 2011; Shagaida 2010; Uzun et al. 2009) or adopt a more historical perspective (Kaz'min 2012; Nikulin 2014; Wengle 2022). A few recent book-length fieldwork-based studies have been published (Billé and Humphrey 2021; Moser 2015), and some monographs published in Russian include fieldwork, among other methods (Kalugina 2015; Nefedova 2014).

13. In contrast to dispersed dispossession, these seem to be examples of state-backed dispossession by force that comes close to conceptual archetypes of dispossession in Marxist theoretical traditions (Levien 2013a).

14. This schematic characterization helps us see how the broader processes of concentration and dispossession in rural Russia differ from the finance-driven global rush on farmland and agriculture (Fairbairn 2020; Ouma 2020), or purer (neo)liberal pathways of agrarian change (Adnan 2013; Levien 2018; Mishra 2020).

15. Other studies emphasize "indeterminacy" (Balazs 2023) and the intersection of slow and more direct forms of violence (Ryabchuk 2023) as an effect of systemic transitions or ruptures. They revisit an older subject in studies of the region—how the disintegration of state-socialist structures has destabilized the present and future horizons (Humphrey 2002; Todorova and Gille 2010)—and show how it lives on through more current reconfigurations that include neoliberalization (Yurchenko 2017) or authoritarian shifts (Mamonova 2019). Postindustrial and further "abandoned" spaces more generally have often provoked similar interpretations and theorization (Biehl 2013b; Carse 2018; Gordillo 2014; Petryna 2002), as have studies on the relationship between direct and everyday forms of violence (Pain 2019; Thompson forthcoming).

16. This clearly concerns the ways respective histories have or have not been dealt with. At a national level, the collective processing of Soviet history has been variously suppressed, and memories of this history are instrumentalized. The more systematic attempts to come to terms with its legacy have been concentrated in some metropolitan circles and NGOs that focused on political repression and persecution more than socioeconomic effects in the peripheries. National and local elites managed to derive relative benefit from the havoc that followed the dissolution of the Soviet system and thus

have little interest in much transparency around these processes. On a local level, the disintegration of institutions and notorious instability arguably also hampered coming to terms with the histories of deprivation systematically. That said, a sense of disorientation and deep insecurity in the face of complex (geo)political ruptures is not unique to the Russian countryside (Genz et al. 2023; Knight 2015).

17. As far as dispersed dispossession resulted in a fragmentation of time horizons and the crumbling of dreams of a great or better future, constitutive for Soviet modernity (Buck-Morss 2000), very different kinds of restoration promises imply the hope of bringing back some future.

18. For a similar point in a study on Romania, see Đunda 2023. For a conceptual reflection on how projects relate to successful and failed foregoing ones, see Barry and Gambino 2024.

19. One can observe similarities to what has been termed the post-Fordist affect (Muehlebach and Shoshan 2012).

20. Most of these ideologies and projects are far right, although a blending with state socialist elements can lead to peculiar ideological constellations.

21. In an article preceding her book, Berlant links her reasoning to Anthony Giddens's concept of structuration. Gidddens (1984, 25) writes: "In speaking of the structural properties of social systems I mean their institutionalized features, giving 'solidity' across time and space. I use the concept of 'structures' to get at relations of transformation and mediation which are the 'circuit switches' underlying observed conditions of system reproduction."

22. A curiosity toward the persisting, abandoned, "uncanny," disintegrating, or recombined infrastructure is evident in much literature on former state-socialist contexts. Such a focus is not without difficulties. Too often have such persistent or crumbling infrastructures been narrowly interpreted or even fetishized as remains of the past, and a focus on infrastructural disintegration cemented an overemphasis on the Soviet system and its collapse (Bennett 2021). Yet there is a plurality of perspectives on crumbling infrastructures. We have seen how rural residents refer to crumbling infrastructures as hermeneutic tools to make sense of a complex present and to link questions pertaining to the past, present, and future. For related arguments, see Dzenovska 2018, Pohl 2021, Vorbrugg 2022.

References

Adam, Barbara. 2010. *Time*. Cambridge: Polity.

Adnan, Shapan. 2013. "Land Grabs and Primitive Accumulation in Deltaic Bangladesh: Interactions between Neoliberal Globalization, State Interventions, Power Relations and Peasant Resistance." *Journal of Peasant Studies* 40 (1): 87–128. https://doi.org/10.1080/03066150.2012.753058.

Ahmann, Chloe. 2022. "Postindustrial Futures and the Edge of the Frontier." *Anthropological Quarterly* 95 (2): 277–309. https://doi.org/10.1353/anq.2022.0016.

Allina-Pisano, Jessica. 2007. "The Two Faces of Petr Arkad'evich: Land and Dispossession in Russia's Southwest, Ca. 2000." *International Labor and Working-Class History* 71 (1): 70–90. https://doi.org/10.1017/S0147547907000348.

———. 2008. *The Post-Soviet Potemkin Village: Politics and Property Rights in the Black Earth*. Cambridge: Cambridge University Press.

Anand, Nikhil, Akhil Gupta, and Hannah Appel, eds. 2018. *The Promise of Infrastructure*. Durham, N.C.: Duke University Press.

Appel, Hannah. 2019. *The Licit Life of Capitalism: US Oil in Equatorial Guinea*. Durham, N.C.: Duke University Press.

Arendt, Hannah. [1958] 1998. *The Human Condition*. 2nd ed. Chicago: University of Chicago Press.

———. 1970. *On Violence*. New York: Harcourt.

Ashwin, Sarah. 1995. "'There's No Joy Any More': The Experience of Reform in a Kuzbass Mining Settlement." *Europe Asia Studies* 47 (8): 1367–81.

Atkin, Carl. 2009. "Investment in Farmland and Farming in Central and Eastern Europe and the Former Soviet Union: Current Trends and Issues." In *Land Grab? The Race for the World's Farmland*, edited by Michael Kugelman, Susan L. Levenstein, and Carl Atkin, 108–19. Washington, D.C.: Woodrow Wilson International Center for Scholars.

Averkieva, Ksenia. 2017. "Simbioz Sel'skogo I Lesnogo Khoziaistva Na Staroosvoennoi Periferii Nechernozem'ia: Opyt Tarnogskogo Raiona Vologodskoi Oblasti." *Krest'ianovedenie* 2 (4): 86–106. https://doi.org/10.22394/2500-1809-2017-2-4-86-106.

Bair, Jennifer, and Marion Werner. 2011. "Commodity Chains and the Uneven Geographies of Global Capitalism: A Disarticulations Perspective." *Environment and Planning A* 43 (5): 988–97. https://doi.org/10.1068/a43505.

Balazs, Anna. 2023. "The War on Indeterminacy." *Focaal* 2023 (96): 32–45. https://doi
.org/10.3167/fcl.2023.960103.

Balibar, Étienne. 2014. *Equaliberty: Political Essays.* Durham, N.C.: Duke University
Press.

Barnes, Andrew Scott. 2006. *Owning Russia: The Struggle over Factories, Farms, and
Power.* Ithaca, N.Y.: Cornell University Press.

Barry, Andrew. 2013. *Material Politics: Disputes along the Pipeline.* Chichester, West Sus-
sex, U.K.: Wiley Blackwell.

Barry, Andrew, and Evelina Gambino. 2024. "Projects of Transition." *Economy and Society,* 1–25. https://doi.org/10.1080/03085147.2024.2364524.

Bartlett, Roger. 1990. *Land Commune and Peasant Community in Russia.* London: Palgrave Macmillan.

Beban, Alice. 2021. *Unwritten Rule: State-Making through Land Reform in Cambodia.*
Cornell Series on Land. Ithaca, N.Y.: Cornell University Press.

BEF. 2008. *Annual Report 2007.*

BEF. 2015. "Black Earth Farming at a Glance." http://www.blackearthfarming.com/pdf
/ataglance14.pdf (website inactive).

BEFL. 2010. "Rossiiskii Rynok Sel'skokhoziaistvennoi Zemli." http://befl.ru/upload
/iblock/5de/5de51c21ab59648a80182016e18fb438.pdf.

BEFL. 2013. "Rynok Sel'khozaktivov, 2005–2013: Chto Kupit i Kak Prodat'? Stsenarii
Vkhoda v Agrobiznes." http://befl.ru/upload/iblock/593/593a23053df1374583c9a8fad
8b8d0df.pdf.

BEFL. 2015a. "Krupneishie Vladel'tsy Sel'skokhoziaistvennoi Zemli v Rossii Na 2015
God." http://befl.ru/upload/iblock/491/49149771547af05ede081aec5f623916.pdf.

BEFL. 2015b. "Reiting Agrokompanii Rossii Po Itogam 2014 Goda." http://befl.ru/upload
/iblock/436/436f54e851e23334a3d047e29a00ab2d.pdf.

BEFL. 2019. "Krupneishie Zemlevladel'tsy Sel'ckokhoziaistvennoi Zemli V Rossii Na
2019 God." http://befl.ru/upload/iblock/652/652a8fa5f787bfb0da685bd8793b875c.pdf.

BEFL. 2020. "Krupneishie Zemlevladel'tsy Sel'ckokhoziaistvennoi Zemli V Rossii Na
2020 God." https://www.befl.ru/upload/iblock/d6a/d6a4b0dde4f8168cdb5dda
65b3910d33.pdf.

BEFL. 2022. "Krupneishie Vladel'tsy Sel'skokhoziaistvennoi Zemli V Rossii Na 2022
God." https://www.befl.ru/upload/iblock/18e/18ebf5c96c935cd71327ce24f5b134ec.pdf.

Benjaminsen, Tor A., Stein Holden, Christian Lund, and Espen Sjaastad. 2009. "Formal-
isation of Land Rights: Some Empirical Evidence from Mali, Niger and South Africa."
Land Use Policy 26 (1): 28–35. https://doi.org/10.1016/j.landusepol.2008.07.003.

Bennett, Mia M. 2021. "The Making of Post-Post-Soviet Ruins: Infrastructure Development and Disintegration in Contemporary Russia." *International Journal of Urban
and Regional Research* 45 (2): 332–47. https://doi.org/10.1111/1468-2427.12908.

Berlant, Lauren G. 2011. *Cruel Optimism.* Durham, N.C.: Duke University Press.

Berlant, Lauren G. 2016. "The Commons: Infrastructures for Troubling Times." *Environment and Planning D: Society and Space* 34 (3): 393–419. https://doi.org/10.1177
/0263775816645989.

———. 2022. *On the Inconvenience of Other People.* Durham, N.C.: Duke University
Press.

Berndt, Christian, and Marc Boeckler. 2023. "Geographies of Marketization: Studying Markets in Postneoliberal Times." *Progress in Human Geography* 47 (1): 124–40. https://doi.org/10.1177/03091325221144456.

Biehl, João. 2013a. "Ethnography in the Way of Theory." *Cultural Anthropology* 28 (4): 573–97. https://doi.org/10.1111/cuan.12028.

———. 2013b. *Vita: Life in a Zone of Social Abandonment.* Berkeley: University of California Press.

Billé, Franck, and Caroline Humphrey. 2021. *On the Edge: Life along the Russia-China Border.* Cambridge, Mass.: Harvard University Press.

Bishop, Matthew Louis, and Anthony Payne. 2021. "The Political Economies of Different Globalizations: Theorizing Reglobalization." *Globalizations* 18 (1): 1–21. https://doi.org/10.1080/14747731.2020.1779963.

Blomley, Nicholas. 2003. "Law, Property, and the Geography of Violence: The Frontier, the Survey, and the Grid." *Annals of the Association of American Geographers* 93 (1): 121–41. https://doi.org/10.1111/1467-8306.93109.

Blomley, Nicholas. 2007. "Making Private Property: Enclosure, Common Right and the Work of Hedges." *Rural History* 18 (1): 1. https://doi.org/10.1017/S0956793306001993.

Bluhm, Katharina, and Mihai Varga. 2020. "Conservative Developmental Statism in East Central Europe and Russia." *New Political Economy* 25 (4): 642–59. https://doi.org/10.1080/13563467.2019.1639146.

Bluwstein, Jevgeniy, Jens Friis Lund, Kelly Askew, Howard Stein, Christine Noe, Rie Odgaard, Faustin Maganga, and Linda Engström. 2018. "Between Dependence and Deprivation: The Interlocking Nature of Land Alienation in Tanzania." *Journal of Agrarian Change* 18 (4): 806–30. https://doi.org/10.1111/joac.12271.

Borras, Saturnino M., Ruth Hall, Ian Scoones, Ben White, and Wendy Wolford. 2011. "Towards a Better Understanding of Global Land Grabbing: An Editorial Introduction." *Journal of Peasant Studies* 38 (2): 209–16. https://doi.org/10.1080/03066150.2011.559005.

Boyer, Dominic. 2010. "From Algos to Autonomos: Nostalgic Eastern Europe as Post-imperial Mania." In *Post-Communist Nostalgia*, edited by Maria Todorova and Zsuzsa Gille, 17–28. New York: Berghahn.

Britzman, Deborah P. 1995. "'The Question of Belief': Writing Poststructural Ethnography." *International Journal of Qualitative Studies in Education* 8 (3): 229–38. https://doi.org/10.1080/0951839950080302.

Buck-Morss, Susan. 2000. *Dreamworld and Catastrophe: The Passing of Mass Utopia in East and West.* Cambridge, Mass.: MIT Press.

———. 2006. "Theorizing Today: The Post-Soviet Condition." *Log* 11: 23–31. http://www.jstor.org/stable/41765180.

Butler, Judith. 2010. "Performative Agency." *Journal of Cultural Economy* 3 (2): 147–61. https://doi.org/10.1080/17530350.2010.494117.

———. 2013. "Dispossess: Kent Klich's Images of Vacated Life in Gaza after 2008." Posted February 20. https://www.youtube.com/watch?v=n-Ie9WHrpg4.

Butler, Judith, and Athena Athanasiou. 2013. *Dispossession: The Performative in the Political.* Cambridge: Polity.

Byrd, Jodi A., Alyosha Goldstein, Jodi Melamed, and Chandan Reddy. 2018. "Predatory

Value: Economies of Dispossession and Disturbed Relationalities." *Social Text* 36 (2): 1–18. https://doi.org/10.1215/01642472-4362325.

Caldwell, Melissa L. 2010. *Dacha Idylls: Living Organically in Russia's Countryside.* Berkeley: University of California Press.

Callon, Michel. 1986. "Some Elements of a Sociology of Translation: Domestication of the Scallops and the Fishermen of St Brieux Bay." In *Power, Action and Belief: A New Sociology of Knowledge?* edited by John Law, 196–229. London: Routledge & Kegan Paul.

Carse, Ashley. 2018. "Dirty Landscapes." In *Infrastructure, Environment, and Life in the Anthropocene,* edited by Kregg Hetherington, 97–114. Durham, N.C.: Duke University Press.

Certeau, Michel de. [1984] 2004. *The Practice of Everyday Life.* Berkeley: University of California Press.

Chari, Sharad, and Katherine Verdery. 2009. "Thinking between the Posts: Postcolonialism, Postsocialism, and Ethnography after the Cold War." *Comparative Studies in Society and History* 51 (1): 6–34. https://doi.org/10.1017/S0010417509000024.

Christophers, Brett. 2014. "From Marx to Market and Back Again: Performing the Economy." *Geoforum* 57: 12–20. https://doi.org/10.1016/j.geoforum.2014.08.007.

Cima, Ottavia, and Lucie Sovová. 2022. "The End of Postsocialism (As We Knew It): Diverse Economies and the East." *Progress in Human Geography* 46 (6): 1369–90. https://doi.org/10.1177/03091325221127295.

Ciută, Felix, and Ian Klinke. 2010. "Lost in Conceptualization: Reading the New 'Cold War' with Critical Geopolitics." *Political Geography* 29 (6): 323–32. https://doi.org/10.1016/j.polgeo.2010.06.005.

Clapp, Jennifer. 2023. "Concentration and Crises: Exploring the Deep Roots of Vulnerability in the Global Industrial Food System." *Journal of Peasant Studies* 50 (1): 1–25. https://doi.org/10.1080/03066150.2022.2129013.

Clarke, Simon. 1992. "Privatization and the Development of Capitalism in Russia." *New Left Review* (196): 3–27.

Collier, Stephen J. 2011. *Post-Soviet Social: Neoliberalism, Social Modernity, Biopolitics.* Princeton, N.J.: Princeton University Press.

Conley, Heather A., and Cyrus Newlin. 2021. "Climate Change Will Reshape Russia." Center for Strategic and International Studies. January 13. https://www.csis.org/analysis/climate-change-will-reshape-russia.

Coulthard, Glen Sean. 2014. *Red Skin, White Masks: Rejecting the Colonial Politics of Recognition.* Minneapolis: University of Minnesota Press.

Creed, Gerald W. 2011. *Masquerade and Postsocialism: Ritual and Cultural Dispossession in Bulgaria.* Bloomington: Indiana University Press.

Crowley, Stephen. 2016. "Monotowns and the Political Economy of Industrial Restructuring in Russia." *Post-Soviet Affairs* 32 (5): 397–422. https://doi.org/10.1080/1060586X.2015.1054103.

Dankelman, Irene, and Kavita Naidu. 2020. "Introduction: Gender, Development, and the Climate Crisis." *Gender & Development* 28 (3): 447–57. https://doi.org/10.1080/13552074.2020.1843830.

Das, Veena. 2007. *Life and Words: Violence and the Descent into the Ordinary.* Berkeley: University of California Press.

Deininger, Klaus, and Derek Byerlee. 2011. *Rising Global Interest in Farmland: Can It Yield Sustainable and Equitable Benefits?* Washington, D.C.: The World Bank.

Deleuze, Gilles, and Claire Parnet. 1987. *Dialogues.* New York: Columbia University Press.

DeSilvey, Caitlin, and Tim Edensor. 2013. "Reckoning with Ruins." *Progress in Human Geography* 37 (4): 465–85. https://doi.org/10.1177/0309132512462271.

Dorondel, Ştefan. 2016. *Disrupted Landscapes: State, Peasants and the Politics of Land in Postsocialist Romania.* New York: Berghahn.

Dudley, Kathryn Marie. 2000. *Debt and Dispossession: Farm Loss in America's Heartland.* Chicago: University of Chicago Press.

Đunda, Dragan. 2023. "Afterlives of Depopulated Places." *Focaal* 2023 (96): 57–70. https://doi.org/10.3167/fcl.2023.960105.

Dwyer, Michael B. 2022. *Upland Geopolitics: Postwar Laos and the Global Land Rush.* Seattle: University of Washington Press.

Dzarasov, Ruslan. 2014. *The Conundrum of Russian Capitalism: The Post-Soviet Economy in the World System.* London: Pluto Press.

Dzenovska, Dace. 2018. "Emptiness and Its Futures." *Focaal* 80 (80): 16–29. https://doi .org/10.3167/fcl.2018.800102.

———. 2020. "Emptiness: Capitalism without People in the Latvian Countryside." *American Ethnologist* 47 (1): 10–26. https://doi.org/10.1111/amet.12867.

———. 2022. "Good Enough Sovereignty, or on Land as Property and Territory in Latvia." *History and Anthropology* 35 (3): 1–19. https://doi.org/10.1080/02757206.2022 .2139253.

Dzenovska, Dace, Volodymyr Artiukh, and Dominic Martin. 2023. "Between Loss and Opportunity." *Focaal* 2023 (96): 1–15. https://doi.org/10.3167/fcl.2023.960101.

Eberstadt, Nicholas. 2010. *Russia's Peacetime Demographic Crisis: Dimensions, Causes, Implications.* National Bureau of Asian Research project report. May 19.

Edelman, Marc, Carlos Oya, and Saturnino M. Borras. 2013. "Global Land Grabs: Historical Processes, Theoretical and Methodological Implications and Current Trajectories." *Third World Quarterly* 34 (9): 1517–31. https://doi.org/10.1080/01436597.2013 .850190.

Edelman, Marc, and Wendy Wolford. 2017. "Introduction: Critical Agrarian Studies in Theory and Practice." *Antipode* 49 (4): 959–76. https://doi.org/10.1111/anti.12326.

England, Kim V. L. 1994. "Getting Personal: Reflexivity, Positionality, and Feminist Research." *Professional Geographer* 46 (1): 80–89. https://doi.org/10.1111/j.0033-0124 .1994.00080.x.

Escobar, Arturo. 2018. *Designs for the Pluriverse: Radical Interdependence, Autonomy, and the Making of Worlds.* Durham, N.C.: Duke University Press.

Ėtkind, Aleksandr Markovič. 2011. *Internal Colonization: Russia's Imperial Experience.* Cambridge: Polity.

Fairbairn, Madeleine. 2020. *Fields of Gold: Financing the Global Land Rush.* Ithaca, N.Y.: Cornell University Press.

Farmer, Paul. 2004. "An Anthropology of Structural Violence." *Current Anthropology* 45 (3): 305–25.

Fassin, Didier. 2014. "The Parallel Lives of Philosophy and Anthropology." In *The Ground Between: Anthropologists Engage Philosophy*, edited by Veena Das, Michael

Jackson, Arthur Kleinman, and Bhrigupati Singh, 50–70. Durham, N.C.: Duke University Press.

Foucault, Michel. [1976] 1986. *The History of Sexuality: The Will to Knowledge*. London: Penguin.

———. 1977. "The Political Function of the Intellectual." *Radical Philosophy* 17: 12–14.

———. 1997. *The Politics of Truth*. Edited by Sylvère Lotringer and Lysa Hochroth. New York: Semiotext(e).

———. 2008. *The Birth of Biopolitics: Lectures at the College De France 1978–79*. Basingstoke: Palgrave Macmillan.

Galtung, Johan. 1969. "Violence, Peace, and Peace Research." *Journal of Peace Research* 6 (3): 167–91.

Gathmann, Moritz, and Stefan Scholl. 2011. "Raus Aus Moskau! Plädoyer Für Eine Andere Russland-Berichterstattung." *Osteuropa* 61 (10): 77–81.

Genz, Carolin, Lucas Pohl, Janina Dobrusskin, and Ilse Helbrecht. 2023. "Geopolitical Caesuras as Time-Space-Anchors of Ontological (In)Security: The Case of the Fall of the Berlin Wall." *Geopolitics* 28 (1): 392–415. https://doi.org/10.1080/14650045.2021.1912021.

Gerry, Christopher J., Eugene Nivorozhkin, and John A. Rigg. 2008. "The Great Divide: 'Ruralisation' of Poverty in Russia." *Cambridge Journal of Economics* 32 (4): 593–607. https://doi.org/10.1093/cje/bem052.

Giddens, Anthony. 1984. *The Constitution of Society: Outline of the Theory of Structuration*. Cambridge: Polity Press.

Gidwani, Vinay. 2008. *Capital, Interrupted: Agrarian Development and the Politics of Work in India*. Minneapolis: University of Minnesota Press.

Gille, Zsuzsa. 2010. "Postscript." In *Post-Communist Nostalgia*, edited by Maria Todorova and Zsuzsa Gille, 278–89. New York: Berghahn.

———. 2022. "The Socialocene: From Capitalocene to Transnational Waste Regimes." *Antipode*. https://doi.org/10.1111/anti.12878.

Glushkov, Igor, Ilona Zhuravleva, Jessica L. McCarty, Anna Komarova, Alexey Drozdovsky, Marina Drozdovskaya, Vilen Lupachik, Alexey Yaroshenko, Stephen V. Stehman, and Alexander V. Prishchepov. 2021. "Spring Fires in Russia: Results from Participatory Burned Area Mapping with Sentinel-2 Imagery." *Environmental Research Letters* 16 (12): 125005. https://doi.org/10.1088/1748-9326/ac3287.

Gordillo, Gastón. 2014. *Rubble: The Afterlife of Destruction*. Durham, N.C.: Duke University Press.

Gordon, Avery F. 2008. *Ghostly Matters: Haunting and the Sociological Imagination*. Minneapolis: University of Minnesota Press.

Grain. 2008. "Seized! The 2008 Land Grab for Food and Financial Security." https://www.grain.org/article/entries/93-seized-the-2008-landgrab-for-food-and-financial-security.

Guldi, Jo. 2022. *The Long Land War: The Global Struggle for Occupancy Rights*. New Haven, Conn.: Yale University Press.

Gunko, Maria, Nadir Kinossian, Galina Pivovar, Kseniya Averkieva, and Elena Batunova. 2021. "Exploring Agency of Change in Small Industrial Towns through Urban Renewal Initiatives." *Geografiska Annaler B* 103 (3): 218–34. https://doi.org/10.1080/04353684.2020.1868947.

Gupta, Akhil. 2012. *Red Tape: Bureaucracy Structural Violence and Poverty in India.* Durham, N.C.: Duke University Press.

———. 2015. "Suspension." Society for Cultural Anthropology. September 24. https://culanth.org/fieldsights/suspension.

———. 2018. "The Future in Ruins: Thoughts on the Temporality of Infrastructure." In *The Promise of Infrastructure*, edited by Nikhil Anand, Akhil Gupta, and Hannah Appel, 62–79. A School for Advanced Research Advanced Seminar. Durham, N.C.: Duke University Press.

Hall, Derek. 2013. "Primitive Accumulation, Accumulation by Dispossession and the Global Land Grab." *Third World Quarterly* 34 (9): 1582–1604. https://doi.org/10.1080/01436597.2013.843854.

———. 2021. "Rural Dispossession and Capital Accumulation." In *Handbook of Critical Agrarian Studies*, edited by Agha H. Akram-Lodhi, Kristina Dietz, Bettina Engels, and Ben McKay, 515–24. Cheltenham, Mass.: Edward Elgar.

Hall, Derek, Philip Hirsch, and Tania Murray Li. 2011. *Powers of Exclusion: Land Dilemmas in Southeast Asia.* Honolulu: University of Hawai'i Press.

Hall, Ruth, Marc Edelman, Saturnino M. Borras, Ian Scoones, Ben White, and Wendy Wolford. 2015. "Resistance, Acquiescence or Incorporation? An Introduction to Land Grabbing and Political Reactions 'From Below.'" *Journal of Peasant Studies* 42 (3–4): 467–88. https://doi.org/10.1080/03066150.2015.1036746.

Hall, Stuart. 1997. "The Spectacle of the 'Other.'" In *Representation: Cultural Representations and Signifying Practices*, edited by Stuart Hall, 223–90. London: Sage.

Hann, Christopher, ed. 2003. *The Postsocialist Agrarian Question: Property Relations and the Rural Condition.* Halle Studies in the Anthropology of Eurasia. Vol. 1. Münster: Lit.

———, ed. 2005. *Property Relations: The Halle Focus Group, 2000–2005.* Halle: MPISA.

———, ed. 2007. *Postsocialism: Ideals Ideologies and Practices in Eurasia.* Reprint. London: Routledge.

———. 2011. "Moral Dispossession." *InterDisciplines: Journal of History and Sociology* 2 (2): 11–37. https://doi.org/10.4119/INDI-949.

Hannah, Lee, Patrick R. Roehrdanz, Krishna Bahadur K. C., Evan D. G. Fraser, Camila I. Donatti, Leonardo Saenz, Timothy Max Wright et al. 2020. "The Environmental Consequences of Climate-Driven Agricultural Frontiers." *PloS One* 15 (2): e0228305. https://doi.org/10.1371/journal.pone.0228305.

Hart, Gillian. 2002. *Disabling Globalization: Places of Power in Post-Apartheid South Africa.* Berkeley: University of California Press.

Harvey, David. 2003. *The New Imperialism.* Oxford: Oxford University Press.

Hirt, Sonia, Christian Sellar, and Craig Young. 2013. "Neoliberal Doctrine Meets the Eastern Bloc: Resistance, Appropriation and Purification in Post-Socialist Spaces." *Europe-Asia Studies* 65 (7): 1243–54. https://doi.org/10.1080/09668136.2013.822711.

Hoppe, Katharina. 2024. "Dependency Denial in Crisis: Revisiting Feminist Critiques of Dualism." *European Journal of Social Theory*: 1–17. https://doi.org/10.1177/13684310241253572.

Hörschelmann, Kathrin, and Alison Stenning. 2008. "Ethnographies of Postsocialist Change." *Progress in Human Geography* 32 (3): 339–61. https://doi.org/10.1177/0309132508089094.

Humphrey, Caroline. 1983. *Karl Marx Collective: Economy, Society and Religion in a Siberian Collective Farm*. Cambridge: Cambridge University Press.

———. 1996. "Myth-Making, Narratives, and the Dispossessed in Russia." *Cambridge Journal of Anthropology* 19 (2): 70–92.

———. 1999. *Marx Went Away—but Karl Stayed Behind*. Ann Arbor: University of Michigan Press.

———. 2002. *The Unmaking of Soviet Life: Everyday Economies after Socialism*. Ithaca, N.Y.: Cornell University Press.

———. 2005. "Ideology in Infrastructure: Architecture and Soviet Imagination." *Journal of the Royal Anthropological Institute* 11 (1): 39–58. https://doi.org/10.1111/j.1467-9655.2005.00225.x.

———. 2007. "Does the Category 'Postsocialist' Still Make Sense?" *In Postsocialism: Ideals Ideologies and Practices in Eurasia*, edited by Christopher Hann, 12–15. London: Routledge.

Ioffe, Grigory. 2005. "The Downsizing of Russian Agriculture." *Europe-Asia Studies* 57 (2): 179–208. https://doi.org/10.1080/09668130500051627.

Ioffe, Grigory, Tatyana Nefedova, and Ilya Zaslavsky. 2004. "From Spatial Continuity to Fragmentation: The Case of Russian Farming." *Annals of the Association of American Geographers* 94 (4): 913–43. https://doi.org/10.1111/j.1467-8306.2004.00441.x.

Ioffe, Grigory, Tatyana Nefedova, and Ilya Zaslavsky. 2006. *The End of Peasantry? The Disintegration of Rural Russia*. Pittsburgh, Pa.: University of Pittsburgh Press.

Izryadnova, Olga, Sergei Drobyshevskiy, Maria Kazakova, Sergey Tsukhlo, Yuri Bobylev, Natalya Shagaida, Vasily Uzun, Natalia Karlova, Renata Yanbykh, and Nadezhda Volovik. "Real'nyi Sektor Ekonomiki." In *Sinel'nikov-Muryvel, Mau Et al. (Hg.) 2015–Rossiiskaia Ekonomika V 2014 Godu*, 185–303.

Jehlička, Petr. 2021. "Eastern Europe and the Geography of Knowledge Production: The Case of the Invisible Gardener." *Progress in Human Geography* 45 (5): 1218–36. https://doi.org/10.1177/0309132520987305.

Jehlička, Petr, Miķelis Grīviņš, Oane Visser, and Bálint Balázs. 2020. "Thinking Food Like an East European: A Critical Reflection on the Framing of Food Systems. " *Journal of Rural Studies* 76: 286–95. https://doi.org/10.1016/j.jrurstud.2020.04.015.

Josephson, Paul R., Paul Josephson, Nicolai Dronin, Ruben Mnatsakanian, Aleh Cherp, Dmitry Efremenko, and Vladislav Larin. 2013. *An Environmental History of Russia*. Cambridge: Cambridge University Press.

Kagarlicky, Boris. 1992. *The Disintegration of the Monolith*. London: Verso.

———. 2002. *Russia under Yeltsin and Putin: Neo-Liberal Autocracy*. London: Pluto.

Kalb, Don. 2009. "Conversations with a Polish Populist: Tracing Hidden Histories of Globalization, Class, and Dispossession in Postsocialism (and Beyond)." *American Ethnologist* 36 (2): 207–23. https://doi.org/10.1111/j.1548-1425.2009.01131.x.

Kalugina, Zemfira I. 2007. "Deprivatsia Sel'skikh Soobshchestv V Usloviakh Nesostoiatel'nosti Sel'skokhoziaistvennykh Predpriatii: Institutsional'nye I Sotsial'nye Mekhanizmy." *Region: ekonomika i sotsiologia* (1): 186–98.

———. 2012. "Inversia Sel'skoi Zaniatosti: Praktika I Politika." *Region: ekonomika i sotsiologia* (2): 45–67.

———. 2014. "Agricultural Policy in Russia: Global Challenges and the Viability of

Rural Communities." *International Journal of Sociology of Agriculture and Food* 21 (1): 115–31.

———. 2015. *Rynochnaia Transformatsia Agrarnogo Sektora Rossii: Sotsiologicheskii Diskurs*. Novosibirsk: IEOPP SO RAN.

Kalugina, Zemfira I., and Olga Fadeeva. 2009. *Rossiiskaia Derevnia V Labirinte Reform: Sotsiologicheskie Zarisovki*. Novosibirsk: IEOPP SO RAN.

Kangas, Anni, and Suvi Salmenniemi. 2016. "Decolonizing Knowledge: Neoliberalism beyond the Three Worlds." *Distinktion: Journal of Social Theory* 17 (2): 210–27. https://doi.org/10.1080/1600910X.2016.1184174.

Karkov, Nikolay R., and Zhivka Valiavicharska. 2018. "Rethinking East-European Socialism: Notes Toward an Anti-Capitalist Decolonial Methodology." *Interventions* 20 (6): 785–813. https://doi.org/10.1080/1369801X.2018.1515647.

Katz, Cindi. 1994. "Playing the Field: Questions of Fieldwork in Geography." *Professional Geographer* 46 (1): 67–72.

Kay, Rebecca, Sergei Shubin, and Tatjana Thelen. 2012. "Rural Realities in the Post-Socialist Space." *Journal of Rural Studies* 28 (2): 55–62. https://doi.org/10.1016/j.jrurstud.2012.03.001.

Kaz'min, Mikhail A. 2012. *Zemel'nye Reformy V Rossii XIX-XX Vv: Uroki Proidennogo Puti*. Moskva: URSS, Knizhnyi dom Librokom.

Khalvashi, Tamta. 2018. "The Horizons of Medea: Economies and Cosmologies of Dispossession in Georgia." *Journal of the Royal Anthropological Institute* 24 (4): 804–25. https://doi.org/10.1111/1467-9655.12918.

Khazov-Cassia, Sergei. 2015. "In Forgotten Karelian Village, Frustration with Moscow Runs High." Radio Free Europe, December 10. www.rferl.org/content/russia-karelia-frustration-putin/27437400.html.

Kilner, James. 2007. "Vodka and Isolation: Welcome to Rural Russia." Reuters. August 9. https://www.reuters.com/article/world/vodka-and-isolation-welcome-to-rural-russia-idUSL07559056/.

Klein, Naomi. 2007. *The Shock Doctrine: The Rise of Disaster Capitalism*. London: Allen Lane.

Knight, Daniel M. 2015. *History, Time, and Economic Crisis in Central Greece*. New York: Palgrave Macmillan.

Koch, Natalie, ed. 2022. *Spatializing Authoritarianism*. Syracuse, N.Y.: Syracuse University Press.

Kovács, Eszter Krasznai. 2016. "The 'Differentiated Countryside': Survival Strategies of Rural Entrepreneurs." In *Rethinking Life at the Margins: The Assemblage of Contexts, Subjects and Politics*, edited by Michele Lancione, 183–95. London: Routledge.

Kovács, Eszter Krasznai. 2022. "Questioning Rural Populism." *Political Geography* 97. https://doi.org/10.1016/j.polgeo.2022.102621.

Kremlin. 2015. "Vstrecha s predstaviteliami fermerskikh khoziaistv." September 24. http://www.kremlin.ru/events/president/news/50362

Kulmala, Meri, Markus Johannes Kainu, Jouku Nikula, and Markku Kivinen. 2014. "Paradoxes of Agency: Democracy and Welfare in Russia." *Demokratizatsiya* 22 (4): 523–52.

Kuns, Brian, Oane Visser, and Anders Wästfelt. 2016. "The Stock Market and the Steppe:

The Challenges Faced by Stock-Market Financed, Nordic Farming Ventures in Russia and Ukraine." *Journal of Rural Studies* 45:199–217. https://doi.org/10.1016/j.jrurstud.2016.03.009.

Kurakin, Alexander. 2015. "When the State Is Shirking: Informal Solutions for Social Services Provision in Altai Villages." *Przegląd Wschodnioeuropejski* 6 (2): 145–59.

Kurganova, Irina, Valentin Lopes de Gerenyu, Johan Six, and Yakov Kuzyakov. 2014. "Carbon Cost of Collective Farming Collapse in Russia." *Global Change Biology* 20 (3): 938–47. https://doi.org/10.1111/gcb.12379.

Kušić, Katarina. 2024. "What's in a Land Grab? Knowing Dispossession and Land in Southeast Europe." In *Epistemologies of Land,* edited by Felix Anderl, 97–113. Lanham, Md.: Rowman & Littlefield.

Kuzio, Taras. 2023. "Imperial Nationalism as the Driver behind Russia's Invasion of Ukraine." *Nations and Nationalism* 29 (1): 30–38. https://doi.org/10.1111/nana.12875.

Kvartiuk, Vasyl, Martin Petrick, Miroslava Bavorova, Zuzana Bednaříková, and Elena Ponkina. 2020. "A Brain Drain in Russian Agriculture? Migration Sentiments among Skilled Russian Rural Youth." *Europe-Asia Studies* 72 (8): 1352–77. https://doi.org/10.1080/09668136.2020.1730305.

Lander, Christopher, and Brian Kuns. 2021. "The Sinking of the Armada: Problems for the Three 'Flagship' Foreign Investment Agroholdings in Russia and Ukraine." *Europe-Asia Studies*, 1–32. https://doi.org/10.1080/09668136.2020.1842330.

Large Scale Agriculture. 2021. "Top 10 Russian Agroholdings by Revenue 2020." March 29. https://www.largescaleagriculture.com/home/news-details/ranking-revenue

Lasseter, Tom. 2009. "Biden Had It Right: Rural Russia Is Dying of Poverty, Neglect." McClatchy D.C. August 5. www.mcclatchydc.com/news/nation-world/world/article24549709.html.

Latour, Bruno. 2005. *Reassembling the Social: An Introduction to Actor-Network-Theory.* Oxford: Oxford University Press.

Law, John. 1992. "Notes on the Theory of the Actor-Network: Ordering, Strategy, and Heterogeneity." *Systems Practice* 5 (4): 379–93. https://doi.org/10.1007/BF01059830.

León, Andrés. 2023. *The Coup and the Palm Trees: Agrarian Conflict and Political Power in Honduras.* Athens: University of Georgia Press.

Leonard, Carol Scott. 2011. *Agrarian Reform in Russia: The Road from Serfdom.* Cambridge: Cambridge University Press.

Lerman, Zvi, and Natalya Shagaida. 2007. "Land Policies and Agricultural Land Markets in Russia." *Land Use Policy* 24: 14–23.

Levien, Michael. 2013a. "Regimes of Dispossession: From Steel Towns to Special Economic Zones." *Development and Change* 44 (2): 381–407. https://doi.org/10.1111/dech.12012.

———. 2013b. "The Politics of Dispossession: Theorizing India's 'Land Wars.'" *Politics & Society* 41 (3): 351–94. https://doi.org/10.1177/0032329213493751.

———. 2018. *Dispossession without Development: Land Grabs in Neoliberal India.* New York: Oxford University Press.

Lewin, Moshe. 1975. *Russian Peasants and Soviet Power: A Study of Collectivization.* New York: Norton.

Li, Tania Murray. 2007. *The Will to Improve: Governmentality, Development, and the Practice of Politics*. Durham, N.C.: Duke University Press.

———. 2014a. *Land's End: Capitalist Relations on an Indigenous Frontier*. Durham, N.C.: Duke University Press.

———. 2014b. "What Is Land? Assembling a Resource for Global Investment." *Transactions of the Institute of British Geographers* 39 (4): 589–602. https://doi.org/10.1111/tran .12065.

Liefert, William, and Olga Liefert. 1999. "Russia's Economic Crisis: Effects on Agriculture Are Mixed." *Agricultural Outlook:* 15–18. Washington, D.C.: Economic Research Service/USDA.

Lindner, Peter. 2007. "Localising Privatisation, Disconnecting Locales–Mechanisms of Disintegration in Post-Socialist Rural Russia." *Geoforum* 38 (3): 494–504. https://doi .org/10.1016/j.geoforum.2006.11.009.

———. 2008. *Der Kolchoz-Archipel im Privatisierungsprozess: Wege und Umwege der russischen Landwirtschaft in die globale Marktgesellschaft*. Bielefeld: transcript.

———. 2013. "Situating Property in Transformation: Beyond the Private and the Collective." *Europe-Asia Studies* 65 (7): 1275–94. https://doi.org/10.1080/09668136.2013 .822698.

Lindner, Peter, and Alexander Vorbrugg. 2012. "Wiederkehr der Landfrage. Großinvestitionen in Russlands Landwirtschaft." *Osteuropa* 62 (6–8): 325–44.

Litchfield, Rebecca. 2014. *Soviet Ghosts: The Soviet Union Abandoned. Communist Empire in Decay*. 2nd ed. Darlington. U.K.: Carpet Bombing Culture.

Lucas, Louise. 2013. "Investors Wary of Going Back to the Land." *Financial Times*. January 27. http://www.ft.com/intl/cms/s/0/afba4574-4b8e-11e2-887b-00144feab49a .html#axzz3hq6MmuvE.

Lundin, Tomas. 2008. "Den Svarta Jorden Lockar." *SVD Näringsliv*. August 17. https:// www.svd.se/den-svarta-jorden-lockar.

Lustgarten, Abrahm. 2020. "How Russia Wins the Climate Crisis." *New York Times Magazine*. December 16. https://www.nytimes.com/interactive/2020/12/16/magazine /russia-climate-migration-crisis.html?smid=tw-share.

Luyt, Ian, Nunos Santos, and Arianna Carita. 2013. *Emerging Investment Trends in Primary Agriculture: A Review of Equity Funds and Other Foreign-Led Investments in the CEE and CIS Region*. Food and Agriculture Organization of the United Nations. http://www.fao.org/3/a-i3474e.pdf.

Mahmood, Saba. 2001. "Feminist Theory, Embodiment, and the Docile Agent: Some Reflections on the Egyptian Islamic Revival." *Cultural Anthropology* 16 (2): 202–36. https://doi.org/10.1525/can.2001.16.2.202.

Mamonova, Natalia. 2016. "Naive Monarchism and Rural Resistance in Contemporary Russia." *Rural Sociology* 81 (3): 316–42. https://doi.org/10.1111/ruso.12097.

———. 2019. "Understanding the Silent Majority in Authoritarian Populism: What Can We Learn from Popular Support for Putin in Rural Russia?" *Journal of Peasant Studies* 46 (3): 561–85. https://doi.org/10.1080/03066150.2018.1561439.

Mamonova, Natalia, and Oane Visser. 2014. "State Marionettes, Phantom Organisations or Genuine Movements? The Paradoxical Emergence of Rural Social Movements in Post-Socialist Russia." *Journal of Peasant Studies* 41 (4): 491–516. https://doi.org/10 .1080/03066150.2014.918958.

Marcus, George E. 1997. "The Uses of Complicity in the Changing Mise-En-Scène of Anthropological Fieldwork." *Representations* 59: 85–108. https://doi.org/10.2307/2928816.

Marx, Karl. [1867] 2015. *Capital: A Critique of Political Economy*. Vol. 1. New York: Penguin Books.

Matasov, Victor, Alexander V. Prishchepov, Martin Rudbeck Jepsen, and Daniel Müller. 2019. "Spatial Determinants and Underlying Drivers of Land-Use Transitions in European Russia from 1770 to 2010." *Journal of Land Use Science* 14 (4–6): 362–77. https://doi.org/10.1080/1747423X.2019.1709224.

Matveev, Ilya. 2019a. "Big Business in Putin's Russia: Structural and Instrumental Power." *Demokratizatsiya: The Journal of Post-Soviet Democratization* 27 (4): 401–22.

———. 2019b. "State, Capital, and the Transformation of the Neoliberal Policy Paradigm in Putin's Russia." *International Review of Modern Sociology* 45 (1): 27–48.

Matveev, Ilya, and Oleg Zhuravlev. 2023. "When the Whole Is Less than the Sum of Its Parts: Russian Developmentalism Since the Mid-2000s." *Russian Politics* 8 (1): 76–96. https://doi.org/10.30965/24518921-00801004.

McFaul, Michael. 1995. "State Power, Institutional Change, and the Politics of Privatization in Russia." *World Politics* 47 (2): 210–43. https://doi.org/10.1017/S0043887100016087.

McGoey, Linsey. 2012. "Strategic Unknowns: Towards a Sociology of Ignorance." *Economy and Society* 41 (1): 1–16. https://doi.org/10.1080/03085147.2011.637330.

McMichael, Philip. 2014. "Rethinking Land Grab Ontology." *Rural Sociology* 79 (1): 34–55. https://doi.org/10.1111/ruso.12021.

Medvedev, Dmitri. 2009. "Brot für die Welt: Russland will sein Agrarpotential umsetzen. Das Ziel: Zusammen mit anderen Ländern ein Garant der Nahrungsmittelsicherheit werden." *Süddeutsche Zeitung*. June 8. http://www.sueddeutsche.de/wirtschaft/landwirtschaft-in-russland-brot-fuer-die-welt-1.444132.

Mignolo, Walter D., and Madina V. Tlostanova. 2006. "Theorizing from the Borders: Shifting to Geo- and Body-Politics of Knowledge." *European Journal of Social Theory* 9 (2): 205–21. https://doi.org/10.1177/1368431006063333.

Mishra, Deepak K. 2020. "Agrarian Crisis and Neoliberalism in India." *Human Geography* 13 (2): 183–86. https://doi.org/10.1177/1942778620935688.

Mol, Annemarie. 2002. *The Body Multiple: Ontology in Medical Practice*. 3rd ed. Durham, N.C.: Duke University Press.

Mollett, Sharlene. 2016. "The Power to Plunder: Rethinking Land Grabbing in Latin America." *Antipode* 48 (2): 412–32. https://doi.org/10.1111/anti.12190.

Moore, Jason W. 2015. *Capitalism in the Web of Life: Ecology and the Accumulation of Capital*. London: Verso.

Moser, Evelyn. 2015. *Postsowjetische Transformationen in Der Weltgesellschaft: Politische Dezentralisierung Und Wirtschaftliche Differenzierung Im Ländlichen Russland*. Bielefeld: Transcript.

———. 2016. "Forms of Communication between Large-Scale Farms and Local Administrative Authorities in Russian Villages: About Benefactors and Sponsors." *Europe-Asia Studies* 68 (8): 1369–95. https://doi.org/10.1080/09668136.2016.1230179.

Moser, Evelyn, and Peter Lindner. 2011. "Dezentralisierung im Zeichen der Machtvertikale: Paradoxien der Einführung einer lokalen Selbstverwaltung im ländlichen Russland." *Geographische Rundschau* (1): 28–35.

Moskvin, Ivan. 2012. "Vladimir Putin: Sel'skoe Khoziaistvo Stalo Odnim Iz Lokomotivov Razvitia Strany." http://file-rf.ru/context/1355.

Motta, Sara C., and Alf Gunvald Nilsen, eds. 2011. *Social Movements in the Global South: Dispossession, Development and Resistance.* Basingstoke, U.K.: Palgrave Macmillan.

Muehlebach, Andrea, and Nitzan Shoshan. 2012. "Introduction: AQ Special Collection: Post-Fordist Affect." *Anthropological Quarterly* 85 (2): 317–43.

Müller, Martin. 2019. "Goodbye, Postsocialism!" *Europe-Asia Studies* 71 (4): 533–50. https://doi.org/10.1080/09668136.2019.1578337.

———. 2020. "In Search of the Global East: Thinking between North and South." *Geopolitics* 25 (3): 1–22. https://doi.org/10.1080/14650045.2018.1477757.

Nasdaq Stockholm. 2020. "Delisting of Agromino A/S from Nasdaq Stockholm (142/20)." https://www.nasdaq.com/press-release/delisting-of-agromino-a-s-from -nasdaq-stockholm-142-20-2020-10-19.

Nazpary, Joma. 2002. *Post-Soviet Chaos: Violence and Dispossession in Kazakhstan.* London: Pluto Press.

Neef, Christian. 2012. "Binsen Nach Tula: Fehldiagnosen Zur Russland-Berichterstattung." *Osteuropa* 62 (1): 101–7.

Nefedova, Tatyana. 2014. *Desiat' Aktual'nykh Voprosov O Sel'skoi Rossii.* Moscow: URSS, Izdanie stereotipnoe.

Nefedova, Tatyana, and Judith Pallot. 2006. *Neizvestnoe Sel'skoe Khoziaistvo, Ili Zachem Nuzhna Korova?* Moscow: Novoe izdatel'stvo.

Nemtsova, Anna. 2015. "Trying to Build Democracy in a Hellish Russian Village Called Paradise." *The Daily Beast,* April 14. http://www.thedailybeast.com/articles/2015/08 /01/trying-to-build-democracy-in-a-hellish-russian-village-called-paradise.html.

Neumann, Iver B. 1999. *Uses of the Other: "The East" in European Identity Formation.* Minneapolis: University of Minnesota Press.

Nichols, Robert. 2018. "Theft Is Property! The Recursive Logic of Dispossession." *Political Theory* 46 (1): 3–28. https://doi.org/10.1177/0090591717701709.

———. 2020. *Theft Is Property! Dispossession and Critical Theory.* Radical Americas. Durham, N.C.: Duke University Press.

Nikulin, Alexander. 2003. "Kuban Kolkhoz between a Holding and a Hacienda: Contradictions of Post-Soviet Rural Development." *Focaal* (41): 137–52.

———. 2011. "From Post-Kolkhoz to Oligarkhoz." *Vestnik RUDN, Serija Sociologija* (2): 56–68.

———, ed. 2012. *Zemel'naia Akkumulatsiia v Nachale XXI Veka.* Moscow: Delo.

———. 2014. *Agrarniki, Vlast' I Selo: Ot Proshlogo K Nastoiashchemu.* Moscow: Delo.

Nikulin, Alexander, and Irina Trotsuk. 2016. "Utopian Visions of Contemporary Rural-Urban Russia." *Third World Thematics: A TWQ Journal* 1 (5): 673–90. https://doi.org /10.1080/23802014.2016.1359065.

Nikulin, Alexander, and Irina Trotsuk. 2022. "Political and Apolitical Dimensions of Russian Rural Development." In *Politics and Policies of Rural Authenticity,* edited by Pavel Pospěch, Eirik M. Fuglestad, and Elisabete Figueiredo, 77–93. New York: Taylor & Francis.

Nixon, Rob. 2011. *Slow Violence and the Environmentalism of the Poor*. Cambridge, Mass.: Harvard University Press.

Novirost. 2013. "RU.S.SIA: Schedule of Large Farmland Holdings." http://www.novirost .com/downloads/Russia_large_farmland_26.12.2013_Novirost.pdf (website inactive).

Oksamytna, Kseniya. 2023. "Imperialism, Supremacy, and the Russian Invasion of Ukraine." *Contemporary Security Policy* 44 (4): 497–512. https://doi.org/10.1080 /13523260.2023.2259661.

Oliveira, Gustavo de L. T., Ben M. McKay, and Juan Liu. 2020. "Beyond Land Grabs: New Insights on Land Struggles and Global Agrarian Change." *Globalizations*: 1–18. https://doi.org/10.1080/14747731.2020.1843842.

Oliver, Adam, and Suzie Horne. 2013. "Eastern Europe Beckons Farmland Investors." *Farmers Weekly*. http://www.fwi.co.uk/business/eastern-europe-beckons-farmland -investors.htm#.UdwJD215f00.

Ouma, Stefan. 2014. "Situating Global Finance in the Land Rush Debate: A Critical Review." *Geoforum* 57: 162–66. https://doi.org/10.1016/j.geoforum.2014.09.006.

———. 2015. *Assembling Export Markets: The Making and Unmaking of Global Food Connections in West Africa*. Malden, Mass.: Wiley-Blackwell.

———. 2016. "From Financialization to Operations of Capital: Historicizing and Disentangling the Finance-Farmland-Nexus." *Geoforum* 72: 82–93. https://doi.org/10.1016 /j.geoforum.2016.02.003.

———. 2020. *Farming as Financial Asset: Global Finance and the Making of Institutional Landscapes*. Newcastle upon Tyne, U.K.: Agenda.

Oya, Carlos. 2013. "Methodological Reflections on 'Land Grab' Databases and the 'Land Grab' Literature 'Rush.'" *Journal of Peasant Studies* 40 (3): 503–20. https://doi.org/10 .1080/03066150.2013.799465.

Pain, Rachel. 2019. "Chronic Urban Trauma: The Slow Violence of Housing Dispossession." *Urban Studies* 56 (2): 385–400. https://doi.org/10.1177/0042098018795796.

Pallot, Judith. 1999. *Land Reform in Russia 1906–1917: Peasant Responses to Stolypin's Project of Rural Transformation*. Oxford: Clarendon Press.

Pallot, Judith, and Tatyana Nefedova. 2007. *Russia's Unknown Agriculture: Household Production in Post-Socialist Rural Russia*. Oxford: Oxford University Press.

Pavlovskaya, Marianna. 2013. "Between Neoliberalism and Difference: Multiple Practices of Property in Post-Soviet Russia." *Europe-Asia Studies* 65 (7): 1295–1323. https:// doi.org/10.1080/09668136.2013.822708.

Paxson, Margaret. 2005. *Solovyovo: The Story of Memory in a Russian Village*. Washington, D.C.: Woodrow Wilson Center Press.

Pearce, Fred. 2003. "Global Warming 'Will Hurt Russia.'" *New Scientist*. October 3. https://www.newscientist.com/article/dn4232-global-warming-will-hurt-russia/.

Pedersen, Morten Axel, and Morten Nielsen. 2013. "Trans-Temporal Hinges: Reflections on an Ethnographic Study of Chinese Infrastructural Projects in Mozambique and Mongolia." *Social Analysis* 57 (1): 122–42. https://doi.org/10.3167/sa.2013.570109.

Peluso, Nancy Lee. 1992. *Rich Forests, Poor People: Resource Control and Resistance in Java*. Berkeley: University of California Press.

Peluso, Nancy Lee, and Christian Lund. 2011. "New Frontiers of Land Control: Intro-

duction." *Journal of Peasant Studies* 38 (4): 667–81. https://doi.org/10.1080/03066150
.2011.607692.

Petrovic, Tanja. 2010. "'When We Were Europe': Socialist Workers in Serbia and Their
Nostalgic Narratives—the Case of the Cable Factory Workers in Jagodina." In *Remembering Communism: Genres of Representation*, edited by Maria Todorova, 127–54.
New York: Social Science Research Council.

Petryna, Adriana. 2002. *Life Exposed: Biological Citizens after Chernobyl.* Princeton, N.J.:
Princeton University Press.

Pichler, Melanie. 2015. "Legal Dispossession: State Strategies and Selectivities in the Expansion of Indonesian Palm Oil and Agrofuel Production." *Development and Change*
46 (3): 508–33. https://doi.org/10.1111/dech.12162.

Pichler, Melanie, Martin Schmid, and Simone Gingrich. 2022. "Mechanisms to Exclude
Local People from Forests: Shifting Power Relations in Forest Transitions." *Ambio* 51
(4): 849–62. https://doi.org/10.1007/s13280-021-01613-y.

Pine, Frances. 2007. "Retreat to the Household? Gendered Domains in Postsocialist
Poland." In *Postsocialism: Ideals Ideologies and Practices in Eurasia*, edited by Christopher Hann, 95–113. London: Routledge.

Pohl, Lucas. 2021. "The Sublime Object of Detroit." *Social & Cultural Geography* 22 (8):
1063–79. https://doi.org/10.1080/14649365.2019.1683760.

Polanyi, Karl. [1945] 2001. *The Great Transformation: The Political and Economic Origins
of Our Time.* Boston: Beacon Press.

Povinelli, Elizabeth A. 2011. *Economies of Abandonment: Social Belonging and Endurance
in Late Liberalism.* Durham, N.C.: Duke University Press.

Prishchepov, Alexander V., Daniel Müller, Maxim Dubinin, Matthias Baumann, and
Volker C. Radeloff. 2013. "Determinants of Agricultural Land Abandonment in Post-
Soviet European Russia." *Land Use Policy* 30 (1): 873–84. https://doi.org/10.1016/j
.landusepol.2012.06.011.

Puig de la Bellacasa, María. 2017. *Matters of Care: Speculative Ethics in More Than
Human Worlds.* Minneapolis: University of Minnesota Press.

Rabinow, Paul, and George E. Marcus. 2008. *Designs for an Anthropology of the Contemporary.* Durham, N.C.: Duke University Press.

Ribot, Jesse C., and Nancy Lee Peluso. 2003. "A Theory of Access." *Rural Sociology* 68
(2): 153–81. https://doi.org/10.1111/j.1549-0831.2003.tb00133.x.

Rigi, Jakob. 2003. "The Conditions of Post-Soviet Dispossessed Youth and Work in
Almaty, Kazakhstan." *Critique of Anthropology* 23 (1): 35–49.

Ringel, Felix. 2018. *Back to the Postindustrial Future: An Ethnography of Germany's
Fastest-Shrinking City.* New York: Berghahn.

Robinson, Joan. 1962. *Economic Philosophy.* London: Watts.

Rogers, Douglas. 2006. "How to Be a Khoziain in a Transforming State: State Formation
and the Ethics of Governance in Post-Soviet Russia." *Comparative Studies in Society
and History* 48 (4): 915–45. https://doi.org/10.1017/S001041750600034X.

Rosstat. n.d. "Trudovye Resursy, Zaniatost' I Bezrabotitsa." https://rosstat.gov.ru/labour
_force.

Rosstat. 2002a. *Rossia V Tsifrakh 2002: Kratkii Statisticheskii Sbornik.* Moscow: Federal'naia sluzhba gosudarstvennoi statistiki.

———. 2002b. *Sel'skoe Khoziaistvo V Rossii 2002: Statisticheskii Sbornik*. Moscow: Federal'naia sluzhba gosudarstvennoi statistiki.

———. 2005. *Sotsial'noe Polozhenie I Uroven' Zhizni Naseleniia Rossii: Statisticheskii Sbornik*. Moscow: Federal'naia sluzhba gosudarstvennoi statistiki.

———. 2010. *Demograficheskii Ezhegodnik Rossii: The Demographic Yearbook of Russia*. Moscow: Federal'naia sluzhba gosudarstvennoi statistiki.

———. 2011. *Sel'skoe Khoziaistvo, Okhota I Okhotnich'e Khoziaistvo, Lesovodstvo V Rossii. Statisticheskii Sbornik 2011*. Moscow: Federal'naia sluzhba gosudarstvennoi statistiki.

———. 2013. *Sel'skoe Khoziaistvo, Okhota I Okhotnich'e Khoziaistvo, Lesovodstvo V Rossii. Statisticheskii Sbornik 2013*. Moscow: Federal'naia sluzhba gosudarstvennoi statistiki.

———. 2014. *Trud I Zaniatost' V Rossii. 2013*. Moscow: Federal'naia sluzhba gosudarstvennoi statistiki.

———. 2015a. *Sel'skoe Khoziaistvo, Okhota I Okhotnich'e Khoziaistvo, Lesovodstvo V Rossii. Statisticheskii Sbornik*. Moscow: Federal'naia sluzhba gosudarstvennoi statistiki.

———. 2015b. *Trud I Zaniatost' V Rossii 2015: Statisticheskii Sbornik*. Moscow: Federal'naia sluzhba gosudarstvennoi statistiki.

———. 2019. *Trud I Zaniatost' V Rossii. 2019*. Moscow.

———. 2021. *Sotsial'no-Ekonomicheskie Indikatory Bednosti: V 2013–2020*. Moscow.

Rutt, Stephen. 1986. "The Soviet Concept of the Territorial-Production Complex and Regional Development." *Town Planning Review* 57 (4): 425–39.

Ruzhkov, Vladimir. 2012. "The Church Has Replaced the Communist Party." *Moscow Times*. September 18. http://www.themoscowtimes.com/opinion/article/the-church-has-replaced-the-communist-party/468302.html.

Ryabchuk, Anastasiya. 2023. "War on the Horizon." *Focaal* 2023 (96): 46–56. https://doi.org/10.3167/fcl.2023.960104.

Rylko, Dmitri, and Robert W. Jolly. 2005. "Russia's New Agricultural Operators: Their Emergence, Growth and Impact." *Comparative Economic Studies* 47: 115–26.

Ryzhova, Natalia. 2022. "Cows, Moonshine, Pheasants . . . Versus Soybeans." *Inner Asia* 24 (1): 53–73. https://doi.org/10.1163/22105018-02302017.

Sakwa, Richard. 1999. *Postcommunism*. Buckingham, U.K.: Open University Press.

Sassen, Saskia. 2010. "A Savage Sorting of Winners and Losers: Contemporary Versions of Primitive Accumulation." *Globalizations* 7 (1–2): 23–50. https://doi.org/10.1080/14747731003593091.

———. 2014. *Expulsions: Brutality and Complexity in the Global Economy*. Cambridge, Mass.: Harvard University Press.

Schepp, Matthias. 2010. "Das Dorf Zukunft." *Der Spiegel*. February 7.

Scoones, Ian, Ruth Hall, Saturnino M. Borras, Ben White, and Wendy Wolford. 2013. "The Politics of Evidence: Methodologies for Understanding the Global Land Rush." *Journal of Peasant Studies* 40 (3): 469–83. https://doi.org/10.1080/03066150.2013.801341.

Scott, James C. 1985. *Weapons of the Weak: Everyday Forms of Peasant Resistance*. New Haven, Conn.: Yale University Press.

———. 1998. *Seeing Like a State: How Certain Schemes to Improve the Human Condition Have Failed*. New Haven, Conn.: Yale University Press.

Shagaida, Natalya. 2010. *Oborot Sel'skokhoziaistvennykh Zemel' V Rossii: Transformatsiia Institutov I Praktika*. Moscow: Institut Gaidara.

———. 2012. "Institutsional'nye predposylki obezzemelivania krestian posle privatizatsii 90-ikh godov proshlogo veka." In *Zemel'naia Akkumulatsiia v Nachale XXI Veka*, 39–57. Moscow: Delo.

Shagaida, Natalya, Nikolai Svetlov, Vasily Uzun, Daria Loginova, and Alexander V. Prishchepov. 2018. "Potentsial Rosta Sel'skokhoziaistvennogo Proizvodstva Rossii Za Schet Vovlechenia V Oborot Neispol'zuemykh Sel'skokhoziaistvennykh Ugodii."

Shanin, Teodor. 1985. *Russia as a "Developing Society": Roots of Otherness—Russia's Turn of Century*. London: Palgrave Macmillan U.K.

———. 1990. "The Question of Socialism: A Development Failure or an Ethical Defeat?" *History Workshop* (30): 68–74.

Shanin, Teodor, Alexander Nikulin, and Viktor Danilov, eds. 2002. *Refleksivnoe Krest'ianovedenie. Desiatiletie Issledovanii Sel'skoi Rossii*. Moscow: MSSES.

Shapovalova, Iualia. 2011. "Exodus Leaves Russia's Villages to Ghosts." Russia Today. August 30. www.rt.com/news/rural-russia-dying-villages-411/.

Shirley, Andrew. 2011. "How the Land Lies." In Knight Frank; Citi Private Bank: *The Wealth Report*, 35–37.

Skul'skaia, Liudmila V., and Tamara K. Shirokova. 2009. "O Problemakh Sel'skokhozi-aistvennogo Proizvodstva I Ego Kadrovogo Obespecheniia." *Problemy prognoziro-vaniia* (4): 87–101.

Smirnova, Vera. 2019. "Territory, Enclosure, and State Territorial Mode of Production in the Russian Imperial Periphery." *Geographica Helvetica* 74 (1): 13–25. https://doi.org/10 .5194/gh-74-13-2019.

Smith, Jenny Leigh. 2014. *Works in Progress: Plans and Realities on Soviet Farms, 1930–1963*. New Haven, Conn.: Yale University Press.

Snyder, Timothy. 2012. *Bloodlands: Europe between Hitler and Stalin*. New York: Basic Books.

Soto, Hernando de. 2001. *The Mystery of Capital: Why Capitalism Triumphs in the West and Fails Everywhere Else*. London: Black Swan.

Spoor, Max, ed. 2008. *The Political Economy of Rural Livelihoods in Transition Econo-mies: Land, Peasants and Rural Poverty in Transition*. Abingdon, U.K.: Routledge.

———. 2012. "Agrarian Reform and Transition: What Can We Learn from 'The East'?" *Journal of Peasant Studies* 39 (1): 175–94. https://doi.org/10.1080/03066150.2011 .652949.

Stark, David. 1996. "Recombinant Property in East European Capitalism." *American Journal of Sociology* 101 (4): 993–1027.

———. 2009. *The Sense of Dissonance: Accounts of Worth in Economic Life*. Princeton, N.J.: Princeton University Press.

Stengers, Isabelle. 2015. *In Catastrophic Times: Resisting the Coming Barbarism*. Lüne-burg, Germany: Open Humanities. http://dx.medra.org/10.14619/016.

Stoler, Ann Laura. 2013. "Introduction: 'The Rot Remains.' From Ruins to Ruination." In *Imperial Debris: On Ruins and Ruination*, edited by Ann L. Stoler, 1–37. Durham, N.C.: Duke University Press.

———. 2016. *Duress: Imperial Durabilities in Our Times*. Durham, N.C.: Duke Univer-sity Press.

Strelnikova, Elena. 2011. "Russian Provincial Life: Down on the Farm." Open Democracy. September 14. https://www.opendemocracy.net/od-russia/elena-strelnikova/russian-provincial-life-down-on-farm.

TASS. 2021. "Agrarian Sector Becomes a Pillar of Russian Economy—Putin." TASS Russian News Agency. October 10. https://tass.com/economy/1347571.

Thompson, Vanessa E. Forthcoming. *Black Socialities: Urban Resistance and the Struggle beyond Recognition in Paris*. Manchester, U.K.: Manchester University Press.

Tlostanova, Madina. 2012. "Postsocialist ≠ Postcolonial? On Post-Soviet Imaginary and Global Coloniality." *Journal of Postcolonial Writing* 48 (2): 130–42. https://doi.org/10.1080/17449855.2012.658244.

———. 2015. "Can the Post-Soviet Think? On Coloniality of Knowledge, External Imperial and Double Colonial Difference." *Intersections* 1 (2). https://doi.org/10.17356/ieejsp.v1i2.38.

———. 2019. "The Postcolonial Condition, the Decolonial Option and the Post-Socialist Intervention." In *Postcolonialism Cross-Examined: Multidirectional Perspectives on Imperial and Colonial Pasts and the Neocolonial Present*, edited by Monika Albrecht, 165–78. New York: Routledge.

———. 2010a. "Introduction: From Utopia to Propaganda and Back." In *Post-Communist Nostalgia*, edited by Maria Todorova and Zsuzsa Gille, 1–13. New York: Berghahn.

———, ed. 2010b. *Remembering Communism: Genres of Representation*. New York: Social Science Research Council.

Todorova, Maria, and Zsuzsa Gille, eds. 2010. *Post-Communist Nostalgia*. New York: Berghahn.

Toto, Rudina, Maja Grabkowska, Peter Nientied, Vera Smirnova, and Sonja Dragović. 2023. "The Uncommonness of Urban Commons in Central and Eastern European Countries." *International Journal of the Commons* 17 (1): 155–73. https://doi.org/10.5334/ijc.1189.

Triantis, Loukas. 2018. "The Post-Socialist Restitution of Property as Dispossession: Social Dynamics and Land Development in Southern Albania." *Land Use Policy* 71: 584–92. https://doi.org/10.1016/j.landusepol.2017.10.056.

Tronto, Joan C. 2009 [1993]. *Moral Boundaries: A Political Argument for an Ethic of Care*. New York: Routledge.

Trubina, Elena, David Gogishvili, Nadja Imhof, and Martin Müller. 2020. "A Part of the World or Apart from the World? The Postsocialist Global East in the Geopolitics of Knowledge." *Eurasian Geography and Economics* 61 (6): 636–62. https://doi.org/10.1080/15387216.2020.1785908.

True, Christopher. 2012. "'Ghost Villages' Haunt Russian Vote." Al Jazeera. March 2. http://www.aljazeera.com/indepth/spotlight/russianelections/2012/03/20123272311679897.html.

Tsing, Anna. 2005. *Friction: An Ethnography of Global Connection*. Princeton, N.J.: Princeton University Press.

Tsing, Anna, Heather Swanson, Elaine Gan, and Nils Bubandt, eds. 2017. *Arts of Living on a Damaged Planet*. Minneapolis: University of Minnesota Press.

USDA Foreign Agricultural Service. 2010. *Food Security Doctrine Adopted*. February 11.

Global Agricultural Information Network. https://apps.fas.usda.gov/newgainapi
/api/report/downloadreportbyfilename?filename=Food%20Security%20Doctrine
%20Adopted%20_Moscow_Russian%20Federation_2-11-2010.pdf.

Uzun, Vasily. 2005. "Large and Small Business in Russian Agriculture: Adaptation
to Market." *Comparative Economic Studies* 47 (1): 85–100. https://doi.org/10.1057
/palgrave.ces.8100078.

———. 2012. "Agrokholdingi Rossii: identifikatsia, klassifikatsia, rol', kontsentratsia
zemlepolzovania." In *Zemel'naia Akkumulatsiia v Nachale XXI Veka*, 126–42. Moscow: Delo.

Uzun, Vasily, E. A. Gataulina, Valerij Sarajkin, Vladimir Bashmachnikov, O. I. Pavlush-
kina, and O. A. Rodionova. 2009. *Tendentsii Razvitia I Mekhanizmy Vzaimodeist-
via Krupnogo I Malogo Biznesa V Agropromishlenom Komplekse*. Moscow: VIAPI
Nikonova.

Uzun, Vasily, Natalya Shagaida, and Zvi Lerman. 2019. "Russian Agriculture: Growth
and Institutional Challenges." *Land Use Policy* 83: 475–87. https://doi.org/10.1016/j
.landusepol.2019.02.018.

Uzun, Vasily, Natalya Shagaida, and Valerij Sarajkin. 2012. *Agrokholdingi Rossii I Ikh
Rol' V Proizvodstve Zerna*. Food and Agriculture Organization of the United Nations.
http://www.fao.org/fileadmin/user_upload/Europe/documents/Publications/Policy
_Stdies/Agroholdings_ru.pdf.

Varga, Mihai. 2023. *Poverty as Subsistence: The World Bank and Pro-Poor Land Reform
in Eurasia*. Stanford, Calif.: Stanford University Press.

Verdery, Katherine. 1996. *What Was Socialism, and What Comes Next?* Princeton, N.J.:
Princeton University Press.

———. 1999. "Fuzzy Property: Rights, Power, and Identity in Transylvania's Decollectivization." In *Uncertain Transition: Ethnographies of Change in the Postsocialist World*,
edited by Michael Burawoy and Katherine Verdery, 53–82. Lanham, Md.: Rowman &
Littlefield.

———. 2003. *The Vanishing Hectare: Property and Value in Postsocialist Transylvania*.
Ithaca, N.Y.: Cornell University Press.

———. 2007. "Whither Postsocialism?" In *Postsocialism: Ideals Ideologies and Practices
in Eurasia*, edited by Christopher Hann, 15–21. London: Routledge.

Verdery, Katherine, and Caroline Humphrey, eds. 2004. *Property in Question: Value
Transformation in the Global Economy*. New York: Berg.

Verne, Julia. 2012. *Living Translocality: Space, Culture and Economy in Contemporary
Swahili Trade*. Erdkundliches Wissen 150. Stuttgart: Steiner.

Visser, Oane. 2008. "Crucial Connections: The Persistence of Large Farm Enterprises in
Russia." PhD diss., Radboud University.

———. 2017. "Running Out of Farmland? Investment Discourses, Unstable Land Values
and the Sluggishness of Asset Making." *Agriculture and Human Values* 34 (1): 185–98.
https://doi.org/10.1007/s10460-015-9679-7.

Visser, Oane, Stefan Dorondel, Petr Jehlička, and Max Spoor. 2019. "Post-Socialist
Smallholders: Silence, Resistance and Alternatives." *Canadian Journal of Development
Studies / Revue canadienne d'études du développement* 40 (4): 499–510. https://doi.org
/10.1080/02255189.2019.1688649.

Visser, Oane, Alexander Kurakin, and Alexander Nikulin. 2019. "Corporate Social Responsibility, Coexistence and Contestation: Large Farms' Changing Responsibilities Vis-À-Vis Rural Households in Russia." *Canadian Journal of Development Studies / Revue canadienne d'études du développement* 40 (4): 580–99. https://doi.org/10.1080/02255189.2019.1688648.

Visser, Oane, Natalia Mamonova, and Max Spoor. 2012. "Oligarchs, Megafarms and Land Reserves: Understanding Land Grabbing in Russia." *Journal of Peasant Studies* 39 (3–4): 899–931. https://doi.org/10.1080/03066150.2012.675574.

Visser, Oane, Natalia Mamonova, Max Spoor, and Alexander Nikulin. 2015. "'Quiet Food Sovereignty' as Food Sovereignty without a Movement? Insights from Post-Socialist Russia." *Globalizations* 12 (4): 513–28. https://doi.org/10.1080/14747731.2015.1005968.

Visser, Oane, and Max Spoor. 2011. "Land Grabbing in Post-Soviet Eurasia: The World's Largest Agricultural Land Reserves at Stake." *Journal of Peasant Studies* 38 (2): 299–323. https://doi.org/10.1080/03066150.2011.559010.

Visser, Oane, Max Spoor, and Natalia Mamonova. 2014. "Is Russia the Emerging Global 'Breadbasket'? Re-Cultivation, Agroholdings and Grain Production." *Europe-Asia Studies* 66 (10): 1589–1610. https://doi.org/10.1080/09668136.2014.967569.

Volkov, Sergei N., Viktor N. Khlystun, and Alexander A. Fomin. 2021. "K 30-Letiu Nachala V Rossii Sovremennoi Agrarnoi Reformy." *Mezhdunarodnyi sel'skokhoziaistvennyi zhurnal* 64 (6): 4–9. https://doi.org/10.24412/2587-6740-2021-6-4-9.

Vorbrugg, Alexander. 2019. "Not about Land, Not Quite a Grab: Dispersed Dispossession in Rural Russia." *Antipode* 51 (3): 1011–31. https://doi.org/10.1111/anti.12523.

———. 2022. "Ethnographies of Slow Violence: Epistemological Alliances in Fieldwork and Narrating Ruins." *Environment and Planning C: Politics and Space* 40 (2): 447–62. https://doi.org/10.1177/2399654419881660.

Vorbrugg, Alexander, Mariia Fatulaeva, and Denis Dobrynin. 2024. "Envisioning 'New Forests' on Abandoned Farmland in Russia: A Discourse Analysis of a Controversy." *Environmental Science & Policy.* https://doi.org/1 0.1016/j.envsci.2024.103871.

Wädekin, Karl-Eugen. 1973. *The Private Sector in Soviet Agriculture.* 2nd ed. Berkeley: University of California Press.

Wang, Chi-Mao, Damian Maye, and Michael Woods. 2023. "Planetary Rural Geographies." *Dialogues in Human Geography.* https://doi.org/10.1177/20438206231191731.

Watts, Michael. [1983] 2013. *Silent Violence: Food, Famine, and Peasantry in Northern Nigeria.* Athens: University of Georgia Press.

Weber, Max. 1922. *Wirtschaft Und Gesellschaft.* Tübingen: Mohr.

Wegren, Stephen K. 2000. "State Withdrawal and the Impact of Marketization on Rural Russia." *Policy Studies Journal* 28 (1): 46–67. https://doi.org/10.1111/j.1541-0072.2000.tb02015.x.

———. 2005. *The Moral Economy Reconsidered: Russia's Search for Agrarian Capitalism.* New York: Palgrave Macmillan.

Wegren, Stephen K. 2009. *Land Reform in Russia: Institutional Design and Behavioral Responses.* New Haven, Conn.: Yale University Press.

———. 2011. "Private Farming in Russia: An Emerging Success?" *Post-Soviet Affairs* 27 (3): 211–40. https://doi.org/10.2747/1060-586X.26.3.211.

———. 2014. *Rural Inequality in Divided Russia*. New York: Routledge.

Wegren, Stephen K., Alexander Nikulin, and Irina Trotsuk. 2018. *Food Policy and Food Security: Putting Food on the Russian Table*. Lanham, Md.: Lexington.

Wegren, Stephen K., Alexander Nikulin, and Irina Trotsuk. 2023. "The Fragility of Russia's Agricultural Production and Implications for Food Security." *Eurasian Geography and Economics* 64 (3): 1–39. https://doi.org/10.1080/15387216.2021.2002170.

Wegren, Stephen K., Alexander Nikulin, Irina Trotsuk, Svetlana Golovina, and Marina Pugacheva. 2014. "Gender Inequality in Russia's Rural Formal Economy." *Post-Soviet Affairs* 31 (5): 367–96. https://doi.org/10.1080/1060586X.2014.986871.

Wengle, Susanne A. 2015. *Post-Soviet Power: State-Led Development and Russia's Marketization*. New York: Cambridge University Press.

———. 2016. "The Domestic Effects of the Russian Food Embargo." *Demokratizatsiya: The Journal of Post-Soviet Democratization* 24 (3): 281–89.

———. 2018. "Local Effects of the New Land Rush: How Capital Inflows Transformed Rural Russia." *Governance* 31 (2): 259–77. https://doi.org/10.1111/gove.12287.

———. 2019. "The New Plenty: Why Are Some Post-Soviet Farms Thriving?" *Governance* 33 (4): 915–33. https://doi.org/10.1111/gove.12456.

———. 2022. *Black Earth, White Bread: A Technopolitical History of Russian Agriculture and Food*. Madison: University of Wisconsin Press.

Werner, Marion. 2015. *Global Displacements: The Making of Uneven Development in the Caribbean*. Chichester. U.K.: Wiley-Blackwell.

Whitehead, Mark, Rhys Jones, and Martin Jones. 2007. *The Nature of the State: Excavating the Political Ecologies of the Modern State*. Oxford: Oxford University Press.

Wolford, Wendy. 2007. "Land Reform in the Time of Neoliberalism: A Many-Splendored Thing." *Antipode* 39 (3): 550–70. https://doi.org/10.1111/j.1467-8330.2007.00539.x.

———. 2010. *This Land Is Ours Now: Social Mobilization and the Meanings of Land in Brazil*. Durham, N.C.: Duke University Press.

World Bank. 1992. *Food and Agricultural Policy Reforms in the Former USSR: An Agenda for the Transition*. Studies of Economies in Transformation 1. Washington, D.C.: World Bank.

———. 2016. *Poverty and Shared Prosperity 2016: Taking on Inequality*. Washington, D.C.: World Bank.

Yurchak, Alexei. 2006. *Everything Was Forever, Until It Was No More: The Last Soviet Generation*. 4th ed. Princeton, N.J.: Princeton University Press.

Yurchenko, Yuliya. 2017. *Ukraine and the Empire of Capital: From Marketisation to Armed Conflict*. London: Pluto.

Zhou, Jiayi. 2022. "Naturalizing the State and Symbolizing Power in Russian Agricultural Land Use." *Political Geography* 93: 102545. https://doi.org/10.1016/j.polgeo.2021.102545.

Zinchenko, Aleksei. 2002. *Sel'skokhoziaistvennye Predpriatia: Ekonomichesko-Statisticheskii Analiz*. Moscow: Finansy i statistika.

INDEX

access: concept, 8, 11, 146; to credit, 9, 11, 154n19; to land, 8,11, 44–45, 132–33, 160n5; to machinery, 11, 13, 31, 45, 53, 132; to markets, 13, 41, 153n7; to means of production, 8, 11, 132, 133; to state provision, 69; to state subsidies, 41, 120

adaptation, business, 99–100, 114, 115–16, 118, 119

agency, 119; collective, 49, 127, 128, 129; constraints to, 18, 87, 124, 143–44, 147; and dispersed dispossession, 21–22, 64, 147–48; as persistence, 58–60, 128–29; regenerative, 21–22, 145–46, 147; mentioned, 148, 151n23, 156n16

agricultural expansion, historical, 4, 16, 73, 139, 155n2

agricultural investment: difficulties, 6, 96, 97–98, 105; failures, 6, 15, 89–90, 92–93, 108; ignorance, 91, 92, 108; paradoxes, 90–92; promises, 5, 91, 92, 93–96, 98, 157n3, 157n4; rationalities, 5, 90–92, 97, 108–9; short-termism, 100

agricultural: commodity markets, 18, 28, 96, 101, 102, 104, 120, 153n7; exports, 6, 9; machinery, 40; market volatility, 41, 70, 96, 104 120; paradox, 4–7; policy, 9, 42, 68–69, 96, 103; production level, 68, 70, 71–72, 73; workers, 68–69, 106, 125–26

agricultural subsidies, 12, 41, 66, 68, 103, 120, 140, 158n12; Soviet-time, 15–16, 72–73, 139

agriculture: disadvantage of, 68, 122–23, 132; modernization of, 10, 13, 106; neglect of, 67–68; potential of, 5, 6; profitability of, 20, 72, 91, 99, 101–2, 120, 122; specialization, 10, 139

agroholding. *See* company: vertically integrated

Agrokultura, 32–33, 93, 100

Ahmann, Chloe, 143

alcoholism, 74–75, 77–78

Allina-Pisano, Jessica, 11, 37, 42, 44, 137

alternatives, 13, 39; lack of, 13, 142, 143

anonymization, 29,151n3

appropriation, 19, 20–21, 88, 138–40; and devaluation, 21, 102, 139, 140, 150n21; village-level, 57, 64

Arendt, Hannah, 87, 118, 158n2

authority, local, 58, 111–12, 113, 117, 128; dependence on, 27–28, 39, 143

Barnes, Andrew, 93, 101–2

Berlant, Lauren, 22, 144, 147–48

Black Earth Farming, company, 94–95, 98, 100

Boyer, Dominic, 62

Buck-Morss, Susan, 14, 84, 162n17

Butler, Judith, 28, 85, 119, 148

Byrd, Jodi, 138

capital, forms of, 90, 121–22, 124, 125, 140

capitalist accumulation, 15, 19, 88, 101, 140, 150n15, 160n7

Clapp, Jennifer, 139

Clarke, Simon, 38

collectivization, Stalinist, 4, 39–40, 149n10, 152n4, 153n8; reversal of, 10, 16, 132, 139; mention, 28, 73, 76, 149n10, 153n8

collective farm. *See* kolkhoz

Geographies of Justice and Social Transformation

www.ingramcontent.com/pod-product-compliance
Lightning Source LLC
Chambersburg PA
CBHW031553280326
41928CB00047BA/248